Harvard Prize Books

T HE PRIZE BOOK of the Harvard Alumni
Association shall be awarded to the outstanding student in the next to the grad-
uating class who "combines excellence in
scholarship with achievement in other
fields."

T HIS Prize Book is offered in competition

by

**The Harvard Club of
Cape Cod**

Name of Sponsor

and awarded to

Elena Roderick

May 31, 1995   **P.H.S.**

Name of School

Date

In memory of Howard Simons,
Curator of the Nieman Foundation,
who always asked the right questions

Q&A:

Conversations
with Harvard Scholars

Peter Costa

Harvard University
Office of News
and Public Affairs

PRINTED BY THE
OFFICE OF THE UNIVERSITY PUBLISHER
HARVARD UNIVERSITY
CAMBRIDGE, MASSACHUSETTS

DISTRIBUTED BY
HARVARD UNIVERSITY PRESS

ISBN 0-674-74000-9

Contents

Foreword vii

Acknowledgments ix

Robert Coles, How children imagine God...................................1

Simon Schama, Life cycles of revolutions................................9

William Alfred, Literature reveals essential truths.....................16

Derek Bok, Strengths of American universities...........................23

Sara Lawrence Lightfoot, 1930s odyssey of a black female M.D. ...31

Sheldon Glashow, Mysteries of matter 40

Joseph Nye Jr., The myth of America's decline...........................48

William Bennett, Winners and losers in dieting 55

Susan Suleiman, Art, avant-garde, and feminist theory 62

James Anderson, On the depletion of ozone 69

David Hall, Colonial religion and witch hunts 76

Persi Diaconis, The mathematics of randomness 83

Henry Rosovsky, Challenges facing higher education 91

Marjorie Garber, On the sublimity of Shakespeare........................99

William Graham Jr., Islam, religion for one-seventh of the world..107

Dudley Herschbach, Ballistics of baseball...............................114

Gerald Lesser, Big Bird and the child's universe.......................122

Florence Ladd, Establishing women as role models.......................129

Charles Maier, Historical perspectives on World War II 136

Bill Kovach, The art, business, and craft of journalism 144

Orlando Patterson, The nature of freedom...............................152

Edwin Reischauer, Japan, myths among mysteries 160

Frederick Schauer, Rules and moral behavior...........................167

Mary Karr, The rhyme and meter of life 174

I.Bernard Cohen, History of scientific discovery.......................182

Jerome Kagan, How to parent a happy child 189

Abraham Zaleznik, Help wanted: leaders, not managers 197
Myra Mayman, Art transforms experience 204
E.O. Wilson, Rain forest destruction threatens biodiversity 211
Jan Ziolkowski, The changing concept of friendship 218
Ronald Theimann, The new spirituality in America 225
J. Allan Hobson, To sleep, perchance to dream.......................233
Stephen Williams, Unearthing archaeological myths 241
Alex Kreiger, City and suburban architecture..........................249
Seamus Heaney, Ancient heroes and the poetry of wonder 256

Foreword

Since the founding of Harvard as a small College in the Yard in 1636, Harvard has been committed to the highest attainable standards of teaching and research. The guarantors of these standards, then and now, are its community of scholars. More than buildings, or state-of-the-art laboratories, or museums and libraries, a faculty of scholars compose the chief natural resource and intellectual treasure of an institution of higher learning. It is through the teaching and research of its faculty that students gain new knowledge and greater understanding.

This collection of interviews by Peter Costa demonstrates the range of interests of Harvard scholars and the depths of their inquiries. From ozone depletion to the spiritual life of children, from poetry to physics, these topics of interest by Harvard researchers and teachers form the basis of this book and give it intellectual energy. But these interviews do more than help illuminate their work; they also tell us a lot about their lives. Not settling for just the reflected gleams of their academic personas, Peter Costa has gone beyond asking the standard journalistic questions in this book to try to probe the workings of their minds.

I am proud to have played a part in making available to the public this fine collection of conversations with Harvard scholars.

Derek Bok
President of Harvard University

Acknowledgments

If I had to cite a date for the genesis of this book it would be 1958 when I sat in a small studio at the radio station where my mother worked and listened to her interview a young senator named Jack Kennedy for her daily program. My mother, the same person who had asked me minutes before if I had remembered to return my library books, was now asking a senator what he would do for public education. He answered her with the same forthrightness I had answered my mother. Who would not? Dissembling was impossible with this honest woman—especially when you knew your friends, your priest, and your potential voters were listening. There was also something empowering about the interview process itself; it legitimized a relationship between my mother the radio journalist and the interviewee whom she had met only seconds before she had asked her first probing question. Later on as a newspaper and wire service journalist, I discovered that I could ask questions of very famous people (some inquiries so bold they would make therapists blush and lawyers bristle) and still expect answers. Often, they would volunteer information that would make me blush.

But even though it was exciting to interview the powerful and the famous, the so-called "glitterati"—presidents, novelists, movie stars, culture heroes—I always enjoyed talking to people more about ideas than personalities. Why do so many kings go mad? What is charm, and why is it so important in subatomic physics? Is playwright Edward Albee right, have the dice become too big to toss? But the key, I discovered, was to ask the physicist about kings, the playwright about charm, and the historian about dice.

Moreover, to find myself as Director of the Harvard University Office of News and Public Affairs placed amid some of the world's greatest scholars and be granted the privilege of asking these questions constitutes the ultimate state of grace for a journalist. I am forever grateful for having had such an opportunity. I am often asked two things about these interviews: do I come up with my own questions and are the interviews rehearsed? All the questions herein are my own and were based on hours of reading and research that continue to make my eye surgeon, Dr. Trexler Topping, scowl. None of the interviews, which were conducted from 1988 to 1991, was rehearsed. The Harvard scholars and researchers were all interviewed in the News Office at Holyoke Center, 10 floors above Harvard Square and the bustling Yard, and parsecs away from their pedagogical travail of preparing lectures, writing research reports, and grading exams. The interviews have been edited for length, but are in essence almost verbatim transcripts. In selecting the interviews for this book, I tried to choose as broad a range of subjects as possible. Because of size limitations, however, many other excellent interviews were excluded. I hope to rectify this situation in subsequent volumes. This book is the product of many hands. First, I would like to thank the more than 130 Harvard scholars for consenting to these interviews and for being so gracious with their time. I also want to thank the following people for their help: Laura Ferguson, Managing Editor of the Harvard University *Gazette*, for her encouragement and work in making the Q&A interviews a regular feature in the *Gazette*; Robyn Spartichino for her tireless efforts in transcribing hours of tapes, with additional help from Katie Lawyer; Rhea Becker for copyediting; Miriam Adkins, Rob Phelps, and Mary Barnes for proofreading; Jessica Stern for design; Jane Reed, Joe Wrinn, Laura Wulf, Lilian Kemp, and Mike Quan for photography; Marilyn McDonnell and Kelly Harvey for handling reprint requests; Grace Choi for providing biographical material and photos; Deborah J. Winsten for helping produce and engineer Harvard NEWSMAKERS, the syndicated radio version of these Q&A's; David Ozeil of the UPI Radio Network for assisting in transmitting these interviews to radio stations in the United States and abroad; and the entire Harvard News Office staff for their help and suggestions. I especially want to thank Derek Bok and John Shattuck for their encouragement and support in this effort. Robert Scott has been a true advocate of the Q&A interviews since their inception, and I wish to thank him for his good cheer and his friendship. Richard Emerick of the University of Maine, Orono, and David Littlejohn of the University of California, Berkeley, were mentors for me and urged me to become a journalist and writer. I would like to express my special gratitude to my mother and father, Esther and Paul Costa, for their love and support. Finally, I would like to thank my wife, Sara, and my daughter, Lucy, for their encouragement, their faith in me, and for their patience in enduring all those times I spent chasing, writing, and editing the news.

Peter Costa
Cambridge, Massachusetts
April 1991

A *conversation with*

Dr. Robert Coles

Dr. Robert Coles is professor of psychiatry and medical humanities and a member of the Faculty of Education. His teaching and research has had a profound impact on all who encounter his work. Volumes 2 and 3 of his Children of Crisis series were awarded the Pulitzer Prize in 1973.

COSTA: *In 1960 you served as a physician in the Air Force in Mississippi and you witnessed the racial struggles of the South, the sit-ins, the protests, the beginnings of the civil rights movement and its effects on the children whom you saw there. Did witnessing these events lead you to your work with children?*

COLES: I had been trained in pediatrics and child psychiatry before I went into the Air Force under the doctors draft when all physicians had to put in two years in the military. This applied to everyone until about 1965. So I was prepared to work with children by training. In fact, the first research I did was with children in the Children's Hospital who had polio. [It was] the last epidemic before the Salk vaccine. In the course of working with them as a pediatrician and as a child psychiatrist I began to notice some of their moral and even spiritual concerns as they lay there sometimes dying or certainly paralyzed and frightened about what would happen to them. I think that prepared me for what I saw in the South.

I witnessed the early struggles of children to get into desegregated schools, often involving the need for them to walk by mobs of hecklers, some of them threatening to kill them. I think it was this earlier training and experience in working with children under stress that enabled me to visualize myself talking with a new group of children under a different kind of stress, namely the horrors of social and racial stress in the face of real tension and enmity between white and black people in Mississippi and Louisiana.

I was in charge of an Air Force psychiatric hospital in Biloxi, Mississippi, then and I used to go into New Orleans to medical, psychiatric, and psychoanalytic meetings and it was these travels from Mississippi into Louisiana that enabled me to witness school desegregation because I drove by one of the schools that was desegregated. I saw hundreds of people massed in front of the school, screaming and shouting and threatening one little black child who went into the school all by herself because the entire white school population was withdrawn by the parents of these children. Here you had a situation out of a Franz Kafka story because you had a little girl all alone in a school building with a mob telling her everyday that they were going to kill her. When I saw that happen, my mind went back to the children I met in Boston who were facing a different kind of ordeal, and to my conversations with them and I thought to myself, maybe if I got to know a girl like this little girl, whose name was Ruby Bridges and who became a heroine of mine and, I would say, a teacher of mine, I would learn a lot from her and maybe I could be of some help to her and her family. This began this work.

COSTA: *Was it Ruby who walked past the angry mob smiling, and when a white women asked her, 'What are you smiling at?' she looked up and said she was smiling at God?*

COLES: Yes, this is the girl. This is the girl whose religious and spiritual interests I heard and took note of, but I'm afraid didn't pay as much attention to at the beginning there in the early '60s as I might have, and perhaps should have, had I not been trained in psychoanalytic psychiatry. [That field] has not exactly been known, at least in the past, for its major interest in religious and spiritual matters, at least interest in a positive sense.

COSTA: *I was struck by an anecdote in your book about the nature of psychoanalysis and what are legitimate areas of inquiry. You were working with a young boy from a privileged family. The boy was a computer freak, quite brilliant and wanted to talk to you solely about computers and information processing and things of the intellect. And you told him that psychoanalysis is not meant to be an exploration of the intellect or the soul. Do you have to set aside your psychoanalytic training to discuss spirituality?*

COLES: There is a growing number of psychoanalysts who see a connection between psychoanalytic matters and spirituality, and for that matter, I think Freud himself implicitly saw this all the time. For instance, his written exchanges with Einstein are essentially moral and spiritual in nature. His explorations of Moses have a spiritual side to them. His interests in creativity and in the soulfulness of certain writers bring him closer to spiritual matters.

After all, he was an intensely moral figure who stood for certain values and principles and made those values and principles very clear to the world, and I suspect much clearer to his patients, than many of his followers have been willing to be with their patients.

COSTA: *You've interviewed thousands of youngsters all over the world in different cultures. Do most children reflect adults' views of God, or did you find any that had original ideas of God?*

COLES: I think original for them in the sense that [these children] were not prepared by studies in theology or philosophy or religion to come up with the thinking they've come up with. In that sense their thinking shows that there is a certain kind of common thinking that perhaps all of us have when trying to struggle with these common problems we all have: mainly, how do you figure out the meaning of life and what do you do with the limited amount of time you have on this planet.

I've found that a lot of children do not learn their ideas about religion and spiritual matters only from their parents, although, indeed, the parents are a major influence. They also have a lot of conversations about such matters with friends, with other relatives, with grandparents, especially, by the way, in certain cultures such as in black families and in Spanish-speaking families in America and in other countries where grandparents have much more significance than they do in many American families. And from teachers, from athletic coaches, from people they meet—adults, and people of their own age—in the course of their lives, and often just from their own musings and speculations. I've talked with children who tell me that they look out the window sometimes, at the stars, the moon, the sun, the clouds, and the configurations of the clouds, and wonder and speculate and think. Some of these speculations I find extraordinary.

I have a longstanding interest in theology going back to when I was taking psychiatric training here in Boston at Massachusetts General Hospital and Children's Hospital. I audited a course that Paul Tillich gave in systematic theology in the '50s here at Harvard. I remember him discussing with us Karl Barth and a lot of his theological interests in not only human beings' search for God, but God's search for us. I thought that was an interesting way of putting it. I've often gone back to those moments here at Harvard when I remember some of the remarks that I've heard from children. I especially think of one girl who said to me, 'You know, God must be very lonely at times and he must try and make friends with some of the people he's going to send down to the earth and then when he does send them down he must miss them and he must try to keep track of them.' As she developed this extraordinary line of speculation about God I thought, 'My lord, this is worthy of Karl Barth.' This child's speculations are, indeed, worthy of Karl Barth, and maybe some other theologians too.

There's a kind of resourcefulness, richness, texture, subtlety, and nuance to a lot of these speculations that you hear from children which I think entitles them to be called in their own right—apart from the influence of their parents and others in the adult world—seekers, pilgrims who are interested in the eternal questions that we all have about life. Here we are with an infinity of time and space before us and after us. We wonder about what we are doing, and this, children are eminently capable of wondering about as much as we adults are.

COSTA: *From a psychiatric viewpoint, do you think having a sense of spirituality or religion or religiousness contributes to a child's health?*

COLES: We all have some sense of spirituality or religiousness even if we are agnostics or atheists and deny an explicit or even implicit interest in conventional religion or conventional dogma as it's handed down by the various religious groups. I go back to those questions, for instance, that Gauguin asked when he painted that triptych of his in 1897 that hangs in the Boston Museum of Fine Arts. He titled it, 'Where Do We Come From? What Are We? Where Are We Going?' To my mind, that's what spirituality is. It's the capacity for awareness that we all have and the capacity through language to ask these important existential questions. In that sense I think every one of us has a religious or spiritual side. We may not practice a religion, we may not believe the dogma handed down, but we ask the questions and we wonder. It's that wondering and it's that musing and it's those philosophical sides that children have as well as adults that I call spirituality.

COSTA: *You asked many of the children to draw or paint God. Did most of the children portray God as a smiling, bearded deity?*

COLES: No. God varies in many ways by the background of the child. I noticed when I was working in Europe that God was blondish with blue eyes in Sweden, and slowly the hair color and the eye color changed as I moved down through Hungary toward Italy. Then when I crossed the Mediterranean Sea I started talking with children in Israel. In Tunisia, God had a distinctly different coloration among those children who were willing to draw God. Of course, Jewish and Islamic children do not draw pictures of the deity.

COSTA: *You never asked a child of Jewish or Islamic faith to draw a picture of God.*

COLES: I could have gotten into some of the difficulties that Salman Rushdie got into. Some of these children were prepared to violate some of these tenets because they were tempted to and had in their own minds pictured God, regardless of the injunctions that they not do so in an engraving sense by drawing or painting. Some of them even wanted to draw a little circle to represent God, at least in a geometric sense.

But they were willing and anxious to draw pictures of Moses and other Hebrew prophets and of Jesus and his comrades. But the child's racial background, religious background, even socioeconomic background, and the child's personal life definitely influenced the way the child thinks of God and will picture God. Christian children were very anxious to draw pictures of Jesus and, indeed, of God. There was a great deal of variation depending on where they lived and what their neighborhood was like and who they usually see and therefore what colors come naturally to them as they pick up the pencils and the crayons and the paints.

In my work over the last thirty years drawings and paintings have been extremely important. I learned long ago when I was training to be a child psychiatrist how helpful it can be when talking with children to ask them to draw pictures. In the book *The Spiritual Life of Children* the drawings and paintings that are part of the book are very important because they really give the reader, even as they gave me, access to the way children's minds' work as they attempt to imagine what—really for all of us—is almost unimaginable, namely, what God looks like. It's quite a task for anyone whether you're a child or an adult to picture what is beyond any human knowledge or experience.

COSTA: *Tell us about the boy who had the interesting visual representation of the Trinity. I think he saw the Holy Ghost as a rainbow.*

COLES: This was a wonderful way of trying to give some visual life to what is obviously the intangible. He said to me once, 'I just don't know what this Holy Ghost is. I've asked the nuns and I've asked the priests and they tell me close your eyes and imagine and it will come to you and if it doesn't, then don't worry about it.' The boy once told me, 'I closed my eyes and I couldn't see anything and then I told my mother and father that I couldn't see anything and I was trying to think about what the Holy Ghost looks like. Then suddenly I thought to myself I know what the Holy Ghost is. The Holy Ghost is a rainbow and my mother said, "Where did you get that idea?"' And he said, 'Well, because the Holy Ghost knows everything and sees everything and a rainbow has all the colors and it covers the whole world because it is a huge arc.'

What this boy was really telling me—we had further conversations about this—is that he had somehow managed to find a concrete symbol for this very, very elusive conceptual matter. I thought to myself this is worthy of anyone I have ever met at Harvard, professor and student alike.

COSTA: *Catholic nuns, as discussed by the young people in your book, got a bad rap—or maybe a deserved one—as being extremely stern. One student said that if the nuns are so strict, then God must be even sterner.*

COLES: I have a great deal of affection not only for the Catholic church but for certain nuns whom I've known very well, and I've spent a lot of my life working in a Catholic workers soup kitchen and knew Dorothy Day very well so I don't come off this with any animus. But it so happens that the Catholic children I worked with most closely in Boston were going to a particular school where they were both getting a lot from these nuns and being very well educated by them. But the nuns were very stern and I think some of their sternness came across in the conversations I had with some of the children. Mind you, they were very respectful of these nuns and very admiring of them in certain ways, but there's no question that the nuns handed on to these children a very stern, tough, demanding, and somewhat ascetic God. And not those nuns alone because some of the children I worked with in the South who came from a fundamentalist Protestant background also struggled with some of that Christian asceticism that they had picked up in Sunday School.

Indeed, when I talked with Jewish children of the Orthodox persuasion in Israel there was a good deal of that there among them as well. This has always been an aspect of the three religions I've studied through children, namely, Islam, Christianity, and Judaism, that ascetic, puritanical side. But, of course, there are other sides to religious life and I've [gathered] that from children as well. The more joyous, celebratory, and sensual side of religious experience.

COSTA: *There was one chapter in your book which I think your fellow psychiatrists and psychoanalysts would worry about, and that was describing those rare but real instances when some children experience a visionary moment. How do you as a psychiatrist differentiate a visionary moment from, say, a psychologically disturbed moment?*

COLES: I remember having a long conversation with Anna Freud about this, and she pointed out to me, 'You know, there's a continuum between the normal and the pathological, and the real issue is how far we walk down that continuum.' Some footsteps are fine, but, of course, as you move further and further away into the realm of the psychopathological then they all start worrying. The visionary side of our lives is not to be confused with the hallucinatory side of disturbed people's lives.

COSTA: *I would be remiss if I didn't ask you this question: How does God look to you?*

COLES: It depends on my mood, it depends on the particular day, maybe even the time of day in my life. I often think of God when I think of my parents. I think of God when I think of my mother's wonderful smile as she put her hands on my brother and me and encouraged us and and handed on to us some of the treasures of her own moral and intellectual life, namely, George Eliot's *Middlemarch* or Tolstoy's *War and Peace*. I think of God coming across to me through my mother's smile and her loving kindness or my father's highly refined moral sensibility. I think of God sometimes when I remember my father in the last years of his life doing volunteer work with fellow elderly people in Boston, and visiting them and bringing meals to them. I think of this as a God-like moment. My father and some other elderly people sharing stories with one another. His goodness being a part of their lives and a lot of what they offered to him being a part of his life.

I think of God when I think of some of the children I've met and what they've said to me, which comes across in this book. I think of God when I think of some of the elderly people I've met whose thoughtfulness and sensitivity gives me pause and gives me some meaning in my own life. In other words, I think of God through his or her people who are in their own ways incarnations of whatever the deity is.

I think of God when I think of some of the teachers that I have had, some of the Harvard professors that I have studied with, such as Perry Miller, Erik Erikson. I think of God when I remember my friendship with Dorothy Day. If God somehow isn't connected to Dorothy Day, then I don't know what God is. And why shouldn't I as a human being in my visual life and in my intellectual life and in my imaginative life and in my emotional life connect God with someone such as Dorothy Day.

COSTA: *You are unique, except for William Carlos Williams, who was your great mentor, to be a literate doctor who can communicate to others in emotional and imaginative ways, and still not jettison the science of being a physician. How did you come to harness those two horses?*

COLES: This has been a lifelong struggle for me. The answer is implicit in your question. I wrote my college thesis on William Carlos Williams, and then Perry Miller, my professor here at Harvard, encouraged me to send it off to Williams with some resistance on my part because I was afraid he wouldn't like it. From [Williams] I got back a little note on one of his prescription pads saying, 'Not bad—for a Harvard student!' Then he added a little footnote: 'If you're ever in the neighborhood, drop by.' Well, a week later I was down in New York, with fear and trembling, calling him up. I got his wife on the phone and she said, 'If you want to come over here, Bill will be coming home and maybe you can have a cup of coffee with him, even some supper if you want to stay with us.' So, of course, I made a beeline for the bus and went over there to Rutherford and that's how I met him.

The next day he took me on his medical rounds and I met his patients in Paterson, the poor, humble, working-class people whom he'd given his life to as a physician, up and down those tenement house stairs, meeting them, knocking on the doors, visiting them, often not being paid by them, struggling to do what he could for them, and struggling with all the problems he had as a hard-working doctor who also wanted to write, and obviously did write. I shifted my whole life around because of this. I became so taken with him and so admiring of him that I thought this is how I'd like to spend my life, at least being the doctor side of Williams because I never thought of myself as a writer and I never thought of myself as having the ability to write other than to write college papers.

So I took the premedical courses and went to medical school and while in medical school I used to visit him a lot and he did become a wonderful mentor in my life. Those conversations gave shape to my whole sense of what life ought to be about. So I went into pediatrics—because he had basically been a pediatrician—and then went into child psychiatry. In fact when I started my work in the South he was still alive—he died in 1963—and I shared with him some of my experiences with some of the first black and white children I met during the school desegregation struggle. He was the one who told me to try to take these observations and offer them to readers as stories. He said, 'Don't write this up in psychiatric jargon, don't write it up as if you were a social scientist. Those children are telling you wonderful incidences. There is a narrative voice in you that I hear as you describe what you've heard from these children and they have narrative voices. You be the intermediary between those children and what they are going through and what they have to tell you and what you have learned from them, and what you have to offer readers.' With that kind of advice from him I think my writing career began because I tried to do what he suggested I ought to do. That's, in a capsule form, a summary of how one particular stumbling, bumbling person trying to find some meaning in his own life happened upon this particular way of combining medical and psychiatric research with a writing life.

COSTA: *You've written more than a thousand articles and more than 50 books. In 1973 you won a Pulitzer Prize for your writing about children. What do you see as your next goal in your work and in your writing?*

COLES: I'm now doing interviews with elderly people who managed, despite their medical infirmities and their vulnerabilities—social, economic, racial—to be independent and live on their own. I'm very interested in independence and resiliency, whether it be in children or other people who are older and I'm trying to do some interviews in the North and the South with elderly people— black, white, rural, urban—to try to figure out how, perhaps against great odds, elderly people manage to live a life of dignity and resiliency. I think this will keep me busy for a while.

I guess, in that sense, I'm continuing a tradition of documentary child psychiatry and documentary psychiatry and mingling the kinds of observations that people such as James Agee, Walker Evans, and Dorothea Lange did . . . mingling that with the kind of medical psychiatric training that I've had and then trying to write it up in some kind of a reasonably coherent and understandable manner.

A conversation with
Simon Schama

Simon Schama is professor of history, member of the Board of Syndics of Harvard University Press, and Mellon Professor of the Social Sciences. Schama's melding of cultural history with biographical research has had fascinating results. His prolific output includes Citizens, *an acclaimed book about the French Revolution, and the BBC series* Landscape and Memory *(to be aired in 1993).*

COSTA: *You wrote in the preface of your book,* Citizens, *the following: 'Asked what he thought was the significance of the French Revolution, the Chinese premier Zhou Enlai is reported to have answered, "It's too soon to tell."' Of course, he said that about 200 years* after *the French Revolution. In Eastern Europe, is it too soon to tell the significance of their revolutions?*

SCHAMA: Yes, I think it is essentially. What we know about revolution and what we remembered when contemplating the 200th anniversary of the French Revolution was the tremendous unpredictability of the phenomenon. What almost all revolutions have in common is an initial phase of extraordinary euphoria. The revolution in the first place concentrates on exploding the symbols of tyranny, of despotism, all the things into which people pour their particular personal grievances. If you were hungry, if you were frightened, if you were nervous about being able to speak publicly under what seemed to be a dark regime, this sudden blaze of light that occurs when a society explosively renews itself seems to bathe everything in an equal radiance.

As I heard somebody say on National Public Radio the other day: the hard part really now begins. One particularly hard part is to build a new society, a new political world, which has room for disagreement. And the contrast 200 years ago was between the Philadelphia Convention, in which the building of a political house that would make disagreements possible without cracking the state apart was the number one item on the agenda, and the experience of the French, which turned out to be rather less fortunate. The concentration there was on unity, on creating a feeling of brotherhood, which would literally mean that men would never be separated. The French were very averse to creating a system of different political parties. I think if we scan the horizon on Eastern Europe, different societies right now have the creation of political pluralism in a different ranking order in their priorities. If you are Polish I think you want to be fed, if you are Romanian I think you certainly want to have a world that is going to be a little bit more decent. If you are in Czechoslovakia, with its earlier experience of political pluralism, issues of how to construct a world where there can be political parties are higher up and easier to contemplate.

COSTA: *Most people in America fail to appreciate what you've just mentioned: the role that economic conditions play in fomenting revolution. More often than not, not having bread is the stronger reason to revolt, than taxation without representation, for example.*

SCHAMA: I think that's right. But another very striking characteristic of most revolutions is that even though being extremely bad off and feeling the pinch in a very acute way is what brings ordinary people who normally don't see themselves as political animals into engagement in politics, those at the top, those who are running revolutions, those who are articulating its long-term goals and even its medium-term goals can't really make a revolution in the name of sausages on the dinner table; it has to be in the name of a somewhat grander ideal. What this does, inevitably, is really confuse the issue of, if you like, freedom and sausages. There is nothing in being allowed to vote or being allowed to write a letter to the newspaper that will guarantee that sausages will be there. The problem is when people are led to believe that one thing will almost certainly follow the other.

I think the present government in Poland and the present regime in Hungary are actually being quite shrewd about lowering people's expectations. Mr. Mazowiecky's government is being extremely brave about exposing the Polish people to this rather alarming shock that they are going to have in discovering the less immediately pleasant aspects of becoming a market economy. The world has no experience on exits from socialism, exits from communism, creating, if not overnight, then really on an urgency basis, a market economy. And it doesn't really help that situation to have lectures from our president, or from Milton Friedman, on the instantaneous virtues and transformations of Adam Smith-style, rugged, individualist capitalism. Interestingly enough, the more sophisticated economies—one thinks of Hungary and Czechoslovakia in that context—are themselves aware of that and are trying to find some difficult halfway house between the mixed economies of Germany and Scandinavia, and American capitalism in the West.

10

COSTA: *How much of revolutionary activity is spontaneous, and how much of it is controlled by what Marxist-Leninists used to call a vanguard elite?*

SCHAMA: The answer is really 'no' to both possibilities. Because societies break down, because their economies fall under terrible stress from time to time—one expects this to happen cyclically in the normal way of things—large groups of people can feel profoundly and violently alienated from the status quo. What they then become part of is a latent pool for rebellion and insurrection. The old regime, the old monarchies that governed Europe for three or four more centuries simply thought of these in terms of food riots. The 'old' regimes of our own times—communist governments—could likewise deal with these isolated pockets of resistance if they were simply in the form of individual strikes, if they took the form of a sporadic sort of looting or something of that kind. In order for it to be much more coherently revolutionary activity, this element of economic disaffection must really receive a much more powerful engine of political articulation, and that political articulation usually comes from cracks inside the regime itself.

COSTA: *As a historian, do you subscribe to the idea of the great man, or great person, as history maker, or the theory that great times forge great persons? For example, do Napoleons, by sheer dint of their personalities, change world events, or is it the social, economic, and political conditions that allow Napoleons to thrive?*

SCHAMA: Thinking in terms about the impact of personalities on history has been regarded with deep suspicion if not total contempt by 'professional' historians, partly because it was thought to be something first articulated by Thomas Carlyle, the nineteenth-century British historian, and it also had overtones of fascism about it. Historians, by and large, are a rather nervous, well-intentioned liberal bunch. In some sense, admitting that immensely powerful personalities could have an impact on history was almost endorsing the possibility that politics should be the collision of great wills.

But of course you don't have to be that nervous. The opposite view is mainly that we are all floating along in an indeterminate soup filled with bits of economic and social matter, and that every so often there will be a chunky piece in the soup which you won't be able to chew on and that chunky piece will turn out to be some sort of political hero or villain. I think that won't do either. The twentieth century in particular has been overwhelmingly affected by the force of single-minded, immensely efficient, often implacably ruthless individuals whose entire lives have been public. One thinks, for better or for worse, of figures like Lenin or Gandhi. There is no doubt when one talks to my own father's generation—I was born in '45—about the impact that Churchill's rhetoric made on the British determination to survive the blitz.

Roosevelt's similar determination, although the product of a much more pragmatic personality, arguably turned the course of the war when he offered lend-lease to Britain. Equally I think Mikhail Gorbachev's reformism has been the permitting condition of change in Eastern Europe.

It would be absurd to deny that these sorts of personalities don't have a profoundly formative impact on history. That said, history isn't entirely a parade like a waxworks museum. We're not just limp putty waiting to receive the impress of powerful personalities.

COSTA: *How much really changed after the French Revolution? You wrote that some of the wealthy actually got richer, and some of the poor became poorer afterward.*

SCHAMA: I think I'm tremendously controversial for being much more modest in my evaluation of the social changes and the economic changes, and in fact being rather negative about the net tradeoffs at the end of the French Revolution. The most controversial part of my book is to imply that the engines of change were grinding away for better or for worse before the revolution, and that the revolution in some sense puts on the brakes. This is a very unusual and difficult view to take, but I stand by it.

However, I don't mean by that to say that nothing changes. I would be the last person to say that a political world of great modernity and dynamism was not created—it was created. There is no doubt that the concept of individual citizens comprising a new kind of state on whose ascent sovereignty depended was a radically new idea—not an absolutely virgin view. Mrs. Thatcher was tactless enough to say that when she came to Paris. Not absolutely new, but essentially it was dramatically articulated and there was some attempt to live it out in France. There was an attempt to say that all males over a certain age with a certain amount of property and education—later on that even didn't stay as a qualification—should have a vote, should have a part to play in the operation of a political society. So one can also recognize the origins of modern political journalism, even political propaganda, political theater, all these things are writ very large, immensely large in the French Revolution and were genuinely new and permanently changed the nature of modern politics.

COSTA: *Many political theorists say that the best time for extremists of either political persuasion, left or right, to take power is shortly after a revolution. Do you agree?*

SCHAMA: There is no doubt that they are presented with dramatic opportunities because the nature of power is bound to be so fluid. It is rather like a young man who falls in love with a girl for the first time having only had the most unrealistic, virginal, and poetic concept of what falling in love really is and then discovers that it's a very mixed experience. Once that happens, revolutionary regimes, like that young man, then often become hungry for change.

I think what *can* happen is once you've said goodbye to a particular kind of sovereignty, which had been graven in authority, political elites can then really say, 'Well, nothing need necessarily stand unchallenged.' That really does often open opportunities for powerful groups of individuals, factions, parties to impose their own prescription.

Another condition that very often characteristically happens in the wake of revolutions—this was true not only in France, but in China and Russia and Cuba—is that revolutions really make a lot of the world so nervous that very often they are faced with a situation of great anxiety on their borders. They are very often in a quasi-war situation, or they see themselves and think themselves into a quasi-war mentality. That very often plays into the hands of, you might say, soldier-citizens, people who say 'Well, that's very nice, all this stuff about liberty, all this stuff about the harmony of brothers, but we need in the first instance to secure our frontiers, to make sure the revolution is not going to be destroyed, and if we have to put in suspension some of these liberties in the name of which we fought the revolution, well, too bad. We promise you we will restore them as soon as the situation has returned to normal.' Then of course the situation characteristically never returns to normal.

COSTA: *The guillotine is the symbol of the French Revolution. Is there some dark need in the human spirit that those who are overthrown must pay for their politics or their dastardly deeds, in some cases, with their lives? For a revolution to be effective, must one have this kind of retribution?*

SCHAMA: There are two kinds of reasons that are given and which were given for the very rapid trial and execution of [Nicolae] Ceausescu. It was a hot topic at the American Historical Association in our session on revolutionary violence. He had been executed the day before and it was impossible to keep him out of the discussion. There are two sorts of reasons given. There is a perfectly pragmatic and rational reason now being given by the government, namely that executing him [and his wife] saved lives, that it was only with obvious evidence of the physical elimination of the tyrant that you could in fact disarm those who were in the process of attempting a counterrevolution. There was something to that, even though my own view said that if a revolution is fought in the name of due process and law, one must absolutely do one's utmost to see that those processes are respected. Even though I feel this, it is very difficult to sit here on the top of Holyoke Center in Harvard Square in an armchair and feel absolutely certain that you would have actually voted for that admirably, idealized view. But sitting in the streets of Bucharest, I'm not sure.

You asked me whether at the same time, quite apart from these pragmatic issues, there is some sense of—the Greeks call it catharsis—psychological purge, some sense of sacrifice that is demanded in these highly emotionally charged situations of revolutionary drama. Whether or not one likes to see it, the fact is that that has pretty much always been the case. It is very difficult to think of a revolutionary situation that has not involved firing squads and show trials and very public forms of vengeance, of punishment.

I think revolutions for most people—not for the leaders, not for people who have always conceived their lives in terms of big public acts—for most Joes on the street, it's an incredibly risky business. You don't know whether it will work. If it doesn't work, you're going to be punished, your children and family are going to be punished. You don't know what is going to happen, so there is a sense in which you are sticking your own neck out, you're putting your life on the line for something, the conclusion of which is still rather vague.

One response to this sense of nervousness and even a little guilt is to try and evacuate your nervousness and guilt by pinning the responsibility on one or a small number of figures who then become a receptacle for your hatred and nervousness. I think that goes back to antiquity. To answer your question, I think that has been a constant in political behavior in Europe and we like to think of modern history as having said goodbye to those sort of things. I'm not sure it has.

COSTA: *Let's talk about the process of writing history. You write 1,200 pages a year, almost setting records for volume. I assume that a historian looks at source documents, journalistic accounts of events, etc., and then tries to synthesize them with his or her own interpretation. How did you go about writing this tome and how does a modern historian do this?*

SCHAMA: I'm a terribly bad person to ask actually about how a modern historian does things because I'm notoriously idiosyncratic. In fact, my books were all written in different ways and at different speeds and with different kinds of methodologies. I'm oddly various, oddly restless about methodology. For better or worse, I have not stuck with one.

The book I wrote before *Citizens*, a book on seventeenth-century Holland called *The Embarrassment of Riches*, was done in a much more long-term, painstaking way. I spent nearly ten years accumulating every conceivable bit of evidence from letters to prints to physical evidence, even accounts of furniture. I chewed it over a lot and then wrote a chapter and then went back to do more research and wrote another chapter.

Citizens was quite different. I had done a lot of research on the French Revolution from my first book, which appeared in 1977, which was about Holland in the period of the French Revolution. Originally it was meant to be a book about the military imperialism of the French Revolution, but I turned the priorities upside down, and it became a book about Holland, about the collapse of the Dutch Republic in the late 1700s. When I came to do this book on the French Revolution proper, I had old dusty, smelly files, thousands of pages of notes.

COSTA: *Will historians of tomorrow go to video archives to do their research?*

SCHAMA: I suspect they will. They will certainly go to tapes and transcripts of interviews. I think all of the electronic means of communication will be not only a legitimate but an indispensable form of source for the future historian. In the period I usually deal with, people wrote letters. Napoleon alone wrote some 70,000 letters in his life. It's difficult to believe he did anything else except write letters. He wrote many of them in his own hand.

Today the overwhelming dominance of the telephone over letter writing has absolutely wiped out letter writing. We use phones to dispatch urgent business and that means that an enormous set of sources is completely lost. So future historians may have a very bizarre and artificial sense of how we conducted our business.

COSTA: *Other historians I have spoken to have said that what us laypeople think about history is mistaken: that historians are particularly equipped to give, with the passage of time, the* accurate view of the era. Could you comment on that?

SCHAMA: I rather agree with that. Again, I am terribly unpopular for saying so. I quoted Zhou Enlai saying in response to the impact of the French Revolution, 'It is too soon to tell.' But then I added in parentheses, 'Maybe it is too late.' Historians for a hundred years or more have exalted the virtues of distance, detachment, objectivity. I think the professional historian—with a capital P and a capital H, a phrase that you can tell I don't really much like—likes to think of himself as an Olympian figure sitting on top of an enormous mountain, his mind quite unclouded by prejudicial passion, able at this distance to really reconstruct the motives of past events, past politics, past societies, with much greater clarity than people closer to the time.

Historians are not people who walk around like vessels filled only with the transparent water of academic virtue. They, too, have their own prejudices. I too have my own. One has to be honest about them, put them on the table, and then say, 'I will try and grapple with reconstructing the human reality.'

What I try to do to the reader in this book is push his nose against the windowpane very hard. I try and use the voices of the revolutionaries, the feel, the sight, the sound, the smell of what is going on in an unashamedly dramatic way. I want to try and bring back the kind of human reality of the event as best as one possibly can 200 years later.

A conversation with

William Alfred

William Alfred is Abbott Lawrence Lowell Professor of the Humanities. Dedicated to his students, Alfred is a playwright and author whose keen sense of metaphor illuminates the nuance of everyday life.

COSTA: *In many societies one's ethnic and religious background is passed on by one's grandmother. As one who has written both fiction and nonfiction about immigrants, do you agree that grandmothers play this special role?*

ALFRED: She wasn't my grandmother, she was my great-grandmother, and she was probably born in the late '40s of the last century. She was the most vivid, imperial woman I ever met. She didn't have any teeth except one, and every once in while when it ached, she'd wistfully say, 'I'll give you ten cents if you knock my tooth out.'

She was amazing because she was a kind of walking library. I knew her until I was nine. She raised me until I was four and a half because my father and mother had to work, so they left me with her. She meant a great deal to me. She would sing old songs. They would bring her back to the 19th century. I can't remember the tunes because I have a very bad ear for music. You never could call her grandmother because she would rather be called by her name, Annamaria. She used to sing, 'Annamaria, Annamaria, Annamaria Jones, she could play the banjo, the piccolo, and the bones.' She was wonderful. She told a lot of family stories. . . . The lady who took care of her when she was dying was the one who told me the real version of *Hogan's Goat*.

16

COSTA: *I'm wondering whether a story I heard about your father, a brick-layer, is true or not. When you brought him to visit Harvard he said he was very impressed with the quality of bricks used in the buildings surrounding the Yard. There is something wonderfully ingenuous about that remark.*

ALFRED: Oh, yes. We went around looking, and he'd explain to me all the bonds. There are all kinds of bonds that bricklayers know about. He came from, I think he said, five generations of bricklayers. His father was English. He came from a town called Alfredston, which is named after their family I guess. His father was a leader of the guild of workmen, and my father was known all over New York as being able to make a chimney that would draw instantly. He was a wonderful bricklayer. One of the most delightful experiences I had was to go for a walk in London with him and [a companion] who loved Victorian buildings, and they compared notes as to the Flemish bond, tapestry bricks, and that kind of thing. It was really rather wonderful.

COSTA: *In preparing for this interview I asked a student, who took a course of yours last semester, if there were any typical William Alfred-type themes I should ask you about. The student said, 'Ask him about life lies and how they affect dramatic literature.' What are life lies?*

ALFRED: He probably got the idea from my lecturing on *The Iceman Cometh*. I'm particularly interested in the definition of the truth that is current nowadays. Nowadays the truth must in some way change the person. That wasn't always that way. And it must, in some way, hurt. In the past, people lived—I suppose it's science that did it—with all kinds of very bad ailments and they never knew they had them. When Walt Whitman died, they realized that he had had very bad tuberculosis as a young man and didn't know it. He got over it. The notion is that the damage of the past must be faced, and, in some cases, by a providential blessing people can forget the damage of the past.

In *King Lear*, which that student will tell you is my favorite play, there is the reconciliation with Cordelia. The reconciliation is a really hard one because the old man has to realize that this woman is just forgiving him without even forgiving him. She just goes back to the moment when she was thrown out of the house, and asks for his blessing as if nothing had happened in all the period between. But it's like a miracle. The old, proud, stiff-necked king kneels to her, and then as they leave, he says something that I think is very important. He says, forget and forgive, not forgive and forget. In order to forgive, you have to forget.

Most people nowadays live by the fashionable principle that they ought to keep going over the time they wanted a sailboat and papa didn't buy them one. There is too much to do in the present moment of life to waste your time and emotional energy that way. So I suppose that is what I mean by the life lie. We all tell lies to ourselves, and most of time we don't know what they are.

COSTA: *Someone said recently that we are what we forget and what we remember. Do you agree with that?*

ALFRED: Yes, I do agree with that. One of the greatest men I have known, and he was a great friend of mine, was Robert Lowell. He could not forget the past and he was what he could not forget. The poems ring with it.

COSTA: *I reread your play yesterday, Hogan's Goat. It deals, of course, with the smoke-filled-room machinations of Irish politicians in New York, circa 1890. Although much has changed in 100 years, much remains the same in politics. Do you think contemporary politicians are appropriate subjects for drama or are their lives—political and personal—played out too much on TV and on the front pages of newspapers? Are they too overexposed for drama?*

ALFRED: In an age where they will follow a man to a motel, it is very difficult for him to make a political deal much less a personal deal. It is very, very difficult. The other thing that troubles me about politics today is that our most distinguished people, for the most part, won't go into it. Harvard, in its early days, taught rhetoric in order to teach its students how to persuade people in what was considered the right path, so that very good and thoughtful people went into politics. But, for the most part, there is a kind of mediocrity in the whole political thing. I'm not saying that a person has to be an Einstein because, of course, certainly Mr. Roosevelt wasn't, but *there* is somebody who had a sense of duty, not only to the country but to the world.

COSTA: *Has the multimedia aspect of our society changed the dramatist's role? Ever since Aeschylus' time one could expect a real insight about one's society from reading a play of a fallen king, and now as you say, with people following politicians to motel rooms, all the drama may already have been vented.*

ALFRED: 'They have the press for wafer, the franchise for circumcision.' That was first said in the 19th century by a man who kept a journal in France. He said that the newspapers really were to literature what the photograph was to painting. It did something in a sense to make less significant a single moment, a moment when you could look at the face of somebody on the street, for instance, like that wonderful picture of the weeping man [taken] when France fell. It had a whole world of meaning in it. But you see so many pictures that you begin to get jaded and you ultimately don't notice. If you did notice all of the things that are thrust on you by the media it would be too much for you.

COSTA: *Sensory overload.*

ALFRED: Yes, that's right.

COSTA: *How is writing plays different from writing poetry? You do both. Or is the process of writing always the same and the only thing that changes is the form of the writing?*

ALFRED: I can't write fiction without writing it in some kind of a verse measure because I began as a poet. That's just a private tic of mine. One of the difficulties about writing in a verse measure that is too much like iambic pentameter is that nowadays actors tend to stress the beat, and when you stress the beat in a play, people listen to the beat and not to the action.

But the French, of course, call all writers for the theater 'poets' whether they write in prose or poetry. And there are two kinds of poetry in a verse play. The most important poetry is what the Greeks call . . . the poetry of the unfolding of the action. That's what I try to work hardest on. Then when I do the revisions I go back to tighten the dialogue, so that you get the highest level of discourse, which is what Frost called writing in sentences.

Frost's example of writing in sentences is in a letter to a man named Bartlett, in which he says you can write in words or you can write in sentences. When you write in words it's all right, but it's like drying laundry by tying the sleeves together. It's bad for the discourse, he said. . . .

For me, the poetry is in making everything ring with the present feeling of the character, and with a feeling that feeds itself into the burden of meaning of the entire play.

COSTA: *I read that you once told some of your students in your playwriting course that while the unfolding action is very important, it's not that important. The thing is to get inside the characters' heads.*

ALFRED: Oh, yes. Much more simply, what I always tell the playwriting class is that you must ask yourself this question from the outset, from the very first sentence in the play: 'Why does this person say this to that person?' and 'Why does that person answer this way?' That's how you get the ongoing motion of human will, human attraction. All of those things work if you just do that. I thought it was a discovery that Archie MacLeish made as a writer. He's the one who really took me in hand when I first began to write verse plays when he was teaching a drama course. He would point to something and say, 'That's a wooden nickel,' meaning, 'Yes, it's pretty, but it has nothing to do with the ongoing action.'

One of the difficulties I have is that I hear an endless music in the streets. The way people talk absolutely fascinates me and I'm trying to find a cadence to capture it in the play that didn't work—and you always go back to the play that didn't work—*The Curse of an Aching Heart*. What I wanted to do was to write a tribute to the poor of New York City. The nearest to 'the Shakespeare of America' is Eugene O'Neill, who said in a wonderfully modest way, 'I wish I didn't write so punk.' He didn't write punk. I think of the cadence in *The Iceman Cometh:* . . . [It] is all New York in one sentence. [In one scene] a man comes in with his girl and points to her and he says, 'Cora wants a sherry flip. It's for her noives.' [The dialogue] also home in on the strain of living in New York. But my difficulty is that the audience members who live in New York and who would understand what I'm trying to do haven't the money to go to the theaters. They are the working-class people.

19

COSTA: *Much of your writing is enlivened by simile and metaphor. Critics love your plays for their wonderful use of language. How did you come by that gift? Is it a lifelong appreciation for the endless music and images or is it something you got from your Irish background?*

ALFRED: Yes, my mother, my father, and my great-grandmother. I remember as a very little boy, my cousin and I tittering in a back room in this brownstone house that my great-grandmother lived in. After her lunch she used to go. in there to lie down. We would throw pillows at her and, of course, we didn't hit her. But she straightened herself up to her full four-foot-eight inches and said to us, 'Go now and break the church windows. Your hands will stick up in the grave.' Now that is what you call strong diction.

When Lindbergh crossed the Atlantic and I saw the picture of the Spirit of St. Louis on the front of the plane with the hand with the sword coming up I thought that Lindbergh had thrown a pillow at his great-grandmother. It was very funny.

The old New York dialect was [wonderful] because what was feeding into it was this cross-fertilization of Italian, German, and Yiddish proverbs and wisdom. It was full of metaphors. 'I need him like a *loch in kop*' is the Yiddish expression. 'I needed him like a hole in the head.' It's absolutely wonderful.

COSTA: *You've had six heart attacks. Could you talk about your meeting with the honors thesis student?*

ALFRED: He was reading a very wonderful thesis. It was on Gertrude Stein. I was in Kirkland House in my rooms there and I had this terrible sharp pain and I fainted. I came out of the faint and he was still reading, and I said, 'Would you come back later? I don't feel very well.' It was a minor heart attack but I didn't even know it was a heart attack. I thought I had a stomachache or something like that. But my first was when I was 16, when I got that awful flu that used to kill people, and that was before penicillin. I got out of bed too soon and had a heart attack. But I've been very lucky. Now the heart's pretty good.

COSTA: *Another thing that a lot of people don't remember about you is that you were in the tank corps in World War II. What was that like?*

ALFRED: I suppose I was probably the most inefficient member of the tank corps. I was first in the 747th and in the 749th medium-tank battalion. And then they transferred me to a headquarters company because they couldn't teach me how to drive. Having been raised in New York City and having been raised poor, my father had the car. Nobody else had the car, so I never knew how to drive. Of course, tanks look enormous and absolutely indestructible, but they are as sensitive as day-old kittens. You do the wrong thing with them and they just give up. It's a wonder to me that [tanks] ever won any kind of a victory, they're just awful. So finally what they did was to make me a code clerk.

COSTA: *Another thing that you'll always be known for is the discovery and promotion of Faye Dunaway's career.*

ALFRED: She was working in Lincoln Center and doing very well indeed; she also was the daughter in *A Man for All Seasons*. What happened was we couldn't get a lead for *Hogan* no matter where we looked. Nobody seemed right. It was the day before the 13th of September 1964, which was a Monday—that's my mother's birthday, that's why I remember it. It was the first day of rehearsals . . . in the afternoon, late, and we heard these heels coming up the stairs—click, click, click, click—and the three of us turned around and this incredibly beautiful creature came in. All you could see were the eyes. We looked at her and looked at each other. You could hear the eyeballs clicking and I wanted to say to the producer, 'I don't care if she's got a harelip, let's take her.' And then she read and she read beautifully, and of course she made the play. I didn't make her, she made the play. She's a wonderful actress.

COSTA: *At this time in one's life, traditionally, people become retrospective. Have you been able to do all you wanted to do or is there something you still yearn to do?*

ALFRED: No. I have never regretted one minute of teaching. But teaching is very time consuming, and I have a play that I have been working on for 18 years; every time I start it something else comes up. I will, with the help of God, be able to finish it, the revision—it's all done except for the revision—this summer. Then I have a kind of a dream: to write a poem from [a number of viewpoints] about Christ. I remember that as a kid of 18 I wrote to Gertrude Stein and said that I wanted to write a poem about the life of Christ from 14 viewpoints because the New Testament in St. Matthew says there are 14 generations and that kind of a thing. She wrote back, 'You apparently are interested in pointed numbers. I'm interested in square numbers and round numbers.' I just want to [write about] the moment on Saturday morning after the crucifixion with all of the people [who were] involved telling what they remember. I have to find a beat to do it in. I don't write poetry, I write verse. Seamus Heaney writes poetry, I write verse. His lines are unforgettable, and mine are just functional.

COSTA: *Can you sum up briefly the thing that you have been devoting your life to and that is to telling young students what they should do about their own writing. What advice do you give them?*

ALFRED: To write every day for two hours, even with four courses, if they possibly can. It's the best advice anybody can give. When you teach a writing course you don't teach it, they teach it to each other. You create a community of people who are really interested in finding what it is that engages their main interests in the life they are living and finding a language that will convey that engagement to other people.

I've been very lucky. Over the years it's been a joy to teach the playwriting course because it's wonderful to watch them realize the first flow of their talent and to gain confidence. So I would tell them to write every day and to believe in what you write. Believe that you are a writer. One of the most difficult things to do in a commercial society is to think of yourself as somebody whose main business is to tell the truth as he or she sees it to the people around him, and to tell it with anger or love.

A *conversation with*

Derek Bok

As the 25th President of Harvard (1971-91), a graduate, and past dean of Harvard Law School, Derek Bok's social, political, and ethical initiatives reflect an abiding concern for greater internationalization of education. He is widely respected as a national spokesman for higher education.

COSTA: *You have written in your book,* Universities and the Future of America *(Duke University Press, 1990), that America is now the nation of choice for foreigners everywhere who are fortunate enough to be able to study abroad. One-third of all such students are currently enrolled in this country. By almost any measure, higher education in the United States has no peer. It has a lead over Europe and Japan and it hasn't diminished; in fact, it has increased over the last twenty-five years. Yet even with our unequaled university system we are not the most advanced industrial nation in a lot of respects. How do you reconcile this discrepancy?*

BOK: I think there are two reasons. The most important one, of course, is that it takes a lot more than universities to put a nation at the top by whatever measure—the productivity or gross national product or the ability to solve important social problems.

The second reason is one that we in universities should pay attention to. If you look at the contributions that universities can make that will matter most in helping us address our most important problems in America, these are often not matters that get a very high priority in universities. So there's no question that we could do more than we're doing. I think that we, along with other institutions in America, need to take stock of what our potential contributions are and ask ourselves whether we are doing everything that we can. This book is intended to try to take that inventory for universities and to consider how we can improve our performance.

COSTA: *You've been a proponent of internationalizing the university to make it more available to international students. The population of foreign students has risen at Harvard. Why is that such a critical mission of yours?*

BOK: Because my sense of where the country is going is that it's going to be more and more involved in other countries. More and more business will be conducted with other nations, more and more problems, like global warming and the [deterioration of the] ozone layer, are going to be problems that nations have to collaborate in order to resolve. More raw materials will be acquired in the United States from other countries, so we have to learn to work more effectively together. I think that the university can be a very good preparation for a much more global existence.

COSTA: *There are some criticisms these days of some of the larger research universities in which professors spend a lot of time doing research. Some critics say the faculty should spend more time teaching. Is this commonly held opinion true, and also what is the role of research at a university that values teaching as highly as Harvard does?*

BOK: We live in a world and a society in which new discoveries and expert knowledge are increasingly important in order to make progress and to solve the most important problems before the country. So research is terribly important and it's recognized by the society as terribly important. That's why billions of dollars are contributed to university research by the federal government out of taxpayers' dollars all the time. The problem is to maintain a healthy balance with teaching because, clearly, educated people are also more and more important to the nation and we need to work hard at giving them the best preparation we can. So our problem here, or at an institution like Harvard, is to try to maintain a healthy balance, to make sure that the tremendous incentives for research that are backed up by money and Nobel Prizes are balanced by internal incentives that reward good teaching and make professors want to spend an appropriate portion of their time worrying about the students and the quality of their instruction.

COSTA: *Tuition costs are very high. Why does it cost so much to attend Harvard?*

BOK: I think good education is inherently expensive, and particularly in the United States where education isn't something you simply get in classes. When you go to college, you have a total experience involving all sorts of opportunities; curricular and extracurricular, cultural, athletic, artistic, as well as formal classroom learning. One important thing to remember is that the tuition, high as it may seem, nonetheless only covers about two-thirds of the actual expense of educating students at Harvard University.

The second thing to remember is if you really break it down it may not be quite so awesome as you might think. Think of it this way: to go to Harvard University amounts to paying a little less than $90 a day. For that you get something that perhaps does not compare with the Ritz-Carlton Hotel but does give you reasonably nice accommodations; you get three meals a day thrown in, you have athletic facilities, you have concert halls, you have stages for your play productions, you have an enormous library, and thrown in as an added bonus, you have a wonderful faculty and an enormous array of courses to take. When you put it that way, I think you're getting quite a good value for your money, especially if you compare it to some other prices in the economy.

COSTA: *There's some confusion about the role of the endowment. Most people think that an endowment is like a savings account, that if you need money in your checking account, you merely go to your savings account and transfer the funds. I wonder if you could speak to the fact that you are charged with the stewardship of that endowment and you must protect it for the future.*

BOK: We have to take the long view at Harvard. We've existed for over 350 years, and we plan on existing for at least another 350. So as we look at the endowment, what we have to do is to balance the needs of the president against the needs of the future. We should not save so much from the endowment that we have more than we should in the future, but we should not spend so much and decide to do everything today that we find we are going to starve future generations. There's already a lot of activity in the United States that seems to me is benefiting the present generation by loading some pretty horrendous debts onto the future. We don't want to add to that at Harvard. So what we have tried to do, over the last 20 years in which I've been in office, is to make sure that the endowment contributes the same portion of our expenses in the future as it did today. I can look back now and say that 20 years ago the Harvard endowment contributed about 20 percent of the operating budget of Harvard. Today it contributes just a shade less than that, so I think that's the perspective we have to look at it with. I think future generations will thank us if we go about our task of using the endowment with that kind of prudence.

COSTA: *Let's talk about ethics and moral education, which is a large portion of your new book. You write that you agree with 5th-century Athens and Socrates on this matter. Socrates believed that one teaches the young to do the proper thing by providing the young with ways to think about moral dilemmas. That way, if the moral scene shifts they can apply these principles in the future. But you also say that's not enough these days. I wonder if you could tell us what is necessary to augment the early thinking of Socrates about moral dilemmas?*

Bok: There are really two aspects to moral development. One is the ability to perceive moral issues and think carefully about them. That is clearly a responsibility of universities and one that we should work at harder. The second part, of course, is to develop the character to put the decisions or the views about what is right into practice in your own life. That's much harder and certainly universities cannot hope to do that job unaided. Perhaps they can't even hope to make a very big contribution. But every contribution helps, even if it's small in nature. So we have to think not only how to teach our students about ethical issues, but how to provide an environment that encourages them to take moral issues seriously and to try to put them into practice in their own lives. And that in particular means working at certain fundamental moral issues such as telling the truth, keeping one's word, or respecting the interests of others; things that all of us in every civilized society agrees with. But trying to reinforce those through all the little messages and actions by which people interpret what an institution really stands for and what's really important, it's a very difficult job, but a very important one as we read in the papers every day that all institutions including universities will work at it in everything they do.

Costa: *You've helped institute ethics programs in the professional schools. Tell us why you think that's important these days.*

Bok: I think that anybody who looks at the financial pages or reads about what's happening in law firms or about the dilemmas in medical practice today recognizes that professional people in all professions are faced with more and more complicated ethical dilemmas and that the inability to live up to them costs society and human beings very gravely. So we think there's a very important educational mission: to teach students in our medical, law, business, and other professional schools how to recognize the rather subtle moral dilemmas that exist in their professional lives and how to think about them productively. And then, as I say, to try to provide an environment that reinforces that and makes them regard these as serious issues that they should work at in their own lives.

Costa: *We have rules and guidelines in all of our faculties about conflict of interest. For example, faculty members should only use one-fifth of their time for outside interests, that they have to disclose any financial arrangements they might have with companies. Another example, if they are in the medical profession and they are developing drugs they have to let their deans know about their financial interests in the companies who will develop and market those drugs. Do you see these guidelines as something that is helping keep our faculties honest and doing the right thing?*

Bok: I think it's very important because faculty members, as experts in fields that are important to the public, are increasingly in demand to advise companies, to advise the government, and to work on a whole host of issues. It's very important to a society that they make their expertise available. But, of course, that does lead to lots of complications. It causes some professors to spend more time perhaps working at these relationships than they should in light of their primary obligations to the university. It causes others to get into financial situations that could cause a conflict of interest and undermine the reputation of the integrity of the faculty and, hence, the university. So we have to work at it.

The point I want to emphasize, however, is that we are trying to strike a balance. Outside activities by professors aren't something sort of unpleasant or illicit that they engage in to get rich. For the most part, they are very important activities that are terribly important in helping knowledge move from the university into government offices, industrial laboratories, and other places where they are needed for human welfare. What we simply have to do is to strike those wise limits and appropriate boundaries that are necessary to make sure that all this does not damage the central role of the university in promoting knowledge and good instruction.

COSTA: *We have public service programs here and, as you write in your book, 60 percent of our undergraduates perform some public service. What can other universities do to get students to devote some of their time to public service?*

BOK: First of all, there are some disturbing trends out there. We have checked what values matter most to college freshmen across the country for 25 years and there's no doubt that the values that are rising fastest are the desire to make money, to achieve fame, and to acquire power over others. The ones that seem to be lagging are the interest in helping the community, overcoming racism and violence, and other problems important to the society. So we need to counteract that by encouraging public service. Fortunately, our experience is that there's a tremendous appetite for that among students. We doubled the proportion of students involved in community service, got it up to the 60 percent level, simply by providing seed money for new programs, and providing better advice and counsel in getting those programs started. The students did the rest with their enthusiasm. I think that almost any campus can do the same thing and *should* do the same thing because it's by exposing young people at a formative period in their lives to the problems of society and showing them how they can make a difference that will carry over later in life to all kinds of civic activity that's absolutely indispensable if the nation is going to prosper.

COSTA: *Some critics think that tenure should be abolished. Why do you think it's so vital to the proper functioning of the university to have tenure? Secondly, what guides you in making a tenure decision?*

BOK: The second question I can answer quickly. What we try to do is to look over the whole world. When we make a tenure decision we try to attract the best available teacher and scholar that we can find anywhere. I emphasize anywhere because maybe a third of our faculty in arts and sciences and in the College were born in and received a lot of their education abroad. When we make that appointment we do give them tenure and I know a lot of people question that. I happen to think it's very important and I think if we did away with tenure at Harvard we would make a great mistake. First of all, if we were endlessly reviewing people to see whether they should we be kicked out, that would consume an extraordinary amount of time that could better be spent in the classroom and in the laboratory.

The second thing, a subtler point that is often overlooked, is that tenure is such an important decision. It involves a commitment for a lifetime to a scholar. People in the academic community take it very seriously and are prepared to make much tougher choices than they like to do in other personnel decisions. So you don't just slide someone along or keep them going because maybe they're going to get better. You can't make that serious a commitment without making a very real effort to figure out whether the person you're giving tenure to is really the best possible person. I believe that if we didn't do that, if we didn't have that discipline, and if the choice wasn't that great, it was just a five-year appointment, we'd just sort of pass people along and say, 'Well, maybe they'll get better in five years,' and then beyond a certain point, we'd begin to say 'Well, my goodness, if we weren't going to keep him or her on, we should have gotten rid of them years ago and so we have to keep them on until they retire.' So we'd end up with less qualified rather than more qualified faculty members. So I think in sheer quality terms, as well as to preserve the morale and the collegiality, and to keep people thinking about how to do their best work and not worrying about whether their peers and colleagues are going to judge them badly and kick them out, I think tenure serves us well at Harvard.

COSTA: *You've also been a proponent of improving teaching methods and have done things to help young teachers become better teachers. I wonder if you could tell us about those programs?*

BOK: I think one has to continuously struggle in a research university to make sure that the teaching function gets all the support that it can. We also ought to be continuously trying to find ways of helping people become better teachers and to do the kind of research that will enable us to know what kinds of teaching strategies are the most effective in helping students to learn. So we've developed the capacity to do all those things and to train increasing numbers of our young instructors or graduate student teaching fellows in how to be more effective instructors.

One of the great aids is videotaping. So we now have hundreds of young teachers at Harvard every year going through a process in which they learn about good teaching, they learn what questions to ask themselves about how to teach better, and they also see themselves in the act of teaching.

COSTA: *At the end of the next academic year, in July 1991, you will have served as the president of Harvard for 20 years—quite a hallmark. What has been your most startling realization in those 20 years?*

BOK: At the risk of seeming undramatic I would say that I spent quite a number of years at Harvard before I became president and so there were fewer surprises perhaps than there would have been if I had come in from the outside. I think one of the greatest surprises is really what a pleasant job it is. There are so many bad jokes about academic politics and all the difficult things that are said to go on. I don't know any place where you could work with such good people and people so interested in doing good in the world as you can in a university like this one. So I would say that the job in many ways proved surprisingly pleasant. Part of that is also because I came in at a time of tremendous student turmoil. There was massive distrust by the students toward the faculty and the faculty toward the students. The only thing that they agreed on was that the central administration was rotten. Since then, fortunately, due in large part to changing moods in the country, attitudes have gotten better and better and it's become an easier environment in which to work.

The other thing that is always a surprise, of course, if you're impatient and you want the best, is the relatively slow rate at which change is made in academic life. One of the joys of having been here 20 years is that over that long a period you can see that the glacier actually has moved a substantial distance. But it is always a bit of a shock to come into these jobs full of things you know ought to be done and to recognize that many of them take years of continuous work in order to bring them about. So there is a pleasant and a slightly sobering surprise, but the net is clear in my case: it's been a wonderful experience.

COSTA: *There must be enormous personal pressure on the president of Harvard. You can't, for example, make a grammatical mistake when you're speaking or standing in a shopping line. You always have to be 'on.' Did you find that to be true?*

BOK: During the first two or three years in office, I've never forgotten the genuine pain I felt on reading an article in the *Boston Globe* in which someone had remarked disparagingly that I didn't know enough not to wear ankle-length socks. The thought that anybody even noticed was rather devastating and the fact that, on the whole, it was probably better not to wear ankle-length socks only rubbed salt in the wound. Since then I've become somewhat more accepting of that and less concerned about it, so I do what I do. I try not to think that I'm on display and not to get too self-conscious about being president of a university, and life has gotten much pleasanter.

COSTA: *What advice would you give a starting president?*

BOK: First of all, don't allow yourself to get drawn so much into the external aspects of the job that you forget that the most important part of the university, really, is the teaching and the learning that goes on inside. Be patient because decisions do take a long time to be implemented. Talk to a great number of people and listen to gossip. By nosing around the university and taking every opportunity to talk to people you can learn a lot of things that can alter your agenda and give you insights on whether the institution is ready for certain kinds of change that you want to bring about. You can also learn about people who may be unexpected allies in helping you bring those reforms to realization.

The last advice I would give is not unique to universities but is common to administrations in any setting; it's often ignored. People who leave the most lasting impact and have the greatest effect are those who have a marked ability to focus and to choose a very few things at any one moment to concentrate on. Try to avoid being distracted in a thousand and one activities that could occupy your time. Keep your attention on those very few priorities until you've got them well on the way to a solution and then add other priorities by choosing them very carefully and sometimes even ruthlessly. Over time, you'll get a lot more done than if you try to do everything at the same time.

COSTA: *Going back to your Stanford basketball days, I hear rumors these days that not only are you beating everyone at tennis but you can still hit from the top of the key with your jump shot.*

BOK: No, the last game of competitive basketball I played was on my fiftieth birthday when I was privileged to lead my administration against the Harvard women's basketball team. It was one of those marvelous days where even though you haven't played for months, everything I threw went in. And anybody who knows me, knows that I shoot much more than I should. In the fourth quarter, I remember driving across the key, throwing up a left-hand hook shot and it went in without touching the rim. I walked off the court saying to myself, 'It will never get better than this,' and I've never looked back.

A *conversation with*

Sara Lawrence Lightfoot

Sara Lawrence Lightfoot is professor of education and a MacArthur Prize-winning sociologist. Her book, Balm in Gilead: Journey of a Healer *(Addison Wesley), has won numerous prizes and is part of the Radcliffe Biography Series.*

COSTA: *To set the context for our conversation, I wonder if you could give us a brief biography of your mother. Later on, we'll try to get into issues of what it means to be a Black woman struggling in a racist society 50 years ago. Tell me something about your mother's origins.*

LIGHTFOOT: Margaret Morgan Lawrence was born in 1914. She was born in New York. Her mother had gone from Vicksburg, Mississippi, where she had been living at the time, to New York because it was a safer place to have a Black child. Hospital care was better for Black folks in New York than it would have been in Vicksburg. After a couple of months of being in New York City, she returned to Vicksburg, and my mother grew up there until she was about 14. She was the daughter of a Black Episcopalian priest—a dark-skinned Black man—and a schoolteacher, who is very important in the story—a light skinned woman who looked 'like white.'

She was the only child but she followed another child who was called 'Candy Man.' He was the first-born son who was golden-haired and light-skinned, the prized child who died after he was about 11 months. He died before Margaret was born, but his presence was critical in the family because

31

he continued to be a very revered, very respected, and very admired person even though he was dead. His picture followed the family around every place they went.

My mother went to the school that was connected to the church that her father was a pastor of, which was one of the three Black schools in Vicksburg—one was a parochial Catholic school and the other was a public school—and went there for the first several years of her schooling and then moved to Magnolia High School.

She was always precocious. She began reading when she was 3 and finished high school—the black high school—in Mississippi by the time she was 14. But she knew that in finishing high school that she was not educated. If she wanted to become a physician—which had been her goal since she was about 9 years old—she'd have to become better educated.

So she decided on her own to move to a fashionable section of Harlem, to live with her grandmother and aunt. [The women] had, by then migrated from Richmond, Va., to New York.

[My mother] went to school at one of the two classical city high schools, Wadleigh High School, the other being Hunter. She passed the [entrance] examinations and went to Wadleigh, which by then was pretty integrated. Perhaps a third of the students were Black. She was quickly seen there as one of the prize students. She was tutored by the dean in Greek and Latin and graduated two years later with the Greek and Latin prizes.

The dean had suggested that she apply to three schools: Hunter, because it would be free in New York; Cornell, because it was a school with a fine reputation, and Smith, because she really thought Margaret should go to a girls' school and not be distracted by the presence of boys. Happily, from Margaret's point of view, she was admitted to Cornell on scholarship, and she went there.

When she arrived, she was the only Black undergraduate at Cornell. This was 1932, and she was not permitted to live in the dormitories. She didn't have enough money to live in the dormitories anyway. I think she arrived on the train in Ithaca with $11 in her pocket and by the time she took the taxicab from the train station up the hilly terrain to Ithaca, she had just a couple of dollars left.

So she was not allowed to live in the dormitories and had to take a job as a maid in the household of a professor. She really lived very much the life of a maid in one part of her life. She slept in a cold, empty attic, she made all the meals, she did all the laundry, she served all the meals, and she ate in the kitchen. But at the same time, she took a full load and graduated from Cornell doing premedical work in four years.

She left Cornell and went to Columbia University Medical School where she did her training. She went from there to do an internship in pediatrics at Harlem Hospital which was one of the teaching institutions connected to Columbia. She went from there to do a masters in public health in epidemiology at Columbia School of Public Health where she had an extraordinary encounter with Doctor Spock and where she was inspired in the direction of combining pediatrics and psychiatry. She taught for a while at Meharry Medical College in Nashville, Tenn., which is an all-Black school and continues to be a predominantly Black school, and returned North, by then, with her husband and three children to do a residency in psychiatry and to train in psychoanalysis. In brief, that is a description of her life.

COSTA: *You've written an entire book, a fascinating book, entitled* Balm in Gilead: Journey of a Healer, *in which you explore every aspect of the moves and the changes in your mother's life. One's parents, some people say, are the strongest forces in the formation of a child's personality. What aspects of personality does your mother display that are like her mother's and which are like her father's?*

LIGHTFOOT: I think it's particularly true when you have an only child, because there is this powerful triangle. Her father was an outgoing, expressive, relational person, who always said the famous line, 'I like that man, he thinks the world of me.' It was always that dynamic: if he was thought well of, he liked that person.

And he reached out to people. As a minister he was ecumenical and he went far and wide to make relationships and to go about his spiritual healing. Clearly from her father, my mother took the kind of responsible role of reaching out to people. And the notion of healing comes from her father. I think she would have been a minister and followed in his tracks if the Episcopal ministry had allowed women. In some sense, being a physician was a second choice because she could manage to become a doctor, even though she was a woman.

So I think the healing tradition comes very much from her father, the reaching out comes from her father, and the relationship issue, the wanting to be in reference to other people and to be responsive and empathetic to other people comes from her father, and to deal with pain and trauma comes from her father.

From her mother comes a very private and restrained side, comes this feeling of wanting to work in very concrete ways—as my mother says, 'with her hands.' My mother's mother was a teacher and was committed to teaching in a very important and dynamic way. But she didn't necessarily like to talk very much about it. She loved the doing of it and the great satisfaction that comes from knowing that you have participated so fully and completely in a person's life. And I think that the concrete aspect of doing work, and the reticence about speaking about it in . . . analytic and abstract terms comes from her mother.

COSTA: *In your book you go into much detail about light skin versus dark skin among blacks and how 50 or 60 years ago lighter skinned blacks enjoyed greater freedom in society and greater respect, even among fellow Blacks. I wonder if you could explain this whole ethos of graduations of skin color and societal pull.*

LIGHTFOOT: I think this is something that is known to the Black community very deeply. But I think, certainly in Afro-American biography, and even in Afro-American social history, this has not been talked about very openly and very honestly. And I think it took some courage for me to raise this as an issue in the life of my mother. It was particularly an issue in the life of my mother, even beyond what the Black community was feeling at that time, because of what her parents represented.

My grandmother, my mother's mother, was a very fair-skinned woman and looked white to most white people. And her father was a very dark brown-skinned man. My mother was a sort of a medium brown-skinned person, who was identified with her father. So in some sense, color was a defining factor in terms of whom she was identified with in her family.

But beyond the contours of the family, was this powerful dimension in Negro society, in Vicksburg, Mississippi, at that time, that has its echoes even in life today. And that is that the more prized people were those with lighter skin and straight hair. That was a very divisive quality of Black life in many Negro communities at that time. A person's status, and often a person's competence was measured in those kinds of ways.

I think that it's not surprising that that's true, because obviously, it is a kind of mimicking of white standards, that is, that those people who looked more white were prized more greatly. So it isn't surprising, but it has been a very damaging aspect of Black life for a very long time. Luckily, much of that is diminished today. These kinds of categories of blacks are not as clear and not as divisive as they were at that time.

COSTA: *You also mention other physical characteristics, one being that your mom had what was called, 'good hair.' What is the importance of that?*

LIGHTFOOT: That's also a derivative of white standards of beauty, for sure. That is that those Negroes—and I'm using 'Negroes' on purpose here because at that time that is what we called ourselves, 50 or 60 years ago—those Negroes who had long, straight, hair like white people were thought to have 'good hair.' And those Negroes who had kinky or nappy hair were thought to have 'bad hair.' That was very much a judgment of one's beauty in the community. It depended upon one's mimicry of white standards. Again, I think there has been amazing progress on that front, but there are still derivative echoes, even today.

COSTA: *Did your mother ever come to completely renounce all of that and say 'I feel terribly oppressed by that kind of false standard of competency'?*

LIGHTFOOT: I wouldn't say that she felt oppressed, but she surely renounced it. In raising her three children she was determined that they shouldn't have any of these feelings related to measuring people, judging them on these physical characteristics. So we were not allowed in our house to talk about 'good hair' or 'bad hair.'

COSTA: *Your mom's life is filled with, what we today would call, outrageous acts of racism that affected her career and her personal life. I'm thinking of the 'well meaning' person at Cornell who told your mom that Black students could live in a nearby house of ill-repute. [This person] didn't know that it was a house of ill-repute, but your mother went there and looked in the window and made that determination. That was a truly outrageous example of racism.*

LIGHTFOOT: Racism is often malignant behavior and innocence combined, so that when this dean—who was the dean of the students at the time—told her that most Black graduate students lived down the hill in this house—and she told [my mother] where the house was—that was an expression of extraordinary innocence. Obviously [the dean] had never gone down there, but the fact that she had never inquired and never chose to look into it meant that it was, it seems to me, a profoundly racist act.

COSTA: *You also mentioned that your mother worked her way through college as a maid, a domestic servant. That must have been particularly poignant for someone who would soon become a physician/psychoanalyst.*

LIGHTFOOT: Yes, I think it was, although she had such a strong determination to become a physician that it's amazing what she was willing to go through. . . . She doesn't look back upon that as a terrible, traumatic time. She looks upon it as the kind of steps she needed to take in order to earn a living, in order to go to school so that she could become a doctor. And she didn't feel it as a personal assault to her dignity, obviously.

Throughout our two years of conversation that went into this book, she kept saying, 'I had a very firm feeling about myself from my parents. So that when someone from the deep South called me 'nigger' I interpreted that always as their problem. Something must be wrong with that person to have to call me nigger, because I'm a strong and good person. And there was that feeling of self-assurance, certainty, and confidence in herself that made her able to be in this relatively demeaned position as maid of a household—that wanted to make sure she felt like a maid—and still maintain her sense of self and her sense of dignity throughout.

COSTA: *There are so many messages in your book and subtle points for non-Black readers, for example, about the trips that your mother took to New York by train and about passing the Mason-Dixon Line. You say in your book that Blacks' spirits brightened when they reached Cairo, Illinois, because they could move up into better seating positions after traveling through the segregated South, little things like that sprinkled through your book.*

LIGHTFOOT: Right, I think what is so exciting about biography and narrative as a form, is that you get a sense of the whole cultural and historical moment through the details of life like that.

COSTA: *Your mom was also denied admission to medical school initially on the basis of race. You write in your book that the dean told her that, although she was extremely qualified to attend medical school, they had admitted a black student 25 years ago who died from tuberculosis, so they thought they wouldn't take a chance on another Black student. That's pretty incredible.*

LIGHTFOOT: Now, *that,* my mother's dignity could not withstand. She went in to speak to the Cornell Medical dean, after quite a superior record at Cornell in premedical work. All of her white counterparts who had done very well were being admitted to medical school and it was considered pretty normal that if you did well in premedical work you would go on to medical school.

She expected reward and applause and adulation from the dean when she went in. When he came out with this, she was in a state of extraordinary shock. She was speechless. She went into a mode that she now describes as 'depersonalization,' just a fog, not knowing where she was or even who she was for several days. This experience was so traumatic: finding out that she couldn't go on to medical school because of this terrible tragedy 25 years ago to some Black student, about an illness that he had obviously no control over.

There are traumas in my mother's life that she identifies as so deep and so profound and so painful that they caused her this sense of fog and not knowing who she was. That was one of them.

COSTA: *She had a similar experience when she was called in while she was completing her own psychoanalysis to become a psychoanalyst. She was asked in by someone to review her being certified as a psychoanalyst and she had a deja-vu-type experience. You might talk about that.*

LIGHTFOOT: She was called in at what she thought was the end of her psychoanalytic training. The dean of the Columbia Psychoanalytic [Clinic] said that the committee, in reviewing her progress, her written work, and her oral work, and her analysis, felt as if she needed to see one of the faculty members first before she concluded her analysis and before she concluded her training. He was very vague and refused to say why it was that she needed to see this person.

Margaret didn't want to see this person because he was known to be someone who had had very ambivalent feelings at best about Black people, who had done major research on Black folks, and who had thought of himself as a real researcher, a white researcher, who really had an understanding of the Black psyche that Blacks didn't have of themselves.

My mother thought that was very treacherous ground and very threatening and refused to speak to him even when the dean said you must speak with him to finish. They had a real conflict about it and finally he agreed that she should speak to her supervisor rather than to this man. It turned out that the dean had heard from this man that Margaret didn't want to work with Black patients. Because she had refused to work with him in his research, he interpreted that as her not wanting to work with Black patients. Of course, her whole career had been designed around one day preparing herself to be the best physician she could so that she could give fully and completely to the Black community. So this was an obscenity to her, this total distortion of her purpose in being there. Once again she experienced this extraordinary depersonalization.

The difference between the Cornell Medical School rejection and this psychoanalytic training was significant because she was able to speak up and to respond to the psychoanalyst. She was able to say, 'No I won't do that, I refuse to do that,' and to work out some sort of negotiated compromise. So she didn't lose voice, she wasn't silenced, she wasn't dumbstruck. She did fight back the second time.

COSTA: *You paint a picture of your mom as a particularly strong-willed person. You mention several times in the book her refusal to conform to what her family thought was appropriate dress. Can you tell us about that?*

LIGHTFOOT: Because she was a brown-skinned girl and because her mother had some negative feelings about that—at least that's what [my mother] experienced—her mother felt as if she should wear browns and greens and dark blues so that her brownness wouldn't show so clearly. My mother, who had a great love for color, wanted to wear yellows and oranges and magentas and reds, and had this conflict with her mother about what colors she might wear.

At one point she just begged and begged to buy an orange dress that was in a window in a Vicksburg store and finally, after begging and pleading, her mother gave in, but only because the dress was on sale. The dress was never taken from her closet, she was never allowed to wear it.

COSTA: *Another example of her spiritedness is the daily ritual she performed of walking 35 blocks, I think you wrote, from high school in Harlem rather than spend 10 cents for bus fare so she could save money for a violin.*

LIGHTFOOT: That was a case of her violin teacher saying that Margaret deserved—because she was getting better and better—to have a good violin. But in order to do that she had to save her money. So she walked that distance and she would join up with a friend and they would both walk. Now part of that was self-sacrifice. The other part was that she loved the chance to be alone, to ruminate, to make plans, to imagine, and to fantasize. Very much of Margaret's life was lived inside her mind.

COSTA: *That's a function of being an only child, isn't it?*

LIGHTFOOT: It's the function of being an only child, I think, but also, temperamentally, she was introspective. She was intuitive and there was a great fantasy life, a great imagining life there which translates beautifully into the life of a psychoanalyst. This mind is very playful, very figurative, very reflective, and interpretive.

I think partly it derives from temperament and partly from a family where she had no siblings to talk to and where she had parents who rarely wanted to talk to their child. Talk wasn't part of the nature of the relationship.

COSTA: *It's extremely difficult to write about someone in one's immediate family. How did you manage to keep your writing from being just an adoring valentine?*

LIGHTFOOT: [Laughs] For years, I have been doing work that requires that I try to pierce through the covers of things. For years, I've been doing research on school, on families, and on communities which requires a kind of inquiry that tries to get below the surface and understand the nature of the underneath, and recognizes always that there are vulnerabilities in goodness, there are always inadequacies and imperfections in goodness. In some sense [my work] seeks to uncover and, in a way, celebrate those imperfections . . . .

So that orientation of recognizing the good, recognizing the limitations of good, the imperfections of good, and vulnerabilities of good is very much a tradition of my work.

In talking to my mother, I very much tried to balance the roles of daughter and inquirer and storyteller, or narrator. If she said something that seemed pretty starry, it was very, very rare because she is a very reflective and self-critical person and recognizes the color and richness and dimensionality of pain and trauma and joy and triumph, all of those things that are integrated into a person's life. Part of what made it easy with my mother is that she . . . does not have trouble, at 74 years old, talking about the pain or talking about the negative feelings and she finds in the darkness luminosity in some way.

COSTA: *Could you see yourself in your mother's world and can she see herself in your world?*

LIGHTFOOT: I think she can most assuredly see herself in my world because she is very much a part of this world. She's still working, she's very vigorous, she's very adventuresome, she takes risks, and she continues to take journeys in her own life and in her own work. So she is very much a part of my world.

More difficult was seeing myself in her world. Part of the struggle of this inquiry was placing myself there, was getting enough sense of the context and the boundaries and the parameters to be able to see the world as she saw it. And she was good at describing the context, always from the interior, I mean. She is a very interior person, so this is a biography written from the inside out rather than from the outside in. But it was important for me to understand enough about the historical and social context so that I could interpret it as she did in those times.

A vivid example is, as she was talking about her life and growing up in Vicksburg, she would [mention many different] people. This was early on in our conversations and I would constantly ask, was that person white or was that person Black? Finally, she said, 'Listen, unless I say otherwise, these are all Black people. My life in Vicksburg was very different from the life you have, in that white folks were largely irrelevant. So unless I otherwise indicate, assume I'm talking about the Negro community in Vicksburg, Mississippi.'

Just that slight insight gave me a sense once again of the context within which she lived, very different from my own.

COSTA: *You outline your arrival at the campus at Swarthmore College and contrast that with your mother's arrival at Cornell. I wonder if you could tell us a little about the difference.*

LIGHTFOOT: My mother arrived at Cornell in 1932 all alone—all dressed up, and all alone. Far away from the family, more than a thousand miles from them on a train, and with very, very little money. No ritual, no ceremony, no easing her in, no support, no hugs, no kisses, no fond farewell.

I arrived with my parents at Swarthmore exactly 30 years later with both my parents there, both of my siblings there, with paraphernalia, with a record player, rugs, and with my paintings to hang on the wall, and with a very ritualized farewell. There was the President's Tea, walking around meeting other parents, and saying everything we had on our minds. It was so sad for me to be going and I was so pleased to be going. And then the farewell, which was tearful, and hugs and kisses and goodbyes, fully supported and fully understood by my parents about all of the tension and strain that went into the departure. It was just extraordinarily different. I recognized my sense of privilege and bounty and abundance in contrast to my mother's lonely arrival.

A *conversation with*

Sheldon Glashow

*Sheldon Glashow is the Higgins Professor of Physics and winner of
the Nobel Prize in 1979. He is the author of* The Charm of Physics
*(American Physics Institute) in which this interview is reprinted. His
aim is to demystify science and make science appealing to
high school students.*

COSTA: *Before we talk about physics, I'd like to talk to you about some of
the personal things you wrote about in your recent autobiographical book,*
Interactions. *In the book you discuss your transformation from a nerd—I
believe that is what you called yourself—at the Bronx Science High School in
New York to a Nobel Prize winner. Throughout the book you credit your dad,
who was a plumber and a craftsman, for instilling in you a lifelong curiosity
about how things work. How do you manage to keep the fires of curiosity
burning after all these years of scientific investigation?*

GLASHOW: That is a difficult question. You mention nerds. Of course, nerds
are an endangered species today, and I'm a great defender of them. I go hunting for nerds because they make promising graduate students eventually.

Now, how could I still be interested? The reason I really got into physics is
because I found it so much more interesting than anything else. I was not very
good at sports . . . so I picked on physics as something that was really a lot
of fun. And it still is. It's very exciting and certainly addictive.

GLASHOW: I think maybe I'm not as smart as I used to be, but I'm certainly at least as much interested in these questions. It's always the same questions. What is it all for? What is it all made of? How does it all work? They still fascinate me.

COSTA: *Did you look at, say, a radio when you were growing up, and want to take it apart?*

GLASHOW: Oh, yes. I took clocks apart, I took radios apart. I could never get them back together again. There would always be some parts left over that didn't fit and it wouldn't work. So that's why I'm not in experimental physics. I had the most marvelous electric train set, vintage 1930s, which I managed to take apart and never get back together again. My experimental life is full of tragedies.

COSTA: *So you kept taking things apart until you reached a subatomic level, so to speak.*

GLASHOW: So to speak, right.

COSTA: *In the book you explain a lot of the intricacies, to us laypeople, about subatomic particles, bosons, and quarks, but you also tantalize us with a story about your dad and how he survived falling into a vat of molten lead. Tell us more about that.*

GLASHOW: He came over from Russia in 1905 and he took all kinds of laboring jobs, construction jobs. At some point, he was building a house or putting the plumbing into a house. They used molten lead on the joints. He simply fell into the tank of lead. He explained to me how he was protected by a little layer of air, so he didn't get seriously burnt at all.

I was impressed by the physics and by the fortuitous accident in which nothing serious happened to my dad.

COSTA: *He also came through Ellis Island during the wave of immigration. What kind of transformation goes on there, that people come in with names that are theirs and come out with names that are not theirs?*

GLASHOW: Our name was Glukhovsky. That was my father's name when he was in Russia—in Czarist Russia, I should say. Neither the immigration person nor my father thought that that name would swing in America. So they had an amicable discussion and they sort of puzzled things out—in a totally friendly fashion, so my father said—and came up with this bizarre name, Glashow. He was the first of them. There are hundreds of them around today.

COSTA: *You also mention the driving force to succeed that often comes from being of immigrant parents. You have two brothers, one of whom is a doctor, and one who is a dentist, both very successful. What happened to you? No, seriously, did the expectations concerning what is success and what is not success in the new world affect you as a boy growing up, with the drive to succeed and to be good at school?*

GLASHOW: Yes, sure. My parents were very concerned that I did well in school, as I am with my own kids. But I don't think so much it was the parental influence as the ambiance in our middle-class, half-Jewish, half-Irish neighborhood in Manhattan. There was a strong desire to succeed, to pull out of this mean existence. It was as much my peers, the other children—who have been very successful, many of them doctors, dentists, lawyers, and scientists and such today—as it was my parents. The whole circumstance was one that emphasized learning.

Just as there is, today, a strong tendency not to stand out, not to accomplish anything, and to not be a nerd, at that time there was not so much the desire to be a nerd, but the desire to triumph in school.

COSTA: *Education was the vehicle for upward mobility.*

GLASHOW: Absolutely.

COSTA: *You've written that there is no intellectual pursuit more challenging than physics. What is it about physics that makes it so difficult?*

GLASHOW: No, no, no. It's not a difficult science. I think modern biology is much more difficult: you have to remember the names of all kinds of god-awful chemicals. You don't need that in physics. The thing about the kind of physics I do, which is fundamental physics, is that we don't know the rules. It's a contest, a game. It's a kind of gambling game where you put your money where your mouth is as to what you think is the way nature did it. Then, if you're lucky, you get proven to be right. There is no greater feeling than to win this bet with nature.

Once upon a time, me and my buddies figured out that there has to exist a fourth kind of quark. Ten years later it was found. That feels pretty good. It's the kind of feeling that I've had a few times in my life. It's a challenge, it's a game. It's like going to a magic show and figuring out how the tricks are done. It's like reading a detective story and trying to anticipate the ending. It's all of these things. It's a very human activity except focused on one simple question: how does it all work?

COSTA: *But to read that detective story, doesn't that presuppose that you have the language of some pretty advanced mathematics?*

GLASHOW: It presupposes the knowledge of not-so-advanced mathematics, but as you say, the sciences depend upon one another. I can't understand physics unless I understand mathematics; I can't understand chemistry unless I understand physics. This is a very important fact because, as you know, all Harvard is divided into three parts: its sociologists, its humanoids, and its scientists.

It's a nice place where we get to talk to these people in other disciplines, but we always have to talk on their turf because theirs are very horizontal disciplines where, in a sense, they have a shallow knowledge of a wide variety of things. But ours is a vertical discipline where everything depends upon everything else. They never know science. We know a little bit about literary criticism, or about history, or about ecology or about sociology. We're always compelled to discuss things or argue things or enjoy conversations on their turf, never on ours, because they lack these skills.

Two societies, an idea that was once introduced, is very true. Actually it's not very true. There is one society: there are the people who are literate and understand things, and then there are the rest who don't, and unfortunately, I must place two-thirds of Harvard in the category of the people who are missing the best part of human knowledge.

COSTA: *Perhaps now is a good time to mention your plea for better scientific literacy among students.*

GLASHOW: Oh, it's a mess. It's not just science, it's not just math, as you know, it's history, too. I would venture to say that less than half the population of this country knows the relative order of the American Revolution and the Russian Revolution in time. Very few people can identify Rome on a map of the world. It's everything.

It's worse in science. People are trying to do things to improve science education. I give some lectures in the summer. The National Science Teachers Association is very ambitiously going to attempt to unify all of science. Here is an example. At some point in school, a kid cuts open a heart, a cow's heart, and sees how it works. At the same time in chemistry class, he or she can be learning about hemoglobin and how oxygen is transported, and what oxidation and respiration are, and all that stuff.

In physics, at the same time, they will be learning about the discovery of air pressure, about pressures of fluid and blood pressure. Then the whole thing can fit into a unified meaningful whole, instead of this awful business we have of teaching bits and pieces here and there.

COSTA: *As you mention in your book, why are there so many talented mathematicians who were originally trained in physics, but comparatively fewer physicists who were mathematicians?*

GLASHOW: Generally the tendency toward abstract mathematics is irreversible. There are physicists who move into more abstract mathematics circles. Einstein is a good example. Heisenberg was another. They begin with down-to-earth questions. They do quite well at solving those problems and then move on to more abstract disciplines. It's very rare that it goes the other way, it's true. Although physicists often move in another direction, there has been a very large flow of physicists into biology, into hands-on biology. Wally Gilbert is an example and there are a dozen others, people who started as physicists and moved into hands-on biology. So we go either way.

COSTA: *Let's turn to the need for university professors to teach as well as do research. You teach a Core course here in physics for undergraduates. I want to tell you a short story that relates to teaching. I studied freshman physics with a friend of yours, Leon Lederman. I remember one of his lectures about the conservationist energy involving a 200-pound brass sphere that was suspended from a wire from the ceiling in the lecture hall. Leon walked to the side of the lecture hall and very slowly and carefully placed his back and the back of his head against the wall. Then he had an assistant move the sphere over to him. He grabbed the sphere between his hands and brought it right to the tip of his nose and very gently released the sphere and let it slip through his hands. The sphere, of course, swung across the room in a great arc to the far wall and swung back and stopped short, in what seemed just microns, in front of his nose. We all gasped and applauded madly. He was always doing things like that.*

GLASHOW: I often wondered where Leon got that funny looking nose . . .

COSTA: *Making physics fun for us.*

GLASHOW: That was a demo I saw in my class in Cornell in 1950, the exact same demo. I do it from time to time.

We also sometimes put a graduate student down on a bed of nails and smash a large cinder block over his chest. Once I hid a plastic container of ketchup on his chest. He would get up covered with 'blood.' I certainly do things like that. It's hard to get graduate students willing to sacrifice their shirts.

COSTA: *In order to reinvigorate oneself for teaching, you say it is important for a teacher to be a researcher to enliven the theory with practice.*

GLASHOW: I don't think there are clear boundaries between teaching, research, and learning. As we teach, we learn, and as we do research, we present that research in our teaching. As we see the responses of our students, we learn how better to do the research. It's all folded together, from the points of view of the students, researchers, and also the teachers. It's all one. That's what major American universities are all about. They mix these activities, and so they should remain.

COSTA: *In the Core course you teach, what would you like your students to walk away from that class with?*

GLASHOW: I would like them to be excited about, and to understand a little bit of, how it is that people have been able to understand to the extent they do, what matter is made of, what goes on in a brick as you get 10 times closer, as you blow it up in size by a factor of 10, then another factor of 10, then another and another and another; to understand exactly how it's put together.

And, conversely, if you imagine lots of bricks, the whole world, the solar system, the galaxy, the universe itself, to also reconcile the birth and evolution of the whole of the universe with the properties of matter on a very elementary scale.

At the moment that's what it is all about: the physics of the very large and the physics of the very small have come together. The snake is in the process of eating its tail, and it's very exciting to be around at this time. Everything is finally being put together.

COSTA: *Could you tell us, in terms that we might understand, something about what is going on in a subatomic level—what the weak force is, are there things smaller than quarks?*

GLASHOW: That is a lovely question. Every time I get asked this question I always, in the back of my mind, wonder 'Does this guy understand air pressure? Does he understand why Boyle's Law is true? Why there is a spring in the air?' Many times the answer is no, and if it's no, it's very hard to go further and explain what the weak force is, what the strong force is. But I'll try anyway.

Once upon a time around about the 1930s or so, we realized that all of the many different displays of force and motion that are absorbed in the world are reducible to just four which we call, briefly, the strong and the weak nuclear force, gravity, and electromagnetism. Actually gravity and electromagnetism are about all you need for most anything you might ever do.

Plumbing, my father's specialty, depended on gravity because water goes down, and it depended on electromagnetism because it explains how you wipe a joint and why copper is and what it is, and everything else about everything you might see, feel, smell, touch, or do. Ultimately you do need these other two forces, strong and weak nuclear forces. They have to do with the atomic nucleus, radioactivity, and all those other dirty words. But they're kind of important because if we didn't have a nucleus, we wouldn't have an atom, and we wouldn't have anything else.

So the strong and weak forces have to do with the atomic nucleus. What we who won the Nobel Prize some years ago (and a number of other people who didn't) did is to realize that two of these four forces are really different aspects, different avatars, of the same underlying equation or system, mainly the weak force and electromagnetism are really one.

So, in a sense, we've reduced the number—and only in a sense—of forces from four to three, suggesting a further reduction from three to two and of course some ultimate unified dream of Einstein, one. But we ain't there yet.

COSTA: *So much of the experimental and theoretical work in physics depends on giant Pharaonic-sized machines. Will these mega-machines help you in your work as a theoretician?*

GLASHOW: We depend on experimental information, and all these wonderful things we know about nature and the universe depend upon our telescopes, our X-ray observatories, our accelerators, and all sorts of other devices. So I am tremendously excited about the new accelerators that are about to come into operation in Europe this summer . . . I'm even more excited about the Waxahachie initiative, the Gippertron, Ronald Reagan's accelerator in Texas.

COSTA: *I didn't know it was the Gippertron.*

GLASHOW: [Laughs] It's the Gippertron, but not officially. It's officially the Ronald Reagan Center for Particle Physics. If it's funded. . . .

COSTA: *Some other scientists think that if we could take some of the billions that might go into that, and put it into something else . . .*

GLASHOW: Well, I don't see why they want to take my money. I would thoroughly agree that science in this country is underfunded and could deal with having its funding doubled. That's just about what we're asking for in particle physics. We can build the SSC [superconducting supercollider] with double the present budget for high-energy physics. As far as the other scientists go who are doing wonderful work, I think their budget should be doubled too. Absolutely. I agree with that. But I wouldn't say I want to build my machine by taking away their money and I doubt seriously whether they want to do their stuff by taking away our money.

COSTA: *Is it more difficult to persuade Congress to support this project because you're not going to get, say, Teflon out of it?*

GLASHOW: The Teflon was pretty good. That came from the atomic bomb project. Did you know that? In separating uranium, which was something necessary to do in order to get U235 to make bombs—which is what we wanted in those days—we did all kinds of experiments with heavy gases, uranium gases. The way you make a gas out of uranium is you combine it with fluorine. We did a lot of fluorine chemistry and one of the things that came out of the Manhattan Project was, in fact, Teflon.

. . . I'm sure that there's going to be all sorts of wonderful technology flowing out of building the SSC: superconducting energy storage, mass transit, tunnel development, all kinds of technologies at the cutting edge.

COSTA: *You talk a lot in your book about finally winning the Nobel Prize in physics. Something I seem to detect is that you were a little bitter about having to share it, unlike in Madame Curie's day when people got the prize solely. Now there seem to be two and three people, like Leon Lederman last year who shared the prize with those who worked with him at Columbia.*

GLASHOW: It's true the person who gets the whole prize gets three times more money than a person who doesn't and has to share it with a couple of other people. In fact, you can even get a quarter of the money.

But the money is not the issue with the Nobel Prize. It's just a queen for a day or a king for a day. It's really quite wonderful, a great honor. It's nice to be honored. But I'm very happy that I shared the prize with two good friends, Steven Weinberg and Abdus Salam who were, and remain, my very good friends.

COSTA: *How are the Europeans doing in theoretical physics compared to us?*

GLASHOW: It's hard to pin that down exactly in theoretical physics . . . Unfortunately, at the moment, the best experimental facilities are in Europe and that's very inspirational to the European physicists, so they do very well. The Italians do superbly, the French do very, very well in condensed matter physics. Everybody's doing well. The Russians are marvelous. It's not a competitive game. It's always been the most international sport of all: the pursuit of physics.

. . . It was, in the 17th century, very international, and so it is today. We treasure our international fellowship very much and we rarely try to say, 'This was done in America, this was done in Europe, this was done in Russia.' It was done by us, working together.

COSTA: *There are very few women in theoretical physics. Is there anything you can do about it?*

GLASHOW: That's changing. Yes, there's everything you can do about it. You just train more of them. The solution is to have women who are interested in physics learn some physics at an early enough stage.

There are lots of women . . . and they do very well. They go into theoretical physics and experimental physics, and they've been eminently successful. So it's changing. We don't have 50 percent women at Harvard, but we have 25 percent or 30 percent women in my field.

A *conversation with*

Joseph Nye

*Joseph Nye is Clarence Dillon Professor of International Affairs,
associate dean of the Faculty of Arts and Sciences, and director of the
Center for International Affairs. Nye has conducted research and taught
in Europe and the United Kingdom. As Deputy Undersecretary of State
during the Carter administration, Nye became a member of
the Trilateral Commission.*

COSTA: *In your new book,* Bound to Lead: The Changing Nature of American Power, *you examine the great debate about the 'decline' of America.
Some think the United States is losing the economic war with Japan, that the
U.S. is losing the education race with the entire Pacific Rim, that it's like
Ancient Rome, which overextended itself with far-flung conquests, that there
are signs of corruption at home, also similar to Rome. Are we really in
decline?*

NYE: I think decline is a misleading metaphor. The United States has lots of
problems: education, savings rates, and so forth. But 'decline' implies that
somehow there are larger forces beyond our control, and that is simply not the
case. If you look at the American share of world product today, it is the same
in 1990 as it was in 1975. After World War II, what happened is that we had
an artificial high, and we did lose our share of world product from about forty
percent of the total to about twenty-three percent of the total for the next
quarter-century. But, basically, then we hit a plateau, which is at about the
same level we were at before World War II. So to portray that as decline is
pretty misleading.

COSTA: *Many people have compared contemporary America to Victorian Britain, and you examine this in your book. You cite four major differences: the degree of dominance the U.S. enjoys, the U.S. is not as dependent on foreign trade as nineteenth-century Britain was, the U.S. has a single continental-scale economy, and the sense of empire is different because the U.S. has different levels of commitment overseas than Britain had. You talk about geopolitical challenges facing the U.S. that are different from those faced by Britain. Could you elaborate on these points?*

NYE: Yes. It's very popular to see the United States as taking Britain's place as the country that's overstretched and in decline. But in practice, our situation is really quite different. In 1914 the British were not the largest economy in the world and not the largest military power—they ranked third and fourth on those two measures. The United States ranks first on those two measures today. Perhaps equally important is the fact that in 1914, Britain was being hard pressed by the kaiser's Germany, which had already passed Britain in both military and economic strength. The United States has a military rival, which is really in decline, the Soviet Union; that's the country that is imperially overstretched. It has an economic rival—Japan—which has made enormous progress, but which is not a military power. Since power is relative, the situations of Britain in the early part of this century compared to its competitors, and the U.S. at the end of this century compared to its competitors, is vastly different.

COSTA: *Are economics and political power linked? Can you be politically powerful and weak economically? And can you be strong economically and weak in the geopolitical world?*

NYE: Over the centuries, different types of resources have produced power. Sometimes military power has been more important, and economic power is obviously important, but what produces it has changed with time. In the seventeenth century we would have looked at gold bullion for Spain, or in the eighteenth century we would have looked at population for France, in the nineteenth century industrial power for Britain.

What we find at the end of the twentieth century is that a science and technology base and its application to an information-based economy is really critical. And there, the United States is still well placed. If you look at scientific citations, the number of engineers, and the amount of money spent on research and development, the United States is still in a leading position. It is being obviously put under pressure by Japan, but the argument that the Americans are finished or not in a leading position in science and technology and in new information-based areas, computers, biotechnology, is simply not the case.

COSTA: *Are there some intangibles that make a nation powerful? For example, I'm thinking of America's cowboy-frontier essence: we take risks as a nation and always have; we are innovators in technology; we look for new ways to do things because of our capitalistic system. Do those intangibles help?*

NYE: Certainly the fact that we have an entrepreneurial spirit and flexibility in our social class system have been important sources of strength. I believe also that one has to look at the United States in terms of the type of society and culture it has. For example, people complain that the United States depends too much on foreigners for our engineering skills. But the other way to look at that is that any society which can absorb people so that a fifth of its engineers are foreign-born and [these people] find themselves at home in the country, has an openness which is a source of great residual strength. The danger I see is that people say the United States should close down and become more like Japan. In fact the openness and flexibility of our society is a great source of strength.

COSTA: *How important was the geography of America to our sense of power? We've been protected, and continue to be protected, by two great oceans. Isn't there a trend among some of the leaders that we should become a fortress America again?*

NYE: In a world of major military threats with a balance of power centered in Europe, the oceans were indeed a great source of security for us. But I think the point about the world today is that these traditional models of one country rising up to challenge another are probably inappropriate, that what we are seeing in the world today is much more a defusion of power as you have a growth in interdependence, which means that oceans don't necessarily protect you.

Many of the items on the agenda of international politics today—whether they be terrorism, drugs, or the spread of epidemics like AIDS—are things that are not susceptible to traditional power resources. . . . Military protection at the borders is much less relevant than being able to organize cooperation with other countries through international institutions or coordination of policies. The oceans, which were indeed a great source of strength for us in the past, are much less relevant for this new agenda of world politics.

COSTA: *You write that the end of the gold-exchange standard in 1971 was a hallmark indicating an end to American hegemony. Can you explain that?*

NYE: The United States was artificially preponderant for a quarter of a century after World War II—basically we had been strengthened by the war while everybody else had been weakened—and it was natural that we eventually would return to a somewhat more normal position and give back some of the marbles we had won, so to speak. You can see it in the statistics from 1945 to about 1970 or so, and there are two big events that, in policy terms, really reflect that. In the political area, the American withdrawal from Vietnam, where it *had* overextended itself politically, and in the economic area, the closing of the gold window and separating the dollar from gold were symbolic of the end of this quarter-century of American artificial preponderance. But it is interesting to note that even when the dollar was no longer redeemable in gold, other countries still chose to invest in the United States and to hold onto dollars, which indicates that their faith in the underlying nature of the U.S. economy was not disrupted or destroyed by this.

COSTA: *As an expert in disarmament, you have spent a lot of time trying to understand the defense of this country and its expenditures. Was Dwight Eisenhower right in his worry about the growth of the military-industrial complex or are military expenditures vital to a healthy economy?*

NYE: In the past, you could argue that military defense expenditures often had a beneficial spillover effect on the economy. I think that's less the case today. In many information-based technologies, it's the civilian area that's leading the military area.

It's worth noticing that in terms of Eisenhower's worry about the military-industrial complex that while pressure groups have always been strong in this area, as well as other aspects of American life, that the key question about the size of the defense budget depends on external events and the public mood. I think the trends are in the right direction, but we can thank Gorbachev rather than Eisenhower.

COSTA: *You have written in your book that in the 1990s we will continue to be a bipolar world in terms of military power because of the nuclear arsenals that the United States and the Soviet Union continue to hold. Could you expand on that thought?*

NYE: There are about 50,000 nuclear weapons in the world today—about forty-eight percent of them in the United States and about forty-eight percent in the Soviet Union. So in that sense—the structure of nuclear weaponry—the structure remains bipolar.

But it will tell you less and less about the rest of world politics because nuclear weaponry is proving to be a not very effective form of power. It's musclebound, it's almost impossible to bring to bear on your political objectives. So while we'll still likely have a bipolar structure of power in terms of the distribution of nuclear weapons, that will be much less relevant in the future in terms of telling you who is able to get the outcomes they want on particular political issues.

COSTA: *How much does the kind of military hardware and capability determine whether one will do adventuristic kinds of intervention in different countries? I'm thinking, for example, of early Britain and controlling the seas. When technology changed, that wasn't so important anymore. And I'm thinking about the muscleboundedness of both the paralyzed superpowers. How much does nuclear armament paralyze us to act in our own interests?*

NYE: I think we're going to have to invest much more heavily in other aspects of power. In the book I distinguish between what I call hard power resources and soft power resources. Hard power resources, the military sort or economic sort, will remain of importance, but there will be an increased weighting in the mix of power resources of what I would call soft power resources, which have to do with the openness of your society, the attractiveness of your culture, your ability to use international institutions. I think that that's an area where we have underinvested in the past, so what one would hope is that you will find some reallocation of resources from the military budget, as the international political climate improves in U.S.-Soviet relations, and a greater investment in areas like information, economic aid, help to developing countries, the building of international institutions, and so forth.

COSTA: *You say in your book that the major roles economically will still be played by the U.S., a revitalized Europe, and Japan. Economists say that the Soviet Union is an economic disaster, and it will spend the next decade trying to get food on its citizens' tables, and will not be able to dominate any other arena until it gets that done. Do you agree that the Soviet Union's role will be diminished as Europe, Japan, and the U.S. continue to grow?*

NYE: Yes, I agree with that. I think the Soviet problem is entering into what you might call the third industrial revolution of an information-based society, and the Stalinist central planning system is all thumbs and no fingers; it lacks the flexibility to adjust to this kind of a world. Just to give you one example, in the mid-1980s the Soviet Union had about 50,000 personal computers in the country, the Americans by that time had about thirty million. So there is a long way for the Soviets to go. I suspect the next decade or two are going to be spent coming to terms with these problems of economic decline. On the other hand, let's remember that sometimes declining countries do foolish things, after all, it was a declining Austria-Hungary that took great risks in August 1914, which led to a disaster. So the fact that the Soviets are in economic decline I think is true, but I think we also have a strong interest in making sure that a declining power does not turn to adventuresome ways.

COSTA: *Let's look at some of the new challengers to American dominance. Let's look at Germany first: it is currently the dominant economic powerhouse of Europe, it has skilled labor, advanced technology, and a very strong currency situation. If it does reunify with East Germany, would it continue its dominant role in Europe despite 1992?*

NYE: I think a reunified Germany is not a direct threat to the United States in any sense. It's worth remembering that even a reunified Germany will only be one-fifth the size of the United States.

The real concern that we have about a unified Germany is its effect on the rest of Europe. An American policy for some time has been to be in favor of German unity, but within the context of strong German ties to the other European states. Keeping Germany vitally involved in the European community is important, and in terms of reassuring its neighbors. So I think the key question on German unification will be how it's done, what sort of institutional ties surround a unified Germany, rather than unity per se. Thus far, the West German leadership has been very clear about its desire to maintain those institutional ties within the European community.

COSTA: *How much should we worry about German history—the two world wars, the horrible holocaust. Forty years have passed, there is a different Germany, times are different, but how much of that worry is realistic and how much is paranoia?*

NYE: As I say to the five hundred students in my Core Curriculum course on international conflict, never forget history, but don't become the prisoner of history either. Germany's location in the center of Europe has always been something that has the potential for instability, and certainly the nature of German society in the past added to that instability. But the things that are different are the fact that Germany now has had forty years of democracy, which it never had before; of the three wars that were caused or at least contributed to by German unification in the center of Europe—1870, 1914, and 1939—none were preceded by a democratic government in the capital of Germany. The other difference is the continued American involvement in Europe, which means that while Germany is larger than the other European states, it is obviously not larger than the United States, and the American presence helps to make a difference from prior historical episodes as well. So, yes, an eye back on history is always wise, but not if you fail to see what's standing in front of you.

COSTA: *Japan, as you have written and as everyone knows, is the world's largest creditor nation. It has invested highly in its young with its celebrated emphasis on education. Its business management and organization are the envy of the world, as is its work force. It also provides more foreign aid than any other nation. Will it grow larger in the decade?*

NYE: I would certainly expect Japanese power to increase. Japanese financial power has already showed a dramatic rise. Japan has become the world's second largest economy. Japan has demonstrated enormous capabilities in many areas of manufacturing. On the other hand, we don't want to cast Japan in the role of the enemy that the Soviet Union has just evacuated because I think what we would be mistaking at that point is the fact that Japan thus far has chosen not to become a military power, and if you look at the balance of power in East Asia, what you find is that the United States is the only country in the region that is both a military and an economic superpower, which means we play a large role in the stability in the area. I'm not convinced that a Japan which became nuclear, and thereby frightened not only the Soviet Union but also China and its neighbors in Southeast Asia, would be a stabilizing factor. We want to make sure that in the process of engaging in various types of economic disputes and arguments that we don't let that get out of hand so it pushes the Japanese in the direction of militarization and the development of independent nuclear weapons.

53

COSTA: *How much of Japan-phobia is real? How serious is their threat economically? Are we at war with Japan economically?*

NYE: I think the metaphor 'war' is mistaken when you apply it to the economic area. There are many things where both sides could win in some larger aggregate sense, which is not true in a war. After all, American consumers do benefit from Japanese cars or other Japanese products, and the argument that it is simply an equivalent of war is wrong.

On the other hand, the Japanese have often been a mercantilist or neo-mercantilist state in the postwar period in which their government has supported certain types of industries targeting American industries while protecting their own at home until they have a position where they dominate the market. There is no reason that we have to agree to that. It seems to me that targeted retaliation and targeted measures in which we respond to this type of Japanese behavior is appropriate. There is a difference between that and a general protectionism. I think that one of the key questions for us in the future is to be able to respond strongly to the Japanese government interference or cartelization of markets, while at the same time, not letting that slip over into broad protectionism because a broad protectionism would just produce inefficient industries in the United States and that really would lead to decline.

COSTA: *Essentially your view is that we are not in decline. We have some areas that need improvement, but we have the spirit, the resources, and the resolve to be a leading nation. Could you summarize your optimism?*

NYE: Yes, I think that the irony for the United States is that it is likely to stay number one, but number one is not going to be what it used to be. And not because there is some other country chasing us, but because of a more general diffusion of power. So the problem that we should be focusing on is not decline and looking over our shoulder to see whether modern Japan is the equivalent of the kaiser's Germany for Britain. What we should be asking is how in a post-cold war world do we invest in new types of power resources—often, more soft power resources—so that we can organize states to deal with the growing issues of international interdependence. The hope I have is that the Americans will not succumb to looking inward and having a protectionist mood, but will realize that they remain heavily interdependent with the rest of the world. We are going to have to think in terms which are very different from those of the cold war. We'll no longer have the Soviet threat to organize our priorities for us anymore.

A *conversation with*

Dr. William Bennett

Dr. William Bennett is a lecturer on medicine and editor of the
Harvard Health Letter. *Popularization of science and medicine has
been the focus of his general writings. Bennett is coauthor of* The
Dieter's Delimma: Eating Less and Weighing More *(Basic Books).*

COSTA: *One of the biggest industries in America today is the diet industry.
More people are spending more money to weigh less and less. Let's define a
few terms: when is a person considered to be overweight by medical criteria?*

BENNETT: The definition of overweight and obesity—both terms are used
and sometimes they are used to mean different things—is difficult because we
are not dealing with a sudden change of state, like from water to ice. We are
talking about a continuous variable. Roughly speaking, at 25 to 30 percent
more than the average level of body fat you start to see at least a statistical
association with medical problems. Obesity, with a greater probability of medical problems, begins somewhere around 70 or 80 percent more than the average amount of body fat. But there's a range in there and I think one of the
most important things that's coming out of current studies is that these judgments have to be individualized. People are in many ways more different than
they are alike. There are some people for whom a certain amount of body fat
seems to pose no problem, others for whom it can be a relatively serious problem.

COSTA: *It used to be that we would look at those life insurance charts that were broken down by size of frame—if you had a big frame then you could carry 25 more pounds—and suddenly all of us had big frames. Those charts are no longer the way we measure health and weight, are they?*

BENNETT: There is a deep problem with the Metropolitan Life Insurance charts, which have been used as you imply, as the standard for evaluating ideal or desirable weight. The original problem with this standard was that the sample who were gathered for measurement were mainly urban white males in the northeastern part of the United States. There is obviously a set of women also because the charts are broken down that way. . . . This is an atypical group to begin with. It was gathered for the first time early in this century and then again around the middle of the century for the more recent version of the tables, which was, by the way, quite different from the first one. It generally upgraded the amount of fat or weight that was regarded as desirable.

So the first problem was that the sample was peculiar. The second problem is that we really don't know how the computations were done. In fact, when the original data were recomputed they looked rather different. Reuben Andres at the University of Maryland and the National Institutes of Health did that.

Finally, the business about frame size is the most peculiar of all. Frame size was never measured on the original sample, and indeed there are no objective standards for frame size and no way of relating frame size to anything else. In fact in the more recent version of those tables a formula for measuring frame size was given, but that formula was never applied to the original sample. We have no conception of what that means. So the second you subtract frame size from the Metropolitan tables you quite often have a thirty-, forty-, fifty-pound weight range that is applicable to people of that height. The tables start to look a good deal more tolerant than they did to begin with. I think the Metropolitan Life tables have to be regarded at this point as a historical curiosity. They can't really be used as the basis for evaluating whether someone is overweight or not.

COSTA: *Recent research shows that there may be a genetic link to obesity. Yet other studies say that the only thing that one can determine from these studies is that if your parents carried weight in certain areas of their bodies you probably will do so too. Could you give an update on this?*

BENNETT: Doing genetic studies on human beings is difficult for the obvious reason that you can't breed them. You have to go out and find, as it were, experiments of nature. These generally involve studies of twins or separated twins, or adopted children who can be compared with their adoptive families and their biological families.

A great deal of work in the last five years has been done, led chiefly by Albert Stunkard in the University of Pennsylvania, which shows, I think persuasively, that there is a genetic component to weight gain, and that this genetic component expresses itself more and more throughout life. This means that we are more likely to look like our relatives at the end of our lives than we are at the beginning. The exact measurement of inheritance is a harder problem to pin down and there is controversy about that. The basic question is how to explain differences. If you and I are different, what percentage of the difference can be explained essentially by the difference in our genes, what percentage by the difference in the environment we share, and what difference perhaps by some ill-defined interaction of those two.

My favorite example for looking at this problem is the Pima Indians of the American Southwest. The Pima are currently a group of people living in their traditional area on the banks of the Gila River in southern Arizona who get very fat by the time they are adults, and are at very high risk of developing diabetes, gall bladder disease, and other associated ill effects of their obesity. It's not so clear that other Native American groups in the same area have the same risk, for example, of diabetes or gall bladder disease. The Pima seem to have gotten a triple whammy with all of this. The Pima live, essentially, a normal life by current standards in their area. They eat basically a beans- and corn-based diet, relatively high in oil, but not fundamentally different from what other people in the same area eat. And they drive trucks and cars, and so on. They have the normal labor-saving, energy-conserving devices that we all use, and of course they are part of a market economy.

If we go back to the last century, we know that the Pima were, by and large, normal in weight except for the older women who showed a clear tendency to get fat, and the [Pima] were already noted to be fatter than their neighbors by comparison. The facts of Pima life at that time were an extraordinarily difficult, hardscrabble existence, eking out a life on the drought-ridden banks of the Gila. Every five years or so their crops would go and they would have to set out across the countryside foraging on foot for their food.

What this story tells us is that the modern Pima are genetically fat with respect to their neighbors. That is, the environment now is virtually identical. They share the same environment, so all we see is the difference in genes. But the Pima are environmentally fat with respect to their own great, great grandparents. There, the gene pool is presumably all but identical and what we are seeing is the permissive effect of modern life: the ability to buy food when you can't grow it, to drive a car to the grocery store rather than go out and hoe or gather, and so on.

There are several morals here. One of them is that the way you look at a gene/environment problem has to take into account the possibility that it can be looked at in either of these ways. The second important moral is that the environment isn't necessarily easier to change than the genes. We walk around with this fantasy that if the problem is only environmental we can solve it. But to solve the Pimas' problem of obesity might require taking away their trucks, excluding them from a market economy and sending them back out to eke out the same old drought-ridden existence in the same old dry fields. That is an unacceptable solution. The kind of facile inclination we have to say, 'Well, this is something we can fix. After all, we know their grandparents were thin,' I think is profoundly misleading.

57

COSTA: *There are also some misconceptions about the degree of obesity that leads to a shortened life expectancy. For example, the famous Framingham Heart Study followed 2,000 people since 1948 and it cited what seemed to be a strong correlation between being overweight and a shortened life span due to heart problems, heart disease, and diabetes. Is this essentially true and is there a level of obesity, which, if one exceeds it, will place one at risk?*

BENNETT: There clearly is a U-shaped curve, meaning that the mortality rate starts high if you're very thin, slides down the descending slope of the U toward some kind of middle range where life expectancy is greatest, and then mortality starts to go up another slope as you get fatter. There has been considerable debate as to where that minimum is. The Framingham data are partially controversial because some of their weight categories don't have enough people in them to make it a firm statistical basis, particularly at the thin end. Thin nonsmokers in Framingham, for example, were not that common in the original sample.

I think it is fairly clear that there is an association. I think it is also fair to say that it's been overstated. Again, the work of Reuben Andres at the National Institute on Aging has suggested that the minimum actually rises over time. That is, the normal phenomenon—gaining weight as you get older—is probably consistent with maximum life span, so that it is hard to give a single prescription. More and more, I think people are inclined to believe that the relatively rapid weight gain that many of us go through in our late 20s and early 30s may be one of the most ominous indicators and that is probably not so much a sign that the weight itself is a problem, but rather an indication that the lifestyle has changed, shifting perhaps toward less activity. We all get busy after we graduate from college. We have other things to do, we stop exercising, we get cars again. It facilitates weight gain and probably a variety of metabolic changes that go along with that.

So weight gain, particularly in that period, seems to be a high-risk factor. Later on in life, the gradual gain that we all go through may be less meaningful and at least part of that may be because by then we are survivors anyway. I would say that trying to extract a simple formula from the data at hand is probably misguided.

COSTA: *This is the first time I think I've ever heard a doctor say that it is dangerous to be too thin. By that, do you mean anorexia?*

BENNETT: Again, it is a statistical association. It is hard for me to say that it is dangerous to be too thin. There is a higher mortality associated with being very thin, not anorexic. Anorexia is a specific condition and people get into bad trouble with that disease. But just being at the thin end of the curve seems to be associated with a higher mortality. There are probably several components there, one of them is clearly cigarette smoking. Cigarette smokers are thinner on average than the general population, not by a great deal, but enough to show up statistically, and they are clearly at higher risk. There is also probably a component in there of people who are getting thin or have lost weight because they are already sick in some kind of subtle way that we will only detect further down the line. One of the most important things to do here is to make sure that you are not looking at people shortly before they get really sick, and fall out of your population. It's terribly important to follow people over time. That radically increases the expense and difficulty of doing the research and that is one reason why our data are so bad.

COSTA: *Let's look at the dieting syndrome. Isn't it true that most people who diet end up putting the weight back on within a couple of years?*

BENNETT: The answer to that question depends really on the relatively few groups that have been responsible enough to report their data. But I can say with some confidence, having looked at that literature, that there is no diet program, plan, procedure, or method in the published literature that shows a simple majority of the people who were less than their starting weight four or five years later, with one possible exception.

The trouble is that these studies do not represent the whole world. It is very hard to tell who is reporting what. What I do know, for example, is that over the last ten or fifteen years, diet studies have tended to be about progressively heavier people. This creates a kind of paradoxical appearance of improvement in the results because heavy people tend to lose more weight even as a percentage of their body weight. Once you adjust for that, it doesn't look like we've made any progress in the last thirty of forty years in the effectiveness of treatment for weight loss. The most effective way to lose weight is clearly dieting. You can make yourself lose weight relatively quickly. Within three to five years, the overwhelming probability is that you will be back at or near your starting weight.

COSTA: *In the 1950s, we used to talk about counting calories as the best thing to do to lose weight. Then, with the fitness craze, counting calories seemed to take a backseat to jogging, getting up to your target heart rate three times a week, and exercise. What does the literature suggest now—a combination? Also, what is the maximum number of pounds per week one should lose to maintain health?*

BENNETT: I don't think it makes sense to lose weight at a rate any faster than one pound a week, and even that is pushing it. By and large, if exercise is possible, I would start there. In fact, I would reverse the usual sequence and start with a period of three to six months of exercise before suggesting that people then try to restrict their intake. The reason for that is that dieting produces a rapid weight loss, much of it fluid. It reinforces a lot of the wrong behaviors and it creates a level of discomfort that makes the long-term behavior—physical activity—less attractive.

For some people, exercise will not prove to be a sufficient method of weight reduction, although often it is a perfectly adequate method of weight maintenance. For them, some kind of intake restriction may eventually be necessary.

The trouble with that is that it's unpleasant and people don't stick with it. Why we go on recommending that people do something we know they will not comply with is beyond me.

COSTA: *What kinds of exercise do you recommend?*

BENNETT: There are some very clear rules for effectiveness of exercise and weight control. The first is that it should be something that you can do at least four or five days a week, and preferably seven. That means that it shouldn't be something so intense that if feels like punishment, because you just won't do it.

Second, it has to be aerobic. That is, it has to be the sort of thing that gets you breathing fast and gets your heart rate up and something that can go on for twenty-five or thirty minutes. Again, it can't be so intense that you won't go on doing it; it has to be something that you can sustain for a period of time.

I've already said the third rule: do something for twenty-five to thirty minutes, and for some people, longer. Those three things are overwhelmingly important. The frequency should be five to seven times a week, it should be aerobic in character, which means fast walking for a great many people, bicycling if they can do it, maybe jogging, which is certainly more intense. Swimming is paradoxical and I don't know why. There are various kinds of data that suggest that swimming is not as effective as other methods. I suspect it's mainly that people don't swim hard enough. It's frightening to be in water over your head when you are out of breath. Then, finally, the duration, the amount of exercise you do over time is undoubtedly critical.

COSTA: *Some physicians believe that some of the more drastic diet regimens actually harm a person's health. I'm talking about those single-substance diets that you read about in the tabloid magazines, like eating only bananas or eating only peanuts. What do you advise about those kinds of regimens?*

BENNETT: The mono diet, whether it is grapefruit or peanuts or whatever, is bound to promote weight loss just because nobody can eat enough of one thing to keep going for very long. They probably aren't as dangerous as they sound only because people don't stick to them. If they did stick to them, sooner or later, all kinds of obvious nutritional deficiencies would begin to develop. Those things are really dumb.

What is more ambiguous are the very low-calorie diets often using a constructed liquid that is supposed to have all of the nutrients and minerals you need. Very low-calorie diets—that is, below 500 calories a day—again, over the short haul, probably don't harm people very much if only because people are pretty durable. But there is a distinct risk if people go on the diet for too long. They will have sudden cardiac arrest and die. This happens less now than it did with the worst formulated diets. We have better formulated diets now, but it still can happen occasionally. It's also important to recognize that these diets have not demonstrated long-term effectiveness even though they have a short-term benefit.

COSTA: *There is near hysteria these days concerning cholesterol. People all around the country brag about their low cholesterol levels. I'd like to know what those magic cholesterol numbers mean and should one prepare one's will if his or her number is more than 200?*

BENNETT: It is reasonable to be concerned about cholesterol. It is ridiculous to start drawing specific cut points for any one person. The cholesterol level that you have has very different significance if you are a man of 20 who is a smoker and has high blood pressure, or if you are a women of 70 who has no other risk factors. Cholesterol should never be interpreted outside a particular person's own context. Saying to someone that mine is lower than yours has no real significance over the long haul. If you have a family history of heart disease, if you are a male, if you have other risk factors, then a cholesterol much above 200 is probably worth working on, but not to the point of obsessiveness that we've reached. Everybody agrees that [being of the] male sex is a risk factor, but there is a point at which you decide that male sex is not worth changing.

There are some people who get their cholesterols relatively low but still have a bad ratio, that is, the proportion of so-called favorable to unfavorable cholesterols still isn't working for them very well. Should they go on throwing themselves into frantic exercise and increased dieting, or should they recognize that they have reached some kind of basic limit of their own and live with that? I obviously am inclined to go for the latter. It is fairly clear on average for middle-aged males that the risk of heart attack begins to rise when there is a cholesterol of about 200. It goes up in a more or less linear way after that. So sure I think it is worth aiming for 200. I think it is also worth being realistic about why we live these lives, and from time to time I am inclined to side with Julia Child, that a life without butter and cream may not be worth living.

A *conversation with*

Susan Rubin Suleiman

*Susan Rubin Suleiman is professor of Romance languages and
comparative literatures. She is past chair of the Committee on Women's
Studies and author of* Subversive Intent: Gender, Politics, and the
Avant-Garde *(Harvard University Press). An essay titled "My War in Four
Episodes" was a vivid description of her clandestine escape from Hungary
and her eventual return visit.*

COSTA: *In your new book,* Subversive Intent: Gender, Politics, and the
Avant-Garde *[Harvard University Press] you link the avant-garde movement
with surrealism. The surrealists, historians tell us, sought to merge the conscious with the subconscious and the real with the unreal to create a super-
reality. Salvador Dali in his famous painting, the one with the melting clocks,*
Persistence of Memory, *displayed those early tenets of surrealism. Is that what
the avant-garde tries to do—to liberate the unconscious?*

SULEIMAN: That was certainly one of the proclaimed intentions of the surrealists, especially of André Breton, who was the recognized leader of the
movement. You used the words avant-garde movement, but in fact there are
avant-garde *movements*. The historical avant-gardes, or so-called 'historical
avant-garde,' would include Dadaism, for example, the immediate precursor
to surrealism and Futurism, which started in Italy before the first world war.
Some people would even include Cubism, let's say, in the broad category of
the historical avant-gardes, and some of the movements in Germany after the
first world war, including German Dada, but other movements, too. So there
isn't one avant-garde, not even one historical avant-garde.

Surrealism, certainly, is one of the most visible of these historical avant-gardes and in some ways I think it's typical of what people have used to talk about the avant-garde because it was an extremely influential movement with a lot of theories, manifestos. It also attracted an incredibly large number of artists, writers, and poets between the two world wars so that it was really present on the international scene.

Now, this question about the conscious and the unconscious and dream and reality certainly was one of the things that they were very interested in, especially, as I say, Breton. Don't forget that in those days Freud wasn't even very much recognized in France. The surrealists were the first ones to read Freud seriously in France. So when they were talking about dream and reality and the unconscious, it was a lot more radical than it might sound now. What happened is that some people eventually tried to make it all seem much more harmless than it really was, to take away some of that radical impetus of the movement by making it into this kind of wispy, willowy desire to merge the real and the unreal. But when they were talking about the unconscious and liberating dreams, they had something quite radical in mind.

COSTA: *Didn't it also have a political component that was linked to the early communist movement?*

SULEIMAN: Absolutely. I think one has to look at all of this in historical context. If you imagine the kind of devastation that was felt in Europe after the first world war, the sense of bankruptcy that a whole civilization [experienced] after four years of carnage, then the movements that grew up after, chiefly Dada—which began in 1916 in Zurich, so during the war—and surrealism—which officially got started in 1924, that is the date of the first surrealist manifesto, but the two movements were more or less merged into each other anyway—if you think of all that and the incredible prestige then of the Soviet Revolution in 1917, which seemed to offer something completely new as an alternative to this bankrupt culture, then you understand why the political component was really very strong.

[There was a] journal published which was called the *Surrealist Revolution* and by that they had in mind both a revolution in everyday life and a revolution in poetry, in writing, and certainly in what they would think of as a political revolution, too. When they said 'we want to revolutionize life,' they meant political life and every other aspect of everyday life.

COSTA: *Were they in the intelligentsia or intellectual cafe society or were members of the avant-garde as visible as counter-culture heroes of today are?*

SULEIMAN: In those days, of course, they didn't have the media hype that exists today. If there had been media hype, they would probably have become media stars. But, in their own little ways, they certainly created a lot of waves. There were not a huge number of people involved. But they were experts, having learned a lot from Dada, in creating what they called scandal. One of the members of the movement was Aragon. He wrote very truculently: 'I love scandal, and I love it for its own sake, and if you think that's terrible then go fly a kite.' He was very insolent and that was their way of behavior: to provoke public scandal. They would invite people to a poetry reading where they would walk out outrageously dressed or carrying herring or they created public trials of writers that they didn't like, condemning them, with someone playing the role of judge, somebody of jury, defendant, and so forth. This whole thing was done to attract attention, and very often it did attract attention.

COSTA: *In your book you quote Mick Jagger of the Rolling Stones on the occasion of his induction into the Rock and Roll Hall of Fame, when he said: 'We are being rewarded for 25 years of bad behavior. First we shock you, then they put you in a museum.' Can you tell us about that?*

SULEIMAN: I was writing there about the way that avant-garde movements have almost a kind of sad fate in some ways, which is to be, as the jargon says, recuperated. That is, they are taken up by the mainstream culture and adapted and adopted by people so that the very things that they wanted to make appear scandalous are—you will see them the next day on billboards and in advertisements. In fact, that has happened to a lot of surrealist photography, for example, which was very radical and innovative and still is shocking in some ways because they do all kinds of weird things with the human body. But you see a lot of those same techniques being used to sell cars or soda pop or whatever. I think you could argue that with the Rolling Stones and with rock and roll that has happened. A lot of the original 'bad behavior' in rock and roll was just taken up and it became very much a part of commercial culture.

COSTA: *Your book is largely devoted to looking at literature and art from feminist viewpoints. You said that most erotic art of the past 400 years has displayed the female form in one way or another. Does this make that kind of art patriarchal or inauthentic for women?*

SULEIMAN: Certainly it's patriarchal if you define patriarchy as that system based on the power and the law of the father; that's what it is etymologically, anyway. Insofar as we—by 'we' I mean women—have internalized all of the modes of thought and all of the unquestioned assumptions of the culture, the first thing we think of when somebody says nude is in fact the image of a voluptuous woman. It doesn't mean that we like it necessarily, and it's not a matter of being condemnatory or puritanical or anything else. What feminist theorists really have accomplished with their work is to make people aware that many things that we consider as natural are really not natural, that they are part of the whole cultural baggage, which needs to be looked at.

If we just assume that women's bodies are the ones that have been displayed because, after all, women are prettier or what's wrong with that anyway, I think that one of the things that feminist theory wants to accomplish is to make people look at some of these assumptions and say, well, maybe it isn't as simple as all that, maybe this has something to do with the relations of power, for example, because the person whose body is displayed is generally somebody who has less power than the person who looks. We know that. The person who looks and is fully clothed is definitely in a position of dominance over the person who is naked and being looked at, whether it's in a photograph or in real life or in a beautiful 16th-century, priceless work of art.

Costa: *You also discuss the concept of the politics and poetics of female eroticism in your book and talk about some literary passages in a very candid way. How does that concept of female eroticism change in books written by women for women?*

Suleiman: Why is it that only male artists and writers should talk about our body, like Henry Miller, for example, or Norman Mailer? Why not have us talk about our body too? That way then we are the ones who have that power of speech because that's very important: who is doing the speaking. The body that's looked at is generally silent and the person who looks is the one who speaks. In this case then, it's a genuine move to take over or to become—in slightly technical terms, but not that technical—what is known as a subject. That is, the agent of speech and the agent of action.

I discuss Erica Jong's book, *Fear of Flying*, as an important book, but not even so much aesthetically. I'm not arguing that it's the great American novel, although it's a very well written, vivid, interesting book, and deservedly was recognized as an important book at the time. But it's not a matter of aesthetic value. It's almost a matter of, in this case, symbolic value about what she was trying to say because I think she is the first woman who used, in serious fiction in English, the famous four-letter word . . . but which had become so much a stock in trade of people like Henry Miller, for example.

Costa: *You write in your book that she used that four-letter word 14 times in 14 pages.*

Suleiman: Or fourteen times in *less* than 14 pages. My point there was that she was doing it 'on purpose.' She was doing it as if to say, 'If *they* can do it in writing about us, why can't we do it?' What would happen when we start doing it? Do things really begin to move, do things change if it's a woman who says, 'Well, I love to have lovers and the more the merrier and I also have desires and I also have a head, so I can be a smart woman and still have sexual desires.' These were really quite revolutionary things to say in 1973 and I think for some people these are still revolutionary things to say.

Costa: *To get into one controversial area and admission in your book, you write that you may suffer from a heterosexual bias and 'the heterosexual woman's fear of being "contaminated by lesbianism."' Can you explain what you meant by that?*

SULEIMAN: In the essay on the poetics and politics of female eroticism where I was discussing what I'm calling the sexual/political implications of some of the writing—in this case, some of the French women writers in the late '60s and early '70s—it seems to me that one of the truly interesting things that was done was the attempt to reverse certain kinds of stereotypes. As I was saying earlier, if a woman uses a four-letter word, that reverses what is expected. It was really shocking and it was meant to be shocking. It's really meant to shake you up and to question who has the right to say certain things and who doesn't.

One of the French writers who was doing this in wonderfully interesting ways is a woman named Monique Wittig. She lives in the United States. She's a very innovative writer and has done several books in which there is a purposeful reversing of stereotypes, which is very easy to do because in French, grammar is all-important and everything is divided into masculine and feminine. So Wittig can become extremely revolutionary by simply substituting 'she' for 'he' in all cases, that is, for all pronouns, and never mind about what's the accepted form or what is grammatically correct.

I think that is very interesting, but what I was criticizing in that particular moment is that in several of her books what is accomplished is that the world becomes exclusively female, whereas the general tendency in the culture is to make everything male. (Whenever we want to say everybody, we say 'he,' right?)

She [even] begins to rewrite the classics. It's wonderful, poetically, but what I was getting to with that particular argument was my discomfort in seeing what I thought were possibly the sexual/political implications of a world that was all female. In other words, if you're going to end up simply reversing the present situation, which is that everybody seems to be male—at least everybody who counts—and you say, well, you're reversing everybody [and those] who count are female, it made me feel somewhat uncomfortable because what I would like is to see a world where you have a lot of males and females all doing interesting things, and not being closed in with stereotypes of any kind.

There were other critics who had very much praised Wittig and I, as I say, admire her and love her work, but we're now talking about some of the political implications. There are a number of critics who have praised her and, very interestingly, precisely for bringing about this reversal and creating a fictional world where it's all female. I said that maybe it is the fact that I envision a heterosexual world, and Wittig's world is recognizably—and she doesn't make any bones about the fact—a world where men have become superfluous.

COSTA: *Erica Jong does do a little reversal in that she makes the sex objects, if you will, male. She writes about them from the female viewpoint with desire, as you say, and she did that early in the '70s. Is there a trend among—and I hate to use the term—women writers for that kind of reversal?*

SULEIMAN: I situated it historically and even talked about its limitations to some extent. I also talked about Rita Mae Brown's work. I don't want to suggest that the only thing that interests me is, let's say, heterosexual fiction because Rita Mae Brown in *Rubyfruit Jungle*, which was her first book, did a wonderfully interesting thing where she simply took lesbian desire and made it into the main subject of her book and did [have] the same kind of shock effect by saying, 'Well, men may be desirable, but women are a hundred times more desirable.' That was her story.

I would say that both of those books are situated at a time when it was important to do that kind of simple shifting. My point is that, later on, many women writers did not simply want to do flip-flops. In other words, not simply say it used to be men on top, now it's going to be women on top, but to envisage new combinations. That's how that essay ends actually [with] this really wild book by Angela Carter, *The Passion of New Eve*, which is just great. There you have combinations that are almost unimaginable. That's what I'm arguing for. Not that in the real world we want to have all kinds of hybrids walking around where we don't know at all what they are, but I think that possibility of envisioning combinations where not everything is locked into a straitjacket of 'This is proper for girls' and 'This is proper for boys,' and 'This is male' and 'This is female,' 'This is masculine,' 'This is feminine,' is a very important idea and, after all, things begin in the head.

COSTA: *Art and literature certainly reflect the culture and in some cases bind the culture or constrain it.*

SULEIMAN: Absolutely.

COSTA: *You have been a proponent for a long time for new programs in women's studies at universities and colleges. A lot of people believe it's time that universities had appropriate women's studies programs.*

SULEIMAN: At Harvard when we passed a women's studies program in 1986, the Faculty voted for it *en bloc* with only one dissenting vote. So I would say that there was a real recognition that the time had come. Harvard, I might point out, was one of the last universities in the Ivy League to adopt a women's studies program. However, once we did it, we did it really well. We have one of the best and strongest women's studies programs around.

Undergraduates can major in women's studies and this was the year that we graduated our first senior class. Out of the 10 people who wrote honors essays—it's a small concentration, so 10 a year is very good, actually—four of them won Hoopes Prizes, which are the most prestigious prizes that can be won by undergraduates at Harvard. That's an incredible number to have, a 40 percent *summa cum laude* rate of graduation for our students. So we had some of the very best students in the University doing this. I think the reason they did it is that this is a very exciting interdisciplinary program, personally tailored, lots of individual attention, and intellectually extremely strong, drawing on people from all over.

COSTA: *I think some of the retrograde pragmatists might say—and I'll play devil's advocate—that women's studies is a difficult preparation for any kind of employment. It implies that one has to go on to further scholarship even though these studies will give one real insights into the world.*

SULEIMAN: I know that when we planned it we wanted very specifically to do the kind of program that will allow people to go on, for example, with graduate study in a specific area, such as history or literature or classics. The fact that they were women's studies majors didn't mean that they wouldn't have a real specialization in an area. So, therefore, I would say that a women's studies major is in just as good a position as anybody else as far as graduate school is concerned.

Your question, though, concerned getting a job after college, and I would say that a women's studies major is in the same position, certainly no worse than, any other liberal arts major and possibly better because our women's studies majors are absolutely obliged to take a wide range of courses. In other words, they cannot just decide to be classics majors and do nothing but classics. So they get a very wide background and I think they could go out and get a job in the same kinds of fields that any English major, history major, social studies major would get in business, publishing, or in almost any area that recognizes the virtues of a liberal arts education.

A *conversation with*

James Anderson

*James Anderson is Philip S. Weld Professor of Atmospheric
Chemistry. His research team spends months in the nether regions
of our continent as well as Antarctica to gather data on one of
the least understood manmade phenomena affecting our planet—
the loss of ozone.*

COSTA: *Let's start with a few basics about ozone. Since you're a chemist,
perhaps you can help us define terms. I know ozone is a colorless gas composed of three oxygen atoms. I know you can even generate it in a lab, and
there is good and bad ozone. Ozone is good only if it's way overhead in the
stratosphere blocking the ultraviolet radiation that we don't need, and it's bad
when it is on the ground because it harms our lungs.*

ANDERSON: Ozone begins with the existence of oxygen in the atmosphere,
which is produced by plants through photosynthesis. In the very early stages
of life there was very little oxygen in the atmosphere and as sea life began to
evolve, oxygen—that is, O_2—began to enter the atmosphere and, of course,
the sun was shining brightly and that began to break down O_2 to form ozone.
It's a chain of three oxygen atoms. The truly unique aspect of ozone is that it
absorbs ultraviolet radiation and it's unique because it's the only molecule in
the atmosphere that does this. So as life began to evolve out of the oceans, it
required the existence of ozone in the atmosphere to remove this last piece of
damaging ultraviolet radiation from the sun.

The other aspect that you spoke of, the damaging aspect, comes directly from its odor. It smells like a chlorine compound or some oxidizing material. Its damage comes through burning the lungs. That is a very dangerous aspect that manifests itself when it's present at ground level in cities and polluted areas like Los Angeles, Denver, and so on.

So it has this remarkable character. It's crucial for life because it protects the surface from ultraviolet radiation, but it's also damaging at high concentrations at ground level. The ozone layer is a very narrow region of the atmosphere that contains the preponderance of that ozone that protects us at the surface. We then, as polluters, create another ozone layer at the ground, if you will, and it is damaging to ourselves because it has this character of burning the lungs.

COSTA: *Does ozone occur naturally? Does lightning, for example, generate ozone? I know in laboratories you can generate ozone with high fields of current.*

ANDERSON: Lightning does indeed produce ozone. In fact, you can smell ozone around very strong thunderstorms. That's not the source for the ozone that protects life. The sun is the predominant source, and the reason for that is that the sun puts out a huge amount of energy compared to lightning or any other source. In fact, the amount of energy required to produce ozone in the stratosphere is 100 times or more the total consumption of energy by man at the surface. So it's being produced all the time by the power of the sun and those events occur a billion times a second in every cubic centimeter of the stratosphere. It's a very dynamic process. We weren't given a certain amount of ozone during the origin of the Earth. It's produced every day, every hour the sun shines on the atmosphere.

COSTA: *Let's talk about some of the research that you and your group have done that has brought you some fame. A little more than two years ago, researchers from your group confirmed that an ozone hole did indeed exist over the Antarctic. You did experiments to show that a vortex there was indeed a widening ozone hole and a dangerous one. What is the status of that Antarctic ozone hole today?*

ANDERSON: First, our research was directed toward understanding the cause of the ozone hole. We didn't discover it. In fact, many researchers have worked on the existence of the ozone hole. The question that we addressed was what caused the ozone hole and, in particular, the specific mechanism that would allow us to predict the future course of events.

[We had] a high-altitude research aircraft that went into the Antarctic ozone hole. That aircraft was equipped with a number of different instruments, and those instruments were designed to test whether the ozone hole was caused by atmospheric motion, by the dynamics of the atmosphere, or by chemical causes. Even within the category of chemical theories, we were looking specifically at the chlorine and bromine contribution. It turns out that the cause of the Antarctic ozone hole was indeed chemical and in fact its root cause was the presence of fluorocarbons in the atmosphere. Our particular instrumentation looked not at fluorocarbons but at the product of the breakdown of those fluorocarbons when they reached the stratosphere. It's commonly discussed as a fluorocarbon/ozone problem. That it is. The fluorocarbons are the fuel that produce the materials that directly attack ozone.

COSTA: *On the opposite pole, in the Arctic, you and other researchers have also found that Arctic air may be primed now chemically for ozone destruction.*

ANDERSON: We were shocked in the Antarctic at the clarity of the situation. When we repeated those high-altitude, aircraft-borne experiments in the Arctic we expected to see a mish-mash of motion and chemistry going on, but in fact we saw a very dramatic situation in which the Arctic is primed—that is, all of those dangerous chemicals are, at present, at levels sufficient to remove ozone in large amounts within three to four weeks—which is exactly what transpired in the Antarctic.

So the Arctic is now our point of greatest concern. We saw very high ClO radicals, and radicals are fragments of molecules and they're particularly important in processes such as this because they enter into what is called catalytic cycles. Just as your automobile has a catalytic converter, which speeds up the cleanup of pollution, so too do these catalytic processes speed up the destruction of ozone by factors of a thousand or more. So a very small amount of a compound can have devastating effects, and very rapidly, on ozone.

So that leaves us with an Arctic region that is a chemical beaker properly prepared for the rapid destruction of ozone. The only reason that we don't see massive loss of ozone today or during the winter period in the Arctic is that this chemical beaker is smashed, allowing the chemicals to spew out over the Northern Hemisphere, unlike the Antarctic. So we were surprised, shocked, and we are now in the process of exploring this phenomenon in much greater detail.

COSTA: *Why is it that the Arctic beaker is, as you put it, smashed? Is it because it is not cold enough to contain a vortex? Is there a spin to the air over the poles?*

ANDERSON: There really is a spin. Vortex is the proper word. It's like a well-controlled washing machine in which instead of water sloshing back and forth, it spins around in a highly defined way. It is simple and beautifully defined in the Antarctic because there are no mountain ranges to create waves. Just as the ocean has waves, so, too, does the atmosphere. And in the Antarctic those waves are very weak, they don't transport heat, and they leave this vortex, which is defined as a wind jet, around the Antarctic continent unperturbed. In the Arctic, with the Himalayas, the Rockies, the larger mountain ranges, you generate large wave patterns that break up this vortex much more quickly. But it still forms. It's still clear and present for a period in January, for example, of every year.

COSTA: *There was some concern that the ozone hole in the Antarctic was spreading. Does that concern still exist?*

ANDERSON: If I were to list in level of importance the immediate questions, the first is: Will an ozone hole form in the Northern Hemisphere? The second is exactly the question you asked: Will the Antarctic ozone hole grow, and how will it and its breakup affect the amount of ultraviolet radiation in the Southern Hemisphere? The Antarctic ozone hole in 1987 lasted past Thanksgiving, which of course is deep into summer in the Southern Hemisphere, and that ozone hole is larger than a continental landmass. It moved out as a unit over mid-latitudes. It moved north out over Australia, Argentina, and Chile and they got pretty serious doses of UV—episodically, because it would pass overhead—but they instigated a policy in which they would provide UV dosage [reports] on the evening news along with the weather report. That's a paradigm for what may happen globally when these large regions of depleted ozone move out over mid-latitudes, particularly in late spring and summer. People will have to know about this because that dosage is a very significant health issue.

COSTA: *Perhaps we should talk about the CFCs. Chlorofluorocarbons are the stuff used in refrigerants like Freon. Clearly, it directly leads to the destruction of ozone. I know that some legislators agree with researchers and would like to phase out CFCs by the year 2000. A colleague of yours, Michael McElroy, told me a couple of years ago that even if we changed our use of CFCs at this very moment, it will take 150 years from now to take effect. Is that correct?*

ANDERSON: That's correct, and that has two components. One is the longevity of the existence of these ozone-depleted regions, particularly over the poles. The second aspect of it is that because of the time delay that you alluded to, we are loading the lower atmosphere with these compounds, which provide a storage bank that supplies the stratosphere for many years to come. So if we never synthesized another fluorocarbon molecule we would realize nearly a doubling of fluorocarbon concentrations in the stratosphere by the end of both the decade and the century. So not only will this [influx] to the Antarctic and the Arctic remain for a hundred years, we haven't seen the worse of it yet— even if we never produced another molecule. Therein lies our greatest concern for the Arctic. These catalytic cycles that I mentioned before are very sensitive to the amount of available chlorine and today we are looking at a period of three to four weeks for ozone to be severely depleted. When we double the amount of chlorine by the end of the decade, we are looking at a one-week period required to contain this beaker, before we see very serious ozone erosion. That's why we believe the simple arguments of the amount of chlorine that's currently there in reactive form—the ClO radical—combined with this inexorable buildup, tells us very simply without any large, complicated computer models that we have a very good chance of seeing an ozone hole within this next decade in the Arctic.

COSTA: *Your research group used a converted U-2 plane, a spy plane, to fly through the ozone hole in the Antarctic. I'm told you're now planning to use a remote-controlled plane to do ozone research. Tell us about both planes.*

ANDERSON: The spy planes fly at 70,000 feet, whereas in a normal aircraft that you fly in commercially, you typically fly at half that altitude—35,000 feet. In the Antarctic we can touch the core of this problem with that U-2 aircraft but we're just barely getting into the region of greatest interest. It's also a feat of remarkable bravery on the part of these pilots because we take off from the southern tip of Chile on the Straits of Magellan, and when I say we, that's the wrong term. The aircraft takes off with one pilot, all of the instruments, and one engine, and it flies south over the roaring forties, over the Antarctic continent. If that single engine ever failed, there is very little chance that the pilot would be saved because the temperatures are so low inside that Antarctic region that the pilot would be dead before reaching the ground, even if the parachute and spacesuit and everything else operated properly. So there's a great deal of danger involved in these missions and that contributes in many subtle ways to the deployment tactics.

What we really need to do is to go into the Arctic and into the Antarctic in the depths of the polar night to much higher altitudes and for much longer periods of time. We need to weave this region together as a basket is woven together so that we sample many different places very frequently and we don't place pilots in life-threatening situations.

Because of that strong motivation, not only for ozone depletion but for global change, for climate studies, for hurricane research, for a lot of issues related to global events, we have to have an entirely new platform for making observations. Satellites are too remote, they smear the picture up too much, they can't address the key diagnostic issues. If you had a terrible disease, I could observe you from across the room but I would really need to take blood tests and all of the rest of the normal diagnostics. The atmosphere is precisely the same kind of patient. We've got to reach into the middle of it and do these very high-resolution cause-and-effect studies, which are impossible from a space platform.

So the unmanned aircraft heralds a new era in these studies. It can get to much higher altitudes, it can fly for days on end, it can traverse from the tropics to the polar regions, it can spend a great deal of time inside these Arctic and Antarctic phenomena. Here we have an overlap with onboard intelligence on these aircrafts because in all of the previous missions the ER-2 was sent along one trajectory that was picked before it took off. The pilot, after all, is in a position of protecting his life. He doesn't have time to analyze data onboard. The right way to do these missions is to have a computer onboard that tells itself what those concentrations are, finds the region that's most interesting scientifically, based on predetermined algorithms, and directs the aircraft toward those areas. Just as a glider pilot searches out thermals, so too can the unmanned aircraft locate the regions of very high ClO concentrations and carve back and forth. In one flight we can achieve many months of critical scientific data by properly establishing the trajectory of that unmanned aircraft based on what it sees.

COSTA: *Tell us a little bit about the other regions that look as if they're going to have the same kind of ozone depletion.*

ANDERSON: The Antarctic ozone hole surfaced in the mid-'80s and, of course, that was both a scientific surprise and also a threat to life in the Southern Hemisphere. So we have now come full circle about learning a great deal about both the Antarctic and the Arctic and, to return to this original hypothesis, to begin to delineate how rapid that erosion is at very high altitude. That's going to require a great deal of research because it's spread out over the globe. It's a much more subtle signature and therefore requires a much deeper understanding of the dynamics and the chemistry combined, and the unmanned aircraft is going to be a major component in those studies.

Another area of immense concern is the region over the tropics. This is somewhat of an irony because you would think of them as being very warm. In fact, because of the strong vertical motion, as you see in thunderstorms and in hailstorms, the vertical motion actually cools the air as it rises very rapidly, and the lower stratosphere over the tropics is nearly as cold as the stratosphere over the polar regions. So all of this, what you might call, counterintuitive chemistry that we've learned about over the polar regions may very well be existing and operating over the tropics. We have a question of subtlety here. We were hit on the head with a hammer in the Antarctic. In the tropics, it's a small ballpeen that is very, very delicate and we have to approach that problem scientifically in a much more complete way than we had to in the Antarctic.

COSTA: *There is very little controversy about ozone depletion. Most scientists agree that it indeed is going on. How does ozone depletion affect global warming trends? I know there's a lot of debate about global warming. Some politicians, among others, don't believe it exists.*

ANDERSON: Ozone depletion is a question of absorbing the ultraviolet end of the spectrum. Global warming is a question of reflecting the infrared or long wavelength end of the spectrum. So they are distinct problems but they become coupled as you begin to look into the details. Ozone is important for global warming because ozone is a very important radiative gas, both for heating and cooling of the atmosphere. So by distorting the distribution of ozone, you change the radiation patterns in the atmosphere. There's also a very strong interplay back from global warming into the ozone depletion problem. For example, we've talked at some length about the Arctic and the Antarctic and how sensitive those regions are to temperature, and while the increase in CO_2

warms the surface, it cools the lower stratosphere and because the polar regions are so sensitive to temperature, the buildup of CO_2 actually creates a more serious problem for polar ozone depletion because it decreases the average temperature of the region. Just a degree or two can have a remarkable effect on the probability of the Antarctic or the Arctic producing an ozone hole.

The second aspect is that global warming is a vastly more complex problem than ozone depletion. It takes in a lot of subtle interaction between clouds and radiation and it should be pointed out that while we talk about CO_2 as the greenhouse gas, water vapor is really the greenhouse gas, and the question is how will the buildup of CO_2 affect the water vapor budget, particularly of the upper lower atmosphere, if you will, from five miles up. . . . Global warming is a very, very complicated subject.

A conversation with

David Hall

David Hall is professor of American religious history and Bartlett Lecturer in New England Church History. His integrated approach to the development of religious belief has illuminated the impact of religion on the establishment of our nation.

COSTA: *The church and the Colonies were severe in their outlook. There were no maypoles or calendars with pagan names of the month on them, as you write in your book,* Worlds of Wonder, Days of Judgment. *Could you describe to us what the Colonial church was like?*

HALL: It was different things for different people, although I argue that there was fundamentally a shared culture that drew together the clergy and the people. First and foremost it was giving sermons by the clergy, hearing sermons by the people. Another scholar has calculated that in a given lifetime a serious churchgoer would hear the equivalent of about 10 college educations in terms of sermons, so, for better or for worse, that was one's experience.

Another is the experience of witnessing or observing or hearing stories about the supernatural, whether stories of witches, or stories of what I have called in my book, wonders, which are everything from mysterious signs of nature to visions to voices. Then I'd finally say that outside the church in daily life there were moments of crisis, illnesses, dying, that people tried to deal with in terms of prayer, ritual structures, confession. So religion was something that penetrated daily life in terms of passages, crises, deeply felt moments that people needed to get through in some fashion and they turned to structures or ritual to do that.

COSTA: *In essence, the Colonial church was, as you point out, a church of the people, whereas the church in England was primarily a priestly theocracy.*

HALL: It was a church of the people; the people were given all kinds of powers. We're speaking now primarily of men, of course, because the women were kept in inferior roles, although they joined the church more often. But it was a church of the people. They could understand, they could participate, they could vote the clergy in or out. There were all kinds of ways in which they were empowered and active, and that wasn't common in Catholic countries and certainly less common in England than in New England.

COSTA: *You write about the importance of literacy in America, and how reading and owning Bibles contributed to a congregational rather than a hierarchical approach to religion. Could you tell us more about that?*

HALL: Bibles were extremely plentiful. People had these Bibles in their heads in ways that there really isn't anything comparable today. Maybe some of us have grandparents who still can recite 19th-century poetry by Browning or Tennyson or Longfellow or something like that, and that's roughly what it was like in the 17th century: People could recite or allude to vast quantities of the Bible or sometimes a verse that was written in imitation of the Bible. So there was a literate culture that was also an oral culture. One part of my work is to try to break down this too rigid distinction. In any case, the end result is to suggest that what people read is what they thought. And what they read had a large influence on their religious sensibility, especially the Bible, [and] all kinds of books that looked like the Bible or talked like the Bible or based themselves on the Bible.

COSTA: *It was also important at this time that the Bible and these godly books, as you call them in your book, were written not in Latin, but in English.*

HALL: That's right. I stumbled on the idea of stories. To think of the Bible or of these godly books not in terms of beginnings and middles and ends, but themselves as telling a story like the story of pilgrimage or the story of weak people made strong. (This is, of course, a classic Christian motif of the weak, the dispossessed, Jesus himself being a humble carpenter rising and overturning the priesthood of the Pharisees.) All kinds of people could tell these stories and, of course, tell them against whomever was in power or tell them to sustain themselves being in power. So these books reduced themselves, in some sense, to nothing more than a tiny number of plots or stories that laypeople told and retold in all kinds of ways.

COSTA: *I'm struck by the fact that the Colonial church, despite its claim to be ruled and organized simply and that anyone could interpret scripture, is the same church that allowed the Salem witch trials of the late 1600s to occur. People were put to death often just for speaking their own minds and interpreting scripture in their own ways. How do you explain that seeming contradiction?*

HALL: There are two ways of explaining it. One is that these people, like everyone in Western Europe and America in the 17th century, thought that there was only one kind of truth, one orthodoxy. The fact that the Catholics had their orthodoxy and the Protestants had their orthodoxy didn't really alter the fact that each one thought that there still was only one orthodoxy. The notion of pluralism was simply beyond the comprehension of these people. So when they're dealing with deviants or people who challenge this one truth, they're quite harsh because, after all, the truth is at stake, God's will is at stake. I think it's common sense to realize that if God's truth were at stake and he got angry because people weren't upholding his truth he was going to punish you, so there was a powerful incentive to reconcile yourself with God by zapping those you didn't like.

Witchcraft is a special case, of course, in two respects. One is that the clergy would say of a witch that this is someone who is affiliated with the devil, who therefore specifically broke with everything that was good. But the more interesting aspect of witchcraft, or witch hunting we should say, comes from the local, ordinary people who poured into these courts by the dozens to complain about somebody.

COSTA: *Who were considered witches and how were they tried? You mentioned trial by water: if they floated they were bad. Also, if they sank they were bad. Of course, everybody floated. Why did the witch hunts end and was there remorse for persecuting these obviously innocent people?*

HALL: Your question is quite apropos because I have a new book coming out in December on witchcraft in New England. Witchcraft is quite different from what we might expect. Our children get dressed up at Halloween in pointed hats and black capes and go around casting spells. We think of the witches of Macbeth over steaming cauldrons. That's not what witchcraft was in New England. Witchcraft in New England was really witch hunting, that is to say, someone accusing another person of doing him or her harm and then using the label 'witch.' Witch hunting grows out of misfortune: you have a child that dies or falls ill unexpectedly or a parent who falls ill, or you yourself fall ill, your cattle are suddenly sick, your chicken falls sick. Over and over again, in hundreds of depositions, the root of the deposition is always some form of misfortune or calamity that can't be explained in ordinary, natural terms, at least not in the terms that these people possessed.

Then there's a very interesting train of thought: why did this misfortune happen to me? The next step in the thinking is: someone wants to do me harm. Then it's laid out explicitly in the depositions that people made before the courts that they think of a quarrel they had with a neighbor—it's always a neighbor—over wanting to borrow something or perhaps it's a quarrel over some commercial transaction, somebody trying to cheat somebody else, and they say, 'A-ha, so-and-so wants to do bad things to me because I would not lend him or her person a keg of beer or some milk or fire from my fireplace or something like that.' It's quite ordinary. There's a tremendous ordinariness about all of this. They come into court and they say, 'I'm sure Goody So-and-So cursed me and that's why my child fell sick.'

There's a whole series of cases in which older women are accused but the husband files a suit for defamation, and the court— caught between these two accusations, the one of witchcraft and the other saying this is slander—will often just drop the case. But there are striking instances of women who were suspected of witchcraft but were never accused when they were married. As soon as they became widows, the case was brought against them. Women were very vulnerable.

COSTA: *Who brings those cases? Would they be brought by other women or by men?*

HALL: Men and women jointly. There is no gender distinction in who actually comes forward to testify. This is a painful lesson for some radical feminists to absorb—that women accuse other women—but it's the truth.

Older women were quite vulnerable, women over the age of forty. It isn't always poor women, although there are a number of cases of women who are town beggars or outcasts in certain ways. If you're a Quaker or a person who isn't fully engaged with the religious system, you're also vulnerable. I think if you're just a plain ordinary crabby kind of contentious person, you're vulnerable.

COSTA: *So we're not talking about people with real organic medical problems like epilepsy.*

HALL: No. There's a separate category of cases, and the Salem witchcraft begins with this kind of event, known as possession. These are invariably young women, invariably girls, from the ages of about 9 to 22 or 23 who experience the symptoms of what, in the 17th century, was called diabolical possession. There's no really good psychoanalytic synonym for that. Hysteria is an old-fashioned word that doesn't really work any longer. [There's] striking testimony by people observing that the devil is literally inside and speaking in a gruff voice from these young women. It's just remarkable. The Salem witch hunt was touched off by a number of young girls who collectively went through a kind of period of hysteria—I use that word in the loose sense here—and then began to name other names. They imagined that certain people were accusing them.

Let me turn to the Salem witch hunt. The Salem witch hunt, on the one hand, was a conventional event. There had been witch hunting since the 1630s, 50 or 60 years of witch hunting in New England, so in that sense there's nothing unusual about the Salem witch hunt. What *is* unusual is that a kind of orgy of accusations occurred in this village, not Salem as we know it today, but Danvers, Massachusetts, and then spread to adjoining villages. Around 50 people—men, women, and children—came forward and actually confessed to being witches. This is almost beyond the bounds of comprehension. Part of the process of confessing was to name other people. If you were the magistrate and someone says, 'I'm a witch,' you would say, 'Well, did you go to witch meetings?' They would pause and not know quite what to say but some would say 'yes.' Then, of course, the logical next question was, 'Who else did you see at a witch meeting?' This [caused] an avalanche of names, so by the end of the trials there were 200 people in jail.

COSTA: *Was it only in the Danvers/Salem area in Massachusetts Bay Colony?*

HALL: Only in the Danvers area, Andover. Actually the largest single number of people were accused in Andover than in any other town. [But they were also accused] in Topsfield, and it spread to Boston a tiny bit. It's not called the Andover witch hunt, it's called the Salem witch hunt and I hear people in Andover are grateful for that.

COSTA: *Is there a European analogue to this?*

HALL: Yes, there are European analogues to this. Essex County, England, in the 1640s where actual torture was used. So it's a little different because torture played only a tiny, tiny role in Salem.

COSTA: *In Salem, how were the witches tried?*

HALL: It was pretty much a hanging jury, that's to say, it was a one-day trial, maybe two days at best. What you had was the accused in a courtroom and people who began to remember all these old quarrels. They remembered them as far back as 20 years before. They poured into the court and they just issued this testimony about so-and-so who 20 years ago uttered a curse in my presence and I'm sure that's why my cow died 20 years ago. Of course, there's no way to verify this testimony in the least, by our grounds of objective evidence. They also were testifying about seeing ghosts—their word was 'specters' or 'apparitions'—of these women coming to them in the night and tormenting them. Then you had this sort of Greek chorus of young girls who would sway and sob and claim that they were being pinched and so forth and so on, and they gave testimony. At the end of the day, that was it—unless you confessed. Ironically enough, if you confessed, your sentence was postponed in the hope that your soul would be redeemed and you might yet tell about other people.

COSTA: *As a background to the Salem witch trials, let's talk about some of the concepts behind why this was happening. The early Catholic beliefs were that heaven and hell and purgatory existed and yet despite the Protestant reaction against those concepts, they seemed to have been retained at this period when witches were devil incarnate. What happened?*

HALL: Protestantism was a strongly dualistic religion in this period, so you had this all powerful God, this very strong emphasis on the sovereignty of God and on what, in Protestant doctrine, was called free grace. This is to say that you don't earn salvation by your own merits, you don't really earn it at all, but it's given to you by the intercession of Christ. This, of course, was a doctrine that worked against some kinds of Catholic thinking. If you have a very strong God, you then still need to account for evil in the world because God is, only in some very general sense, the author of evil or misfortune. So it can be said as a truism that doctrines of a very strong God tend to generate doctrines of a very active devil. So this period of Protestant history is one in which the devil and hell and terror are omnipresent as part of the religious system.

COSTA: *Another aspect of this, as you write in your book, is that people in Colonial times were always having supernatural visions and given to confessing everything. They were given to dream interpretations that would impress even Sigmund Freud. What was it in the culture that permitted that kind of activity?*

HALL: It still eludes me entirely to explain this because it calls out for a nonrational explanation, and here we are rational people trying to write rational history, but a couple of things can be said. The Bible is full of people who dream. We all know stories from the Bible: Jacob's ladder and a million dreams that take place. So the Bible sanctions a great deal of phenomena that still carry on in America and in some parts of people's religious heritage. And these people didn't have to go any further than the Bible to say, 'Yes, God still provides prophetic dreams, prophetic visions. There are still signs from heaven of what he's thinking, still natural signs.' Right through the Renaissance all this Greek lore about signs, a kind of natural history, carries right on to the Puritans. That's why I called them Elizabethans in the book. They're really not moderns, they're really backward-looking people who inherited an awful lot of debris or junk, old stuff from the past. That's one historian's explanation.

COSTA: *Is it also true that a lot of immigrants in the last century came here, brought their culture here, and kept it and remained isolated?*

HALL: That's right. I actually read part of this book to a group of people in New York City, most of whose grandparents had come as immigrants from the Old World and from more conservative parts of the Old World, and they had no trouble understanding this at all because they had heard their grandmothers talk about believing in the evil eye. These were things that my ancestors, who were Protestants, gave up a long time ago. But Southern Italians, Eastern Europeans still held some of these beliefs although their children didn't. [This] culture collapsed with the coming of the Age of Reason in the 18th century.

COSTA: *I'd like to talk about faith healing and a modern parallel. Recently in Massachusetts a couple was found guilty of involuntary manslaughter in the death of their son, whom they treated with faith healing. Unfortunately he died because no medical intervention was allowed. In the 1600s most colonists believed that illnesses and sins were linked and people constantly confessed to sins they committed in hopes that such confessions would make them physically well again. Can you tell us some more about that practice?*

HALL: Samuel Sewall was a man who kept a very extensive diary in Boston at the end of the 17th century, so we can follow his actions and his thinking quite precisely. It's striking that when his wife was going into labor, he rises in the morning, he hears that his wife is crying and in pain and his first act is to pray. His next act is to send for two or three ministers to come, who were predictably good prayers, to come and help him pray, and only then does he send for a doctor.

Everyone knew stories of how prayer had healed or prayer had worked some kind of cure. I cite a case in which prayer supposedly deflected an Indian's arrow from hitting somebody. These were stories that were told but, of course, we can't verify these stories. The Puritans did not exclude the professional medicine of their day. God had sanctioned both. God had sanctioned prayer and God had also sanctioned, let's call it, scientific medicine. So you might start with the first, but you'd move fairly rapidly to the second, if it were available. So there wasn't a principle, as there is with Christian Science, of opposing the one and sanctioning the other. That's the difference. But the extent of confidence in prayer that people had is extraordinary.

A *conversation with*

Persi Diaconis

Persi Diaconis is professor of mathematics. Featured in Mathematical
People *(Birkhäuser), Diaconis is an expert in statistics, probability,
and paranormal phenomena. He is currently working on books about
coincidences and mathematical "magic."*

COSTA: *You recently made a discovery about card shuffling and randomness
that surely will shake the gambling capitals of the world. You found that one
needs to shuffle a deck of cards seven times in order for the cards to be in random order.*

DIACONIS: The finding was joint work with David Bayer at Columbia University and it is based on a lifelong interest in the question of how long do you
have to shuffle a deck of cards to mix it up? My original interest in the question was due to my previous life as a magician and my current life as a professor of mathematics, with a specialty in probability.

Probability has its roots in gambling. The earliest discoveries of probability
are all based on questions of gambling, and the question of how many times
do you have to shuffle a deck of cards seemed to be a basic one and one that
none of us could really nail down. That's how I started out on it.

One has to say a little bit about what one means by 'mix it up.' I'm thinking of the fifty-two card deck, a normal deck of cards, and by shuffle I mean:
cut the deck in half and give it a riffle shuffle. And they're not perfectly mixed;
they are just kind of interleafed. What one finds is, first of all, that a few

shuffles—four or five—are not enough to mix up a deck. That is, there is a very strong pattern that persists. But in order to say a pattern persists you have to know where the deck started.

If you are playing in a card game and you see how the cards fell after the last hand, you know something about the deck's initial order. My claim is, for example, if you shuffle a deck of cards four or five times, enough of that initial order persists so that it really isn't well mixed and it makes an enormous difference in practical play of card games. After you shuffle six, seven, eight times and in that range the deck goes from being quite ordered from being very close to perfectly disordered. The remarkable part of the finding is that the transition from structure to random happens in such a short time period. You might think as you mix a deck up more and more it just gets more and more random—what else can happen? That is not the way it works at all.

I have an image of a clear glass bowl, which contains black and white beads. At the beginning, all the black beads are at the bottom and all the white beads are on the top. If you picture stirring the bowl with a canoe paddle, when you started to stir it there would be big streaks and the bottom of the bowl would still be mostly black. That persists for a while and then all of a sudden it gets gray and it stays gray. That's been a finding throughout studies that I have done on a number of ways of randomizing.

The thing that's new is that we can actually prove it as a theorem. It is not 'I think' or 'I guess'; it's a theorem that this phenomenon of the order of cards being intact to being essentially random happens right at seven shuffles.

How many shuffles is enough? There is a sense in which nobody can really answer that question because in order for the deck to be perfectly mixed you have to shuffle it infinitely. But the way I think about it, if you were trying to make use of that information in a casino or a card game it wouldn't be worth the wear and tear after eight or nine shuffles. Seven really is enough for most practical purposes.

COSTA: *Heretofore, most people would shuffle a deck three or four times and consider that adequate.*

DIACONIS: Yes. Bridge players often say three or four times, casinos often five times. By the way, one nice thing about having developed a theory is not only that we know the answer for fifty-two cards, but we know the answer for any size deck. So in Germany one of the big games is called skat and they play with thirty-two cards. For thirty-two cards, five or six shuffles is enough. In casinos they often play with four decks and then you might ask, suppose you played with more cards? Does the number of shuffles double? Well, our theory says the number of shuffles grows like the logarithm of N, that bane of young people in high school. So for two decks of cards, nine shuffles or so is enough and for four decks of cards, thirteen shuffles is where this cut-off point happens and we can tell you the answer for any deck that you'd like.

COSTA: *Have you had word from any of the major gambling houses across*

America or across the world that they are going to start shuffling more because it makes their house odds better?

DIACONIS: Over the years I've studied shuffling, first in work with Jim Reeds at Bell Laboratories and then in work with David Aldous at the University of California at Berkeley. It was the result of months of work in an area called group theory, which is one of the things that I specialize in. At first we knew that twenty or so shuffles was enough for fifty-two cards and then with Aldous we knew that twelve shuffles was enough, and every time I would tell somebody, I would get letters both from casinos and from blackjack players and from interested bridge players asking what we knew and how we knew it and exactly what it meant. So there is a keen interest in it. On the other hand, casinos tend to think that they know it all. I don't know exactly what will happen.

COSTA: *I know that computers played a role in this research. How did you go about using computers? Did you have to write an algorithm for the computer? There is no off-the-shelf shuffling software.*

DIACONIS: One wonderful thing about this problem is that you can't solve it with a computer. Let me explain. The computer has changed the face of the areas of mathematics that I work in. Problems that before were only accessible to years of theoretical work can nowadays just be run on a computer and we get the answer.

Well, fifty-two cards doesn't seem like so many but the number of ways of arranging fifty-two cards is an enormous number. It's about ten to the 68th, ten with sixty-eight zeroes following it. Never will a computer be able to run through all of the arrangements of a deck of cards. . . . So it's not a problem that could be solved by computer. On the other hand, I couldn't have done it without a computer. The breakthrough came when David Bayer, who is an algebraic geometer, was visiting Harvard toward the end of last year, and we started talking about shuffling. David is, among many other talents, a computer wizard. What he did was to try to guess what the answer was by getting the computer to shuffle small decks of six, eight, and ten cards. Even with ten cards, there are three and a half million different arrangements, and if you start shuffling many times and try to keep track of it, it's almost beyond what one can do to make sense out of results that are that computationally heavy. David did manage to look at a formula and guess it and once you know the right answer, that helps a lot. Then we were able to push through by using a very different kind of mathematics, really geometric arguments. We were able to push through and give an exact formula for the chance that the deck is in any given arrangement after any number of shuffles. Having a neat simple formula made the approximations easy and anybody could do them.

COSTA: *Many people think that mathematicians eventually will be replaced by computers. A lot of us know that this isn't true. Could you explain why this isn't true?*

DIACONIS: The shuffling problem is one nice example of that. Even with as humble a problem as shuffling a deck of fifty-two cards, the number of arrangements gets so large that the computer just simply can't handle it. So there are many, many problems to begin with that are just too large for any conceivable computer. Even if every atom in the universe were a computer that was the size of the biggest computers now, it's just very easy to change a fifty-two- to a one hundred-card deck and the [computers] couldn't handle it.

The second thing is that so many of us who have to look at the output of a computer know the computer will just churn out hundreds or thousands of pages of output and how does the human mind make sense out of that kind of output? The only thing I know is to try to organize it, find a theory, and find underlying rationales. That's the job of mathematics: to look at the world around us and find patterns and try to see regularities. There is a mass of data and you have to make sense out of it. Theory is the only way to make sense out of masses of data.

COSTA: *You are also a magician. Is there a hidden intersection between math and magic?*

DIACONIS: I seem to find magical results that have mathematical content and which ask questions that mathematicians have a hard time answering, myself and a number of others included. I think that there is mathematical content in anything, and if we start talking about cooking food or taking the census or almost any area, because I am a mathematician and a statistician, I can find math problems in there. I don't think that there is anything special in magic, but over the years I have found lots of magic tricks that require mathematics in order to make sense out of them.

COSTA: *I know that ancient mathematicians from Euclid's time were fascinated with explaining the real world via mathematics. There also was a great deal of mysticism among early mathematicians. I'm thinking about Pascal's triangle, and of course the mystical followers of Pythagoras around the fourth century B.C. Have you ever investigated any of that?*

DIACONIS: I have been fascinated by a couple of areas that touch on that. One is parapsychology, where I have done an awful lot of work debunking, looking critically at the results of modern parapsychological research and finding that people more or less are finding patterns in noise. A second project, which is very much alive, is one I'm doing with Fred Mosteller of Harvard's Department of Statistics. We are writing a book about finding numeralogical coincidences and patterns in the Bible and lots of other sources, which are often interpreted as the results of a higher power. These are just the kinds of things we like to slice into little pieces.

COSTA: *There is a certain time in the traditional educational cycle of a young person when one knows fairly soon and fairly definitively whether or not one is going to be a mathematician or a scientist. I wonder when that happened for you. Some of the physicists and mathematicians I have interviewed have told me that they knew early on they would become mathematicians or scientists and they also knew that most discoveries are made by people in their youth.*

DIACONIS: I feel as if I am living proof that that's not right. I didn't get at all interested in mathematics until I was 24 years old, when I went back to college after a career of doing something else. In my first three courses in calculus my grades were C, C, and D. Then I got interested and things happened. When I was a kid, I invented card tricks that had a mathematical flavor to them, but I don't feel as if I'm a math whiz kid and I hope that you don't need to be one in order to contribute.

One of the exciting things about being at Harvard is that we really do have wonderful, talented youngsters and I can remember coming here as a graduate student—I was 26 or 27—and at Harvard the people who take graduate courses in mathematics, the first year ones, mostly are undergraduates. I was in the statistics department and didn't know the material, and there would be these kids, these wonderful, gifted youngsters and boy, did I find that depressing. They would understand things so much more quickly and, I thought, deeply than I ever could. I can remember slaving for twenty hours on a homework set and coming in the next day and talking to some kid I was friendly with who was a sophomore or something, and I said smugly, 'Did you get that homework problem?' And he'd say, 'Oh, yeah, and you can see where it comes from and where it goes, and it was sort of cute.' That kid happens also to be a professor here at Harvard; Joe Harris, who is a professor in the math department now. I found it very intimidating, but I kept going. I think that having your own way of looking at things—and my particular strength happens to be finding mathematical problems in the real world and trying to relate the beautiful discoveries of mathematics to real-world phenomena—also has a place. But, boy, I'm sure happy we have whiz kids.

COSTA: *Psychologists talk about in the sciences and in mathematics, particularly, what they call an 'aha' experience: suddenly you look at a problem and say, 'Aha, there it is.' Have you had that kind of insightful experience?*

DIACONIS: I do have aha experiences and they are a great joy. They don't happen very often, and I think hard about them, and I have come to the following conclusion, and this is armchair psychology: I'm sure that my subconscious mind is in there working all the time, and I've become more and more sure of it as time goes on. What I think happens is that I'm stuck on a problem, I either sleep on it or I do something else, and I can find that it can even be hard to carry on a conversation because I'm churning away inside. I'm really not aware of what I'm doing and then I come back to it, not knowing that I've made some progress inside and then, aha, the answer just leaps to mind. That has happened to me enough that I've actually come to have faith in it.

At the moment, for example, I'm learning a new area, the mathematics of group theory. I don't know why I'm learning it, and I am spending many hours a day studying just like a student does. I don't have a problem I want to solve; it just feels right. Every time I have done this in the past, it seemed like I was doing the right thing. It has worked out for me in the past and I just have faith it will work out again. But I think something subconsciously knows some other problem I want to work on and says these are the tools, go learn them, but those links aren't connected or clear for me. It is one of the great joys when it happens, and if you want to experience it, you just work on easier problems.

My friend Martin Gardner, who is one of the great science writers in America, wrote a beautiful little book called *Aha Insight*, and it is a list of problems, which if you think about them, do seem to come to most people after a few minutes. It is almost like an optical illusion, that is, you can't see it and then it just pops into mind. So it is possible to experience if you want to work at it.

COSTA: *I once interviewed a mathematician several years ago who used to do what you did. While he drove he would ruminate about problems and he'd get to his place of work, which was a seventeen-mile drive, and not know how he got there. He said if he ever wanted to make a bumper sticker for mathematicians it would be: 'If you think, don't drive.' I think there is something to that. Your field of statistics, even for a lot of people who are gifted in mathematics, is a difficult field. Can you explain why many people have difficulty with statistics?*

DIACONIS: It is true that statistics is not such a widely understood part of modern mathematics, but I think that that is just a historical accident. Statistics is a relatively young discipline, eighty years old or 100 years old in its modern venue, and it simply isn't a part of most math departments. One exciting thing about the department I'm part of is that it is a very, very alive department, so I've come, the first probabilist that they have ever had at Harvard and I taught a graduate course in probability and I had six faculty sit in on it. I think I taught them how to see probability and I hope I taught the students something too. But I do think that you have to be around somebody for whom it's a living subject and then you can learn it.

I had a similar experience in the subject that I'm now studying, which is group theory, which is the opposite of statistics—it's the mathematics of symmetry. I've never been around a real, live group theorist; Harvard doesn't really have one right now and I learned it from books and I learned it from people who learned it from books and I never really got it. I happened to be visiting the University of Chicago last quarter and there is a group there so I sat in on some courses and I just heard them speaking a language in which they knew what they were talking about, they knew what it all meant, they knew the roots and the extent of it and it became a living subject for me. I think that the trouble that most people have about statistics is because we haven't trained enough statisticians and it's not an integral part of the discipline now. It is quite a young science. The department at Harvard that I came out of, for example, is 25 years old. Mathematics is, I don't know, thousands of years old. I don't think it's a time to judge and certainly I don't think that there is a deep reason that people can't learn statistics. If you haven't been exposed to it, it looks funny to you.

COSTA: *That seems odd to me, since the buzzword today is competitiveness. I would think that statistics for industry would be important in helping do everything from quality control to predicting results of assembly lines. Why isn't there a greater emphasis in higher education on statistics?*

DIACONIS: Statistics is a spectacularly successful field for its age and its size. The department at Harvard, for example, has four senior people in it. It's a tiny little department and of course Harvard is a university with splendid, tiny little departments. But the statistics graduates get two and three job offers and the world is very eager to beat a path to their door. I just think that it's a question of the world learning that it is a hot, exciting field. I think it is hard to realize but it really is a field that is just starting and just finding its way in the world. After 100 years I think that statistics will have integrated itself in a much more basic way than it has now.

COSTA: *Let's talk for a moment about that ten-year period from age 14 to 24 when you were a traveling magician. What was that like and would you do it again?*

DIACONIS: I would certainly hope that I would do it again. It was a great, great experience. It gave me roots and a base that I draw upon all the time. I had a wonderful opportunity when I was 14. The world's best magician, the best sleight-of-hand guy in the world, a guy named Dai Vernon called me up one day and said, 'Hey, kid. Do you want to go on the road with me?' I said, 'Sounds good,' and he said 'Meet me tomorrow on the West Side highway at 2 o'clock.' I did and off we went, and I never went back.

For a couple of years I traveled around with him, pulling the curtain and learning. He's a great guru. He's out on the West Coast now. We split up about after about two years and he went out to found what is called the Magic Castle in Hollywood, a marvelous showplace of magic in America, and I went back to New York, where I worked as a magician and I wasn't a great star or anything. Being a sixteen-year-old magician in New York with no other source of income isn't the easiest life.

COSTA: *Were there any tricks that you studied and studied and never could understand how they were done?*

DIACONIS: My old mentor Vernon used to torture me with things like that. He would never tell me so. He'd get up and he'd say 'Well, I've been thinking about sleight-of-hand all my life and I think I have discovered the essence of true sleight-of-hand and I can say it in a single sentence.' My ears would perk up and then he'd say, 'But I've decided that I'm never going to say that sentence out loud.' Some of those sentences I don't know to this day. He would similarly tell me about tricks that I don't know about to this day. By and large, any tricks that I've actually seen performed eventually I've figured out.

A *conversation with*

Henry Rosovsky

Henry Rosovsky is Lewis P. and Linda L. Geyser University
Professor, acting dean of the Faculty of Arts and Sciences, and a
Fellow of Harvard College. An economist, his most recent book is
The University: An Owner's Manual *(W.W. Norton). Rosovsky was*
instrumental in establishing the Core Curriculum at Harvard.

COSTA: *Your new book is entitled,* The University: An Owner's Manual. *I*
am interested in how you came about that title?

ROSOVSKY: Many people have asked me about that because it's a slightly
unusual title. The title has two sources. The first one has to do with the fact
that I happen to love automobiles, therefore I've read many owner's manuals.
I am a member of the Saab Club of America, I'm a subscriber to *Road &*
Track magazine—in fact my picture was once in *Road & Track* magazine. So
that was one reason why I had thought of the genre, owner's manual.

The other reason is the serious one, I suppose. I felt that universities were
broad public institutions and many people claimed 'ownership' of these institutions. Students often say that they are the university, the faculty believe that
they own the university, the administrators often behave as if they own the
university. The press, the public, everyone seems to think that somehow it
belongs to them. So I wanted to write a book that addresses each one of these
constituencies and explains to them what their responsibilities are, where they
fit into the greater scheme of things. As I said in my book, I use the word

'owner' in the sense of saying, 'This is my country.' Well, the country doesn't belong to anybody, but it is my country nevertheless.

COSTA: *You will forever be known as the 'former dean' of the Faculty of Arts and Sciences. As the former dean, how do you define an educated person?*

ROSOVSKY: A good many years ago now, it must be around eleven or twelve years ago, at a time when I was very actively thinking about these issues, I once tried my hand at defining an educated person. We were then discussing curriculum and I thought that it was impossible to approach this topic without having some notion of what a liberally educated person is. I said at that time that first of all an educated person had to be able to communicate effectively. By that I meant reading and writing and expressing him- or herself orally in an effective and, one hopes, even an eloquent manner.

Secondly, I thought that an educated person would have to have, I think I called it, a critical appreciation and informed acquaintance with the main ways in which mankind gains knowledge about ourselves and our universe. In the sciences this is done by the use of mathematical and experimental methods. In the social sciences, it is done largely by historical methods and to some extent also by quantitative means. In the humanities, it is done by studying great traditions. So that's the second aspect.

A third aspect is to avoid being provincial when emerging with a liberal education. I was very struck by the fact that American students know very little of the outside world and I wanted to be certain that they had an acquaintance of other parts of the world and other cultures. I also felt—and this is the fourth point—that a student should have in their liberal education a serious encounter with moral and ethical issues. That used to be done at home, by churches, by organized religion, but I felt that in our time, in the 1970s, '80s, and '90s, this was no longer done effectively. I didn't think that the curriculum could do it by itself, but I thought that [ethics] should be represented. And, finally, I also believed that liberal education can't only be informed acquaintance and critical appreciation, but it also has to include in-depth learning. I thought that that would be the role of the concentration, or the major. That was my definition of a liberally educated person.

COSTA: *As a professor of economics and as a dean, you've dedicated your life to a concept that this university believes in: that a faculty member at Harvard has to do two things very well—teach and do research. A lot of people don't believe that that's the case. They question teaching at a research institution and wonder if teaching isn't done better at a small college where a professor doesn't have to divide his or her time between the two callings. What's your current view of this?*

ROSOVSKY: I'm interested in the fact that, at least so far, one of the parts of my book that has attracted the most comment is the brief section in which I try to explain why people might have an incentive for being taught by people who do research. Let me make clear what I mean. First of all, some colleges do research. That's a very important point to remember. There is now a whole group of very fine colleges that specialize in having faculties that do a certain amount of research. The emphasis is more on teaching, but nevertheless, they also have an important research component. Furthermore, I never said that a research university is for everybody as an undergraduate. I recognize that people have different needs. Indeed, that is, for me, one of the most intriguing aspects of American education: the great amount of choice that it offers to people in terms of everything—cost, location, emphasis. It is a very rich mix for people to choose from. But for some people, and I think particularly for people who are highly self-motivated, who are very curious, who are intellectually ambitious, maybe even for those who are intellectually precocious, there is an enormous advantage in being taught by a research-oriented faculty. Research and teaching are, emphatically, not a zero-sum game. A lot of people say that; they often say it about Harvard because I think that it's difficult to compete with Harvard, so the easiest thing is to say that our professors don't like to teach, or teach badly. I think the evidence for that is quite the contrary. I once did a little survey that showed that ninety percent of the senior Harvard faculty teach at least one undergraduate course a year. I keep repeating that, but nobody believes it because the myth is very often more important than the evidence.

The reason I think research enriches teaching—to start with the most obvious—is that it prevents burnout. I think that's a very good point because teaching the same thing all the time, not enriched by research activity, is deadly. That's one reason, by the way, that teachers in primary and secondary education burn out so much more than teachers in higher education. It must be a great chore to go into the classroom year after year and repeat what you've said before.

But the most important point to me, and I deeply believe this, is that research is an expression of optimism about the human condition. I think it's better to be taught by people who have a fundamentally optimistic point of view about their surroundings than people who may be more cramped because they are not refreshed by new ideas and research. I say 'optimism about the human condition' because when you do research, you have to believe that there is something new to be discovered. That's hope. You've got to believe that you've got something to say that hasn't been said before. You can be a critic, you can revise, you can move in another direction, you can open up. All these are things that make for a kind of intellectual optimism and excitement that is absent when there is no research. By the way, that does not mean that I approve of occasionally irresponsible behavior of people who want nothing to do with undergraduates, or all of the bad things that we know do, on occasion, exist.

COSTA: *Tell me what it's like going from being a world-class economist doing cutting-edge research to suddenly having to worry about having class-rooms painted, and so on.*

ROSOVSKY. It was a very interesting transition. The most interesting thing about it is that one is totally unprepared. One of the unusual aspects of academic administration is that the people who are selected for these tasks have no previous experience. It's almost as if previous experience is held against an individual. My successor had been a department chairman for one year. My predecessor was a very distinguished labor economist, but he certainly had no particular experience at faculty administration. I came in at a time when there was quite a major economic crisis at Harvard. This was in the early 1970s, in the Carter years, there was inflation and all the problems associated with this, and I promised the Corporation that when I became dean I would eliminate the deficit in three years. We were running a large deficit at the time. I used to sit at night and worry about whether we were spending too much money. I would ask myself, 'Is there enough money in the bank to pay our bills the next day?' I conceived of it from the point of view of a household economy. Our budget was about $200 million and it took me a long time to realize that two years would go by before anybody had the figures in a budget of that size to know what was really going on. So I had a kind of terror. You asked me what it was like? I hate to say this because I always get a lot of flack, but I compared myself to a dentist because I said, 'Half-hour interviews with a fair amount of pain.' When I said that, it somehow got into the papers and I got a letter from the president of the American Dental Association accusing me of contributing to the bad name of his profession. So I don't say that anymore.

It is a very, very sharp change of lifestyle. I must say I enjoyed it very much while I did it. I have no regrets at all having left it. At the time, it was fun and it was very stimulating because you meet an enormous number of people that you otherwise would never get to meet—alumni, faculty, students, all sorts of people. It's very stimulating. Something else that I've said frequently is that being dean of the Faculty of Arts and Sciences at Harvard is like being the curator of a national treasure. I really do think that's what it is. I'm not saying that it is unique, that it is the best, but it's one of our national treasures and I like to think that I approached it in that way.

COSTA: *Why does higher education cost so much?*

ROSOVSKY: I knew that sooner or later someone was going to ask me that question. The whole cost question is a peculiar one, but let me talk about it a little bit because I think it's one that is widely misunderstood. Recently, the president of the University of Rochester wrote a very interesting memoir in which he pointed out that in the late 1950s a Pontiac automobile cost about $2,200 or $2,300. Then he said that a year of college at that time—at Harvard in fact, I checked the Harvard figures—was exactly the same (in 1959). And today, a Pontiac automobile, middle level, costs about $22,000, just about the price of a year at Harvard College. That's worth thinking about because it is much easier, surely, to have gains in productivity in industry and in manufacturing, than in education. Not only does the cost of an automobile compare pretty well with what's happened to the cost of higher education, but, in fact, most people have more than one automobile, and in 1959 they didn't. I think that's worth remembering. And, finally, I say this with some hesitation, but maybe I can say it being a car buff, people have been very critical of the quality of higher education but I think very few people will claim that we have done as badly with quality as the American automobile industry.

In America there is extraordinary choice in terms of what kind of education one can purchase: expensive private schools, less expensive private schools, much cheaper public schools. Quality is not uniquely related to price at all. You can get a superb education in the United States throughout a very wide price range. Another point is that in the very expensive private schools— Harvard, Stanford, Yale, Chicago, places of that kind—enormous sums of money are going into scholarships. I think at Harvard about sixty percent of the students get some scholarship aid. Finally, it's also true, as any economist knows, that not all prices rise at the same rate. That is, relative prices change over time. Some things are more expensive at certain periods, others are less expensive. I'm saying all this because I'm not in agreement with the trendy notion that the cost of higher education is out of control. I would like the cost to rise less. I think it is our social obligation to keep the costs from rising anymore than is absolutely necessary, but I don't think the simple notion that it is rising all that much makes a great deal of sense.

COSTA: *You've written in your book that the dean's greatest responsibility— and I think you also said the president of a university's—is to recruit the best faculty in the world. Why should that responsibility remain number one?*

ROSOVSKY: Because I believe that the faculty is the hub of this particular wheel. The quality of the faculty is the most important determinant of the quality of the university. It determines the kinds of students we get because, basically, the students are drawn here by the quality of the faculty. You may think that students come to Harvard because of some romantic notion, because their parents came here, because of its history. All of these things matter, but basically people are drawn to Harvard because they know that the quality of the faculty here is among the very best anywhere. That's what draws people here from all over the world. So that's one point: it attracts the best students. Furthermore, it then produces the best alumni, and those are the alumni that support us. Also, the best quality attracts research funding.

The whole life of the university ultimately depends on the quality of the faculty because it determines all other things. Therefore, it is the most important obligation for presidents, deans, and anybody who administers the institution to worry about.

COSTA: *Your life is a symbol of what Harvard believes in, and that's diversity. You are appointed to the ruling board of the university. That is, you are a Fellow of Harvard College. Tell me how Harvard has changed; it is no longer a bastion for the privileged the way it was fifty, sixty, seventy years ago. How are admissions policies reflecting a commitment to diversity?*

ROSOVSKY: There has been much criticism of higher education in recent years. While I understand many reasons to be critical, I've always been struck by a paradox: as I say in my book, two-thirds of the best universities in the world are located in the United States. Now that's a small number—we're not talking about 3,500 institutions. But I'm talking about 50 to 100 institutions, and I think that's recognized widely throughout the world. That's why everybody is flocking here. But I'm struck by this paradox because, as I said in the piece I wrote some time ago, of what else do we have two-thirds of the best? Of steel mills? Automobile factories? Banks? I don't think so. Somebody said to me, 'hospitals.' Well, maybe, and that's probably the hospitals that are affiliated with our great universities.

I've been looking at what our critics have to say. I feel that many of them are extremely nostalgic and I think that's one of their greatest flaws. I admit that some good points are made, but these good points are indelibly flawed by an overwhelming sense of nostalgia. Forty years ago, when I was young, civilization was at its height; it has been in decline ever since. A lot of people believe that, I suppose, in every generation. Graduates of every college believe it. But the trouble is that now some critics have given voice to these nostalgic feelings and I think they are rather misleading. When I think back to the Harvard that was here when I came—I came to Harvard as a graduate student in 1949—or when I think of my alma mater, William and Mary, I'm not particularly attracted to the institutions at that time. I don't think that they were bad, but I think it's a travesty to suggest that we are less good today.

People always talked of the beauty of common learning at that time. By 'common learning' I think people mean that there was a kind of consensus, an intellectual and educational consensus. But it was a very easy and not particularly interesting consensus. It was a consensus that was largely based on whites, very often on white gentlemen, very often on white gentlemen from a very narrow socioeconomic base. There were hardly ever any blacks, very few women, Jews were well controlled. It's not a particularly attractive consensus in retrospect. As I said in my book, some people have the picture that we all sat around a kindly Socratic figure, drinking milk and eating cookies, and discussing late Beethoven quartets. That was not the picture I had. We may, for example, not have had drugs in those days, but we had an enormous amount of drunkenness and we had many of the ills of society that have not, in any significant way, changed.

The situation is much more complicated today. We have become much more diverse. We have brought in different cultures. This has become in many ways much more of a proportional representation society. . . . I think that the university has reacted quite creatively to these challenges and I think that the university today—I'm talking about the universities across this country—is, in many ways, more attractive places than they were forty years ago. As I said in my book, I like the university better today than when I was a student. I think what's most distinctive about my book is that it is optimistic and positive. I think it may be the first positive book that's been written about higher education in 25 years.

COSTA: *In the last few chapters of your book you offer advice to deans and presidents at other universities. I was intrigued by one of your principles of deaning in which you say that it's often appropriate to say 'no comment' to the media about various institutional issues. As a university spokesperson I often feel that my role is to give professors, deans, even the president, their Miranda rights. I tell them: 'You have the right to remain silent; anything you say can and will be held against you on page one tomorrow.' Do you agree with that practice?*

ROSOVSKY: I always used to tell President Bok to remember one thing, and that is that today's newspapers are used to wrap tomorrow's fish. The trouble with that is that almost nobody buys fish wrapped in newspapers anymore, so they don't really know what I'm talking about. But I think that that's a very important lesson.

In general, I always talked to the press, probably more than most people. When I was dean, I hardly ever refused to talk to the press, and to the *Crimson* [Harvard student newspaper] in particular, because I think that they're entitled to hear what we have to say. But there are important moments when you have to say yourself that no comment is required, that silence is golden on certain occasions. One difficulty with professors—and the *Crimson* capitalizes on this—is that they don't deal with the press very much, so they'll say anything because they really don't have very much experience. I think dealing with the press takes training just the way everything else does.

COSTA: *You defend and also criticize tenure in your book. Could you give us an evaluation of the tenure process at a research institution, why it's important to have tenure, do you think it should be changed, and what do you think of mandatory retirement?*

ROSOVSKY: Let me begin with tenure. I do defend tenure and I have always been puzzled by the great hostility toward academic tenure in our society. Tenure exists in many different fields. Not long ago I happened to have lunch with a former chief justice of the United States, and this very eminent jurist and I started talking about tenure. He attacked me in the most harsh manner, not personally harsh, but obviously he had very strong feelings about it. He thought that academic tenure was terrible, should be gotten rid of, and so on. And I said, 'Chief, what about your own profession?' And he said to me, 'That's totally different.' I think people have that kind of attitude.

The defense of tenure normally takes the form of academic freedom, and various other reasons. But I think the most important reason is what I call 'tenure as social contract.' When we bring people into academic life, these are people who should have high talent. And their talent is usually of a rather general kind: they could be lawyers, doctors, businesspeople, but they want to do something else and we want them to devote their lives to a different pursuit. That has many rewards. But it also requires sacrifices.

I think that being a professor is a very good life in terms of income, family, obligations of this kind. We are certainly, in no sense, poor. Our salaries are quite respectable, but they do represent a definite sacrifice for many of us vis-a-vis the outside world. I think one reason we agree to choose this life is because we join a kind of extended family. That's the way I like to think of the university. I know that this family will examine me most rigorously before allowing me to become a permanent member. But once I'm a member, it's a kind of marriage. That means that professors should have a sense of security, should not worry about people changing their minds about them, about what they have to say, and so on. I know of a case at Harvard of a professor who wrote very little for a period of some fifteen years, and people started whispering and asking what's going on. Then he published a book that has become, perhaps, the most important work published in his field during the last generation. If we understand that and we understand that no one ever said anything to that individual either in terms of tenure or salary advancement, etc., you see the university at its best.

There has been introduced into all of this a great complication, and that is the lifting of the retirement age in, I believe, 1994. I find that very worrisome because I think that particularly at institutions like Harvard where the students are good, the working conditions excellent, the work itself a pleasure—no heavy lifting and you don't have to stand on your feet all day—that the incentive to stay will be irresistible. Now you could say, what's wrong with that? There will be, in the 1990s, a great shortage of Ph.D.'s. We know that; I think that's been shown. Now, shouldn't we allow older professors to stay? Well, not necessarily, because academic life uniquely depends not only on the inflow of the young, but on giving the young responsibility. In other words, I think it's very important that the choices in this and other universities be in the hands of younger people, and not older people continuing to control who gets appointed, who is selected, who is good, who is not as good. Academic life changes all the time, fields progress, and it's a simple fact that older people cannot understand these things as well as people who are right at the top of their field who are generally in early middle age. So I'm very worried about that.

A conversation with

Marjorie Garber

Marjorie Garber is professor of English. Her mission as director of the Center for Literary and Cultural Studies is to provide a "locus for interdisciplinary discussions." Several of her books illuminate aspects of Shakespeare's works; she is the author of Vested Interests: Cross-Dressing and Cultural Anxiety *(Routledge).*

COSTA: *Since you are our leading expert on Shakespeare, what is it like to teach 900 students at once, and why does Shakespeare continue to be so popular even with today's kids who are hooked on video?*

GARBER: Teaching 900 students is exhilarating. It's a daily education. It's exhausting but it's also immensely inspiriting. Teaching them in Sanders Theatre, which is a beautiful, flexible lecture hall, very much, in some ways, like Shakespeare's Globe [Theatre], is itself very gratifying. The opportunity to talk about theater in a theater to students who are interested in theater as well as literature is very exciting.

COSTA: *Is Sanders Theatre bigger than the Globe Theatre?*

GARBER: It's smaller in terms of the numbers of persons within it. The Globe Theatre, we think, held between 2,500 and 3,000 people, and Sanders holds about 1,100. But the tier system—the rows of people on top of one another—is very similar in the sense of being surrounded by auditors. Certainly the fact that it's made of wood and that it's designed as a theatrical building is all to the good in teaching this kind of course. The short answer is, I love the course.

COSTA: *What feedback do you get from the students who take the course? Why is it so popular? Why are they studying Shakespeare?*

GARBER: For lots of different reasons. Shakespeare is that which to a certain extent defines the modern sensibility in Western culture—English and American speaking culture, also in certain European cultures—and has done so truly since the 17th century. Shakespeare keeps being reinvented and rediscovered by every age and re-recognized in every age, so that you have . . . German speakers in the 19th century writing about *unser* Shakespeare, our Shakespeare, as if Shakespeare were a German author. The world Shakespeare congress this coming summer will be held in Japan, which has produced a large number of Shakespearean scholars doing a great deal of publishing and, of course, has produced some of the most brilliant of Shakespeare movies, in the movies of [Akira] Kurosawa. Shakespeare is an international phenomenon. Shakespeare studies are a language.

Most students come to Shakespeare as if for the second time. Whether or not they have read *Hamlet*, they feel as if they have because *Hamlet* has been disseminated into our common language. At a time when the literary canon is expanding, Shakespeare represents something of a common experience for students, whether they have studied him previously or not. I think there's a sense both of discovery and recognition for students coming to Shakespeare for the first time or the twelfth time, for undergraduates and for graduates. It's also the most exciting teaching one can do. Talking about Shakespeare in the classroom is an enormously rewarding thing to do. I know this not only from my own experience but from that of my graduate students, even those who are not primarily Renaissance scholars.

COSTA: *Critics say that Shakespeare in the late Renaissance seemed to write for more of a mixed public. Critics also say that playgoers of that era may have been more trained to be listeners than we are; reading was done by a smaller group of people back then. Do you agree with this and do you think that Shakespeare pandered a bit to his audiences because of the listening aspect of it?*

GARBER: Different scholars have had different views about what kinds of persons were in Shakespeare's audience, whether it was an educated populace, whether there was more of a social mix, what kind of a place the Shakespearean or Renaissance playhouse was. We know that it was much more of a social nexus than today's theater might be considered to be. There was less of a sense of a hush coming over the assembled multitude; it was more like going to a ballgame. The people came in and out, oranges were sold, there was a good deal of dalliance in certain segments of the theater. It was a place for society to *take place*.

I don't know what would be meant exactly by saying that Shakespeare pandered to his audience. He was a very successful theater manager and man of the theater as well as playwright. He clearly wrote plays which his audiences enjoyed, and that was one of his principal motives, we would think, in doing so. No document exists that tells us what his motives were in writing plays.

Some plays were performed for private audiences, some in front of royal groups, noble groups, in private theaters, others were produced mostly for the public stage. One of the most exhilarating things about looking at the plays is just to look at the ways in which various theatrical moments can play to more than one audience at a time. Certainly the history of the reception of Shakespeare plays has been one in which different qualities were valued by different time periods.

We think we know what the greatest of Shakespeare plays were, but *The Tempest*, for example, was immediately rewritten, and held the stage for a century in a form wholly unrecognizable from the form that it is in right now. *Macbeth*, for many years, was played with additions written by another hand, which changed the play quite materially. Probably everyone knows about the famous revision of *King Lear* in which Cordelia and Edgar marry at the end of the play and do not die. The tastes change, and Shakespeare seems to change with social and theatrical tastes.

It's not really possible for us to recapture fully what it would have been like to be in the 16th- or 17th-century audience. A lot of quite brilliant work has been done in reconstructing what the audience may have been like, and who may have been at particular kinds of performances, and which actors were in what roles, and so on. But to avoid the sense of museum Shakespeare, of merely trying to do Shakespeare in quotation, there is a sense in which we both need to know [the history] and also need to look at Shakespeare through our own contemporary eyes.

COSTA: *A high school English teacher I know once told me that she often took her students to the American Shakespeare Festival Theater in Stratford, Connecticut. Some of her students said after they had heard all those famous lines that they didn't like Shakespeare because he was full of cliches. Is that a common misconception for young people—not realizing that he originated those phrases?*

GARBER: Oh, sure. 'Oh, that's where that comes from!' That response is very common. One thing to bear in mind is that Shakespeare himself is in fact quite consciously in some cases writing down cliches that he's famous for: his 'All the world's a stage' that goes in the mouth of Jacques in *As You Like It*. At the time that Jacques is speaking that he speaks it in a context which makes it clear that it is a cliche, that people kind of hem and haw on the sides of the stage when he delivers it. Shakespeare, taken out of context, is often credited for presenting an originality of things, which he is fact encoding as cliche.

The wisdom of Polonius is another good example of this. Polonius, you might like to know, is the Shakespearean speaker most frequently quoted in the *Congressional Record*. 'Neither a borrower nor a lender be,' and so on, all of these truisms, which are presented as truisms in the Shakespearean context, are cited by lawmakers as not truisms, but true.

But the experience of recognizing Shakespeare, which we spoke of earlier by talking about what it is that brings students to study the plays, the sense of recognizing pieces of their own culture and putting the pieces together, seeing the context in which these pieces represent themselves is often very startling for students and very gratifying: to see the way in which a line that they have known or think they have known all these years, in fact, fits in an ironic or critical context within the plays and may have shades of meaning quite different from the meanings that they seem to have in Bartlett's or in the *Congressional Record.*

COSTA: *You're the director of the Center for Literary and Cultural Studies here at Harvard, which was founded in 1984 with a grant from the Mellon Foundation. Can you tell me what the mission of the Center is?*

GARBER: The Center was founded to foster interdisciplinary and cross-cultural work by faculty, students, and independent scholars, not only at Harvard, but in the Greater Boston and greater New England area. It has coincided in the years of its operation with a tremendous flowering in exactly this kind of work that moves from discipline to discipline, combines philosophy and literature, art history and history. We found that we had a lot of people coming to the Center and showing us new work which precisely exists on the margins of disciplines, people who are doing work quite similar to one another who would not know normally what department to seat that work in. People whose background is anthropological, for example, might come together with people in a seminar on politics, literature, and the arts and find people in humanities departments who are doing work which is very germane to theirs. We function as a place in which people can share work, network, and also have a sense of where various disciplinary inquiries are going.

COSTA: *It seems to parallel the current trend to try to get young students to be less specialized and to follow a subject across disciplines. Is that, in essence, what's happening here?*

GARBER: Yes, it is, though not in a programmatic way because what we exist to do is to function as continuing education, so to speak, for faculty, young professionals, and graduate students. This is a place in which instead of teaching, people come to learn and to share work. The organization of the Center is not one of teacher and student, but that of a shared or collective enterprise in which a paper will normally be distributed by mail to all who request it, and then on a given day, some group of between twenty and a hundred people will get together who have read the paper and meet with its author and hear a few words setting the context of the paper and then discuss the ideas contained in it. It's less directed than a class would be. It's more a result of individual people's initiatives and [there are] some twenty-two headings in which we currently field seminars.

COSTA: *Is there any resistance to this approach? Scholars since Plato's time used to concentrate on a narrow area and pursue it in great depth. Does one militate against the other?*

GARBER: No, I don't think so. I think that most of the work we're seeing and hearing at the Center is work which is done in considerable depth. It's just that the academic disciplines do change over time. The history of the field of English studies, for example, has a very recent history. English studies as an academic discipline was really founded at the end of the last century. Already the question of a national literature is under some inquiry in curricular as well as noncurricular places. What the Center is doing is essentially riding the crest of the wave of where intellectual inquiry is, which will naturally be in a slightly different place from where academic departments or disciplines may find themselves because they exist to codify and to teach. . . .

COSTA: *Does the Center have any stance on the controversy concerning core curricula these days and the canon?*

GARBER: The Center is comprised of some 4,000 people who receive our newsletter and who attend one or many of our twenty-two seminars on [subjects] from politics, literature, and the arts to Celtic literature, medieval literature, and feminist literary theory or 18th-century literature and cultures. Our first annual conference, some years ago, was on the literary canon in the institution. It was very well attended and professors from a variety of scholarly disciplines spoke on what they thought the status of the canon was within their own discipline and what the impact of that was pedagogically. I think it may be time for us to return to that question since it's an ongoing and fascinating question for anyone in the teaching business, anybody who is either a teacher or a student in an academic situation today.

COSTA: *Do core curricula have anything to do, as some Allan Bloom types might say, with fad? There are some authors from Western civilization who should be read forever and the current controversy shouldn't limit reading those people; perhaps we should add to the list, but keep a core list, the argument goes.*

GARBER: I have a couple of answers to that question. One is that I think that the reading of Shakespeare, Spenser, Milton, Dickens, Joyce, Jane Austen, and Virginia Woolf is very unlikely to go out of style. These are not endangered species. This is the bread and butter of any English literary training.

But also 'fad' and 'trendy' are peculiar words that are themselves rather faddish. If you consider, for example, that the poetry of John Donne was out of print for 200 years before the edition of 1912 and T.S. Eliot's famous review of that, which made Donne, again, canonical and one of the most often-taught poets in English literature concentrations today. In 1900, Donne might have been considered a faddish notion. It would have been considered strange to consider him as a cornerstone or building block of an English education.

I think we're in a situation where opening up the canon is a way, on the one hand, of rectifying the sometimes inadvertent omissions of the past. But [it also has] installed within the center of new curricula, crucially important, crucially valuable writers and artists who were neglected for [various] reasons—some of them social and political, some of them historical reasons. The popularity of a black woman writer, Zora Neale Hurston, for example, who is now so often taught in so many literature courses, is a relatively new phenomenon but I think that there's a general sense that this is brilliant and very important work. And there's work that was simply unavailable to our students a few years ago.

COSTA: *To switch subjects, you're doing research on the phenomenon of cross-dressing. Could you tell us how you got interested in that, and what you are finding?*

GARBER: I just finished a book called *Vested Interests: Cross-Dressing and Cultural Anxiety*, which is going to be published by Routledge in the fall of 1991. I no longer remember how exactly I got into this work because I've been [studying] it for a number of years. Certainly one thing that intrigued me was not only the presence of a number of cross-dressers in Shakespearean plays, but a lot of work that has been done on the boy actor and about transvestism as a cultural issue not only in Shakespeare and Renaissance drama but in pamphlets inveighing against it at the time. There's been a lot of interesting social and cultural work on the presence of cross-dressers not only in the plays but in the streets at the time.

But I really became very interested in the question of the way in which cross-dressing has caught the popular cultural imagination, so the book discusses things like why Peter Pan has always been played by a woman and it discusses the play *M. Butterfly*, the story of an extraordinary romance of a French diplomat with a Chinese opera star whom he thought to be a woman and whom he discovered to be a man, [and so on]. I got quite interested in film and contemporary culture. I've done some work on Madonna and Michael Jackson.

COSTA: *Madonna doesn't cross-dress.*

GARBER: Yes, she does. In her 'Express Yourself' video she cross-dresses in a man's suit and a monocle. I have a whole section in which I talk about the monocle as a gender signifier in the early part of the twentieth century. She very clearly is recapitulating [this] in her videos. Of course, she wears a bustier and garters underneath that so she exactly explodes the phenomenon of cross-dressing by being both at once. But in her most recent show, in this Blonde Ambition tour, she also has men wearing bras. She's extremely interested in deconstructing gender conventions in clothing and the power structure that goes with it in the music business, so she shows up at several points in my inquiry.

I also got quite interested in the phenomenon of transsexual surgery. When I started to do this project I was quite convinced that transvestism and transsexualism were quite different, and indeed they are, both from a psychological a from social point of view, [and] there are certain people who would define themselves as transvestites and certain people who would define themselves as transsexuals and they're quite different populations. But from a political point of view, there's a lot that these groups have in common. They meet with many of the same kinds of social questions, they have some of the same difficulties passing, shopping, and being accepted for persons who transgress a certain kind of social norm. There are, I discovered, around the country and around the world, lots of groups that are for transvestites and transsexuals, which are social support groups, which involve in many cases, supporting spouses because, contrary to what is sometimes thought, many transvestites are heterosexual. In fact, their statistics suggest that most transvestites are heterosexual.

I became very interested in the [social place of] drag in culture; and transvestite shows on the stage (of a historical nature); the question of all the women, for example, who played Shakespeare in the 19th and 20th centuries, who played Shakespearean men, who played Iago, who played Hamlet; the recent production in which a woman played Falstaff; the ways in which people are experimenting with these highly gendered characters and in which the literature of analysis is somehow following this cross-dressing trend to find feminine aspects in Falstaff or feminine aspects in Hamlet. There's a famous 19th-century scholar and indeed a 20th-century German film which argue that Hamlet was, in fact, a woman and that a lot of his problems stem from this misunderstanding.

The project really ranges widely and tries to investigate the contemporary cultural fascination with cross-dressing and why it is that you can hardly pick up a copy of *Time* or *People* magazine or the *New York Times* and not find something about [an instance of cross-dressing], why these things seem to be all over our culture right now.

COSTA: *Was there a greater instance or acceptance of cross-dressing in Elizabethan times?*

GARBER: No, because Deuteronomy claims that it's a violation of propriety and God's law to wear the dress of the other gender. This was the claim of Puritan pamphleteers against the stage altogether because boy actors played the parts of women on the English stage and this meant that they, in their professional capacity, had to cross-dress. This was one of the main points being argued against the appropriateness of the stage.

I think over time a more flexible attitude toward cross-dressing on the stage has evolved, but the stage has always been the safe space for cross-dressing, whether you're talking about Divine or drag shows or [a character from Shakespeare], whether you're talking about what we call high culture or what we might call popular culture. The stage has been the place which has allowed that, and has allowed that instead of permitting it in the audience or in the ordinary culture. What we're beginning to see, not only in unisex clothing but in a more flexible sense of the proprieties of gender dress altogether, is a change in that, though not a complete reversal.

COSTA: *Even Milton Berle did lots of things in drag.*

GARBER: Yes, Milton Berle or *Some Like It Hot*, the extraordinary classics of film—Cary Grant in *Bringing up Baby*. But Milton Berle's a good example of someone who routinely played women almost every Tuesday night on the Texaco show. In some article of his that I read not too long ago he was asked why he ran around after women so often. He said that 'Since I cross-dressed so often I had doubts about my own masculinity and I wanted to prove myself in this way.'

But this is a whole mainstream phenomenon in American popular culture. It's not confined to any subsection of the population. The question of why it's not commutable, for example, why it is that men dressed as women are funny, whereas women dressed as men are not automatically funny but may be threatening or may be elegant or seductive. The [effect] is quite different when you're looking at men dressed as women than women dressed as men. Those are the kinds of questions that have concerned me in the book.

A conversation with

William Graham

William Graham is professor of the history of religion and Islamic studies. His scholarship has resulted in numerous theological papers and presentations; a recent book of his, Beyond the Written Word: Oral Aspects of Scripture in the History of Religion, *was published by Cambridge University Press.*

COSTA: *There seems to be a rekindling of interest in the study of religion, especially comparative religion. To what do you attribute this renewed interest on campuses across the country?*

GRAHAM: I'm not sure it's renewed. It might be new in some ways. We saw in the early 1970s, particularly, an upswing and interest in India and in Far Eastern religions. Now I think what one is seeing—as I go to other universities and talk with colleagues I think I see something of this on a wider scale—is the study of religion in a global context, something that is relatively new to the American university scene in the last 30 years as a widespread phenomenon. We're seeing it become an accepted part of the liberal arts context. We're seeing students—here and at other institutions—finding that one very good way to learn about the wider world is to study the religious communities of the world. There are obviously other ways: through literature, through history and other cultural phenomena. But I think now religion is a much more accepted subject than it probably was 30 years ago when religion was understood to be, for most people, Christianity, and maybe even only one brand of that, and, secondarily, Judaism for what it had to say about Christianity, and everything else was called 'the religions of the world.' I think that has changed.

COSTA: *Let's talk about the history of Islam and its underlying effects in the Mideast. You wrote that the popular notion of Islam as a religion of the desert is largely untrue. It began more in commercial centers and first flourished on an agricultural, oasis base. Could you tell us some more about the origins of Islam?*

GRAHAM: It's certainly a fact that in the two towns of Mecca and Medina where we have the career of the prophet Muhammad in the early 7th century being played out that one had fairly developed communities there. There were two different kinds of communities. In Mecca [there was] a commercial community [where] you had tribes that for a good length of time had been settled in what could safely be called an urban environment. And in Medina you had an agricultural community. When I wrote that originally, in a history textbook, I was also thinking more about the ongoing development of Islam. Islam from early on tended to focus in the cities, both [in] the old cities of the Byzantine Empire or the Persian Empire that Islam displaced [and] in new cities that were set up first as army camps and then gradually became major cities and centers. One thinks of Cairo, for instance. It began as one of the Islamic army camps, al-Fustat, and later became one of the great cities of the Islamic world.

The tradition as such really flourished best in these urban centers that became the hubs for the gradual dispersion of conversion, which took place over a number of centuries. The initial Islamic conquest, or the Arab conquest one might say, did not bring conversion of all the [region], but it did set up centers with strong Muslim ruling populations—small but strong because they were the ruling populations—and from there one had a diffusion of Islamic life and Islamic practice over the next few centuries.

COSTA: *What is the etymology of the word 'Arab,' and what does it mean to be an Arab?*

GRAHAM: It's odd; one would think that that's an utterly straightforward problem, but a lot of people more intelligent than I have written about the difficulties of exactly defining 'Arab.' There are a variety of meanings for the term even within the Arabic-speaking world itself. Certainly early on in the Islamic era, 'Arab' was the word most often used for the Bedouin, and it even became at times—and has even remained until the modern period—a term of disapprobation used by the better educated, more urbane, city dwellers for the helter-skelter nomad tribes, which were always a minority in the Islamic world after the first couple of decades.

There are a lot of changes that can be rung on the word 'Arab.' I think it would be wrong to identify 'Arab' with some sort of ethnic group. It's not really an ethnic term. It has basically to do with the use of the Arabic language. We don't tend popularly to make much distinction between, let's say, the adjective 'Arab' and the adjective 'Arabic.' But in fact 'Arabic' should more properly be used for linguistic aspects of the world of the Arabs, whereas 'Arab' should be used to refer to the history and to the people themselves. The latter are defined pretty much as those who speak Arabic and share a sense of being part of an Arab cultural world, and, of course, this has changed quite radically from the time that Arabic was spoken in Muhammad's era just in the peninsula. It spread across North Africa and displaced other languages around the Mediterranean—Latin to some degree, Greek in the eastern Mediterranean—most of all it displaced Aramaic, which was the sort of *lingua franca* of the ancient world before [Arabic] came along. It went out, of course, into the area that we know now as Iraq, as an elite language of letters, religion, and administration, and even into Iran. Because of the Koran, which was originally God's revelation specifically to the Arabs, it has been perpetrated even in non-Arabic-speaking environments to the present day as a scholarly language much as Latin was into the last century in the Western European world.

It's something of a problem to say who the Arabs are. They are those who I suppose today call themselves Arabs and who speak the Arabic language and identity with Arabic culture, and beyond that I don't think we can be very specific.

COSTA: *When Muhammad came to religious dominance in the 7th century he was the last in a long line of prophets, according to the Koran, chosen to bring God's word. Was there tolerance of other prophets before him?*

GRAHAM: There certainly was an incorporation, if you like, of previous religious leaders and peoples into what we might call the Islamic view of history or the Islamic salvation history [*Heilsgeschichte*], to borrow a term from Christian scholarship. That is, the Koran itself reminds the listener of God having sent [prophets] from time immemorial—literally from the first human being, from Adam himself, who is often viewed as the first prophet. The story of Adam and Eve is spoken of in several places in the Koran.

There was thus a series of prophets, most of whom we know as the patriarchs of the Hebrew bible, but a number of whom are not mentioned in the Bible. There are what we might call Arabian prophets who are mentioned, prophets whom we don't find in the Bible. If one looks at the sort of theology of divine revelation that one finds in the Koran and then finds elaborated throughout Islamic history, there is a notion that God has never left any human people without guidance. This guidance has come, if one reads the Koran, in successive ages to successive peoples and usually what has happened is what we might call the fumbling of the message by each community. There are also a number of other common characteristics that we can find repeated in the stories of each of the prophets. Each prophet is usually rejected by his own people and is not listened to in every instance. This is a theme that we know as well from the Hebrew bible, but it's very strong in the Koranic retelling of the prophet stories.

There has been this progressive history of revelation. Each people gets a revelation, but even if they then repent and listen to it, or if only a minority listens to God's word, they ultimately, in writing it down, in transmitting it, allow falsifications to creep in. I think the fundamental Muslim view has been that the Bible and the other scriptures before Muhammad have become adulterated with things that are not from God. People have changed the material that God has given them. So the Koran is seen as having been sent one last time through one last prophet to try to correct what has gone before, not to negate what has gone before but to try to correct what has gone wrong. It's a very logical and consistent view of revelation.

Finally, it's particularly important that the Koran and Islamic thinking pick up particularly on the figure of Abraham. It's fascinating to me because that's exactly what the Apostle Paul had done in the early Christian community, and we find in Paul the same sort of attempt to appropriate the figure of Abraham and say this is Abraham, the father of the Christians after the spirit as he was father of the Jews after the flesh. And, in a way, the Koran is doing the same thing, saying that Abraham was the first true monotheist and stands out as the paradigm of faith for Muslims just as he does for Christians. Looking at it as a historian of religion one sees a very similar kind of effort being made by Muslims to appropriate this great monotheistic patriarch as their prophet, and I think he could stand as a symbol for all of the other prophets in a lot of ways.

COSTA: *I know it's probably impossible to summarize the Koran, but I did take a sentence from one of your writings that the message of the Koran was that the prophet was warning of idolatrous worship of false gods, and against all immorality, especially injustice to the weak and less fortunate people, the poor orphans, widows, and women in general. Is Islam essentially a religion of the poor, the so-called disenfranchised people?*

GRAHAM: There is a strong element of that in the Koranic preaching. There is what I would call a social gospel in Muhammad's message and in the message of the Koran that is really unmistakable. The Prophet was someone who was deeply moved by the plight of the less fortunate. [Muhammad] himself had been an orphan and I think his experience in the merchant community in Mecca led him to see that certain people had fared much, much better through the commercial activities of the major tribes there than did those who did not have access to the sources of wealth. I think all of this made a deep impression. I'm sure there were also elements of Christian influence and Jewish influence as well on this concern for the downtrodden, on this concern for justice in a way that maybe had been less evident in the pagan traditions of pre-Islamic Arabia. But I certainly think it would be fair to say that that was one of the major emphases, not the only one, but one of the major emphases in the early preaching of the Revelation and the Prophet.

COSTA: *Getting back to something you said about the Arabic language as defining and linking the Arab peoples, you write about how some of the early tribes even had poets who proclaimed the strengths of their tribe and simultaneously insulted their enemies with wonderful poetry. This bond of language does not seem to obtain between Iraq and Iran. Is that because more Iranians speak Farsi?*

GRAHAM: Yes, Farsi—or Persian, to give it its English name—is a totally different language, and from a different language group. It's a language that is cognate with our own Indo-European languages such as Greek and Latin. It's also cognate with Sanskrit. That being said, however, one must remember that modern Persian is an Islamic language in terms of its vocabulary, a large percentage of which is Arabic. Certainly in vocabulary and in cultural usages there are many, many affinities between the Arabic-speaking world and the Persian-speaking world.

On the other hand, I think the sense of what one might call national or ethnic identity of the Persian peoples has been something that again and again in history has proven very, very strong and has often manifested itself in ways that put the Persians over [or] against the Arabs per se, even though both might be Muslims.

You have to remember that the Persians have a great pride in a heritage that goes back minimally to the sixth century B.C. and the first of the great Persian empires, three empires that lasted over a thousand years. Indeed, it was only the coming of Islam that finally wiped away the [last empire]. So there is a strong cultural memory there of the greatness of ancient Persia, of ancient Iran, and that has often been called upon as a basis for national consciousness. It happened in the early Islamic era when you had movements that tried to bring Persian letters to the fore after it looked as though Arabic were going simply to inundate the culture of the Persians. And Arabic never did, even though the intelligentsia, particularly the religious scholars in the Iranian world, have always continued to learn Arabic because of the Koran. On the other hand, they've written some of the greatest works of Islamic culture in the Persian language. I would have to say that the Persian language alongside the Arabic language, and perhaps one could add the Turkish language as the third to that group, have been the major cultural languages of Islamic history.

We've seen in the modern era, not so much in the linguistic sense but in the political sense, the attempt of the Pahlevi family, the Iranian shahs of the 20th century, to reinstitute the glories of Persianate culture from the pre-Islamic period. This was, of course, received with great ambivalence by the more religious sectors of the Iranian population. So, yes, there is a certain—I wouldn't say antagonism, that would be the wrong word—but a certain cultural competition between the Iranian and the Arab or Arabic culture in particular down through the centuries, and it continues today.

COSTA: *We read pronouncements about pan-Arabism which incite Arabs to make a holy war. Is that possible with the multiculturalism in the Arab world today, to have that kind of unifying principle?*

GRAHAM: We tend to forget, as often the Arabs tend to forget, that most of the Islamic world is non-Arab. By far, the majority of the Islamic world is non-Arab and, indeed, today the preponderance of Muslim populations live on the other side of Karachi, Pakistan, from the Arabs. The largest Muslim country in the world is Indonesia. There are substantial Muslim populations not only in Indonesia and in South Asia—which far outnumber the entire Arab world put together—but also very substantial Muslim populations in Africa and the Turkish and Turkic language-speaking worlds of Asia and of Anatolia, as well as southeastern Europe, Western Europe, and the Americas. All that being said, to come back to pan-Arabism, if one, let's say, ignores the fact that a military *jihad* is fundamentally a struggle against infidels and not a war that is legitimately declared by one Muslim community against another—although there have been instances of that certainly in Islamic history, but for a Muslim to declare a particular struggle to be formally 'in the cause of God,' the enemy should be an enemy of God's proper rule in this world and therefore an enemy of, let's say, a Muslim social order and political order, and that is rarely the case in some of these more modern conflicts within the Islamic world itself.

The Arabs themselves in terms of pan-Arabism clearly have a lot of problems presenting a united front to the rest of the world, and I don't think we'll ever see that happen. I think the Arab world itself is too diverse. On the other hand, I don't think one should underestimate the importance of the symbolic unity of Arabic-speaking peoples, of the Arabs, if you like. I think that is a very, very strong fact of the modern world. It's also true that most Arabs are Muslims—some are Jews, some are Christians, some are other things, but by far the great majority of Arabs are Muslims. And, of course, the Islamic bond that links them all and in fact spread the Arabic language to them all is central. I don't want to minimize that by saying that there is even often a confusion between Islamic goals and Arab goals. It goes without saying that the two are very naturally brought together in any sort of pan-Arabic rhetoric. . . .

I think it would be wrong for Americans or Europeans or anyone else in the world to presume that there is some sort of pan-Arab menace or some sort of possibility that the Arabs would close together into a united Arab state. Attempts have been made at this, but rarely with any more than regional success, and I don't think that's going to change.

COSTA: *What do you see as the future of Islam?*

GRAHAM: Part of the growth of Islam results from the fact that the Islamic peoples make up a large proportion of what we call the Third World, or the underdeveloped world. As a result, population growth in these areas automatically brings new numbers. . . . . . [Also we're seeing] greater access of greater numbers of the population to education and, indeed, to modern technical education. You're getting changes in the expectations of many Muslim populations just as you are of many other populations throughout the developing world. I think all of these things are going to mean that Muslims are going to be speaking with a greater self-confidence, and perhaps going to be making themselves heard in asking for their rights in a global society where we're going to have to share a great deal more of the Earth's resources than we have in the past. I think we're going to have to listen to these voices because they're easily a seventh of humankind, maybe more. Certainly Muslims will have to be listened to a great deal more than the Judeo-Christian Western world of the last three centuries has been able or willing to do up till now.

That's why I believe it to be terrifically important that we study and spread the knowledge of this part of the world: because they're one of the major groups that we're going to be rubbing shoulders with. They're certainly not the only one, but I think the fact that many Muslims see links with Muslim societies in totally different geographical and political contexts [is important]. They see links that often majority Christian countries don't see with each other in different parts of the world. We're also going to have to pay attention to Islamic voices not just in the religious arena and not just in the cultural arena, but I think also in the political arena.

A *conversation with*

Dudley Herschbach

Dudley Herschbach is Frank B. Baird Jr. Professor of Science.
He became one of Harvard's 33 Nobel Prize winners when he was
honored for his chemistry research in 1986.

COSTA: *There seems to be a blurring of disciplines these days in the natural sciences. Much of what chemistry researchers seem to do looks a great deal like what physicists do. A lot of research occurs at the molecular and even subatomic level. The work is intensely mathematical, very much like physics. The devices used by chemists look to the average person much like the scientific equipment used by physicists. Tell us about this blurring of disciplinary lines between the two fields.*

HERSCHBACH: First, I should say chemistry is a vast domain. There are people in chemistry doing very, very different things. Growing mice on one end, doing nothing but pure mathematics on the other end. So it's not surprising that there is overlap with the techniques, outlook, or approach of physics in part of the spectrum of chemistry. A field which has been represented very strongly at Harvard for more than 40 years is called chemical physics, and that's the area in which I work. It's true, for instance, that in Europe almost all the work in this area is done in physics departments. At meetings of chemical physicists even in this country, large factions of people come from physics departments. So there is an overlap.

But there is an interesting cultural difference even in the field of chemical physics. I like to put it this way: it took me a long time to understand why most people find chemistry particularly difficult, even more difficult than physics in a certain sense. It goes like this: chemistry is an impressionistic painting; if you stand close to such a painting, it's meaningless dabs of paint. That's what the physicist tends to do, because [the physicist] is trying to reduce it to first principles. But the most wonderful aspects of chemistry are in the impressionistic painting sense. That is, you put together parts which may be in some cases physics, but it's not enough to deal with the phenomena that are characteristic of chemistry.

COSTA: *Most of us who took chemistry in high school learned about the elements from the periodic chart and learned how to mix compounds to do everything, even explode sometimes. But that kind of cookbook chemistry is a thing of the past, even at the high school level. How has this changed? Has it been brought about because of the new chemistry, which is changing the way high school chemistry is taught?*

HERSCHBACH: Not changing as much as one would hope. It's part of the sad state of our high school science education in this country that more and more students are being taught in a somewhat abstract or mechanical way without the chance to deal directly in laboratory experiments, with what goes on in a very modest, down-to-earth way.

[Young scientists] should make some of the simplest kinds of observations and think about them in their own terms without receiving it as predigested dogma handed down, because that is antithetical to the nature of science. I'm afraid there is a tendency toward that because so often high school teaching prepares students for standardized, usually multiple choice exams. This just takes the whole life out of things.

COSTA: *Is it also a budgetary thing? I know labs are expensive to set up. A wet lab here costs millions to set up on the university level. High schools suffer from Proposition 2 1/2 and all of those other budget restraints. Is that a reason or is it just an excuse for the scientific illiteracy that seems to be everywhere in high schools today?*

HERSCHBACH: I don't think it's primarily money because the kinds of experiments I think are most suitable for the high school level are not especially expensive in terms of the substances you have to buy. They can be very mundane, prosaic things.

There is a longing to have the most fancy equipment possible, but it isn't necessary. In fact I would say it's a mistake at that level because you want students to see that everyday things are involved with this. It's not something super-special that only a kind of high priesthood could be expected to deal with.

COSTA: *What do you think is the most important skill or characteristic a scientist should have? Is it curiosity or perseverance or analytical skills or something else?*

HERSCHBACH: All of those are important, but if you ask me to say the single most important one—certainly not unique to science—but the most important one is the capacity to fall in love. To get excited, enthralled, obsessed with some question or problem and helplessly give themselves over to their destiny.

COSTA: *Like the mad scientist.*

HERSCHBACH: I don't think it's a mad scientist so much. I think it's fulfillment of human potential to experience this kind of thing in your life, to be fascinated by some questions. It's very much manifest in many scientists I know, but also artists and musicians. You know how many of those people struggle. Our society undervalues them enormously and yet they are in love with what they are doing. That is why they do it at all costs. I think that is the most important single thing.

COSTA: *When did you fall in love with chemistry? Tell us about your odyssey from your early interest in chemistry to the Nobel Prize.*

HERSCHBACH: I know exactly when I fell in love with science, to the moment. I was nine years old and visiting my grandmother, which I always looked forward to because among other things she had *National Geographic* magazine with all those beautiful photographs. This particular issue, the current issue, had an article on the constellations, beautiful star maps. The article was by a scientist from the Harvard College Observatory. I grew up in San Jose, California. It was certainly the first time I had ever heard of Harvard, and of course I had no inclination to have anything to do with the institution.

But I was fascinated by these beautiful star maps so I began making my own maps. I would sneak out at night and climb up a locust tree in the backyard and look at the stars. So that got me started. Within a year or two a teacher had lent me a book that talked about the mechanics of our solar system. So I became intrigued with those things and it was the reason that I took math and science in high school and found I enjoyed them immensely. Then in junior high school I took chemistry. It was my first contact with chemistry per se. I had a fabulous teacher. Again and again I find this is true of other chemists: there was a high school teacher who made all the difference. And this teacher was absolutely wonderful.

Then I went to college. This is something that I never expected to do, but when I found that my high school teachers and coaches all expected it, I began thinking that way. I never expected to go because I came from a family in which no relative had ever gone to college.

When I went to college I didn't know what I should major in, but I put down chemistry as a possibility because of a high school teacher. I was assigned a freshman adviser who was another wonderful chemist, Harold Johnston, and that kind of clinched it.

By my sophomore year he invited me to be a laboratory assistant in his research group and I got to interact with the graduate students, and became intrigued with the whole subject. In fact it was Harold Johnston who defined the problem that I fell in love with, that really led to the work that I pursued, even up until today.

COSTA: *That reinforces what we've been reading about so much today in education: how key it is to find those teachers who inspire young people in high school. Especially in science, where you need a mentor.*

HERSCHBACH: That's right, absolutely.

COSTA: *Going back a number of years, C.P. Snow wrote a book that we all read in college. It was about the two cultures and how they intersect and how they diverge: science and the humanities. There does seem to be some dynamic tension between the two cultures today and there's a great misunderstanding of science in particular. In fact, even quite educated people view science today as a clear and present danger. Critics cite nuclear power, mapping the human genome, biotechnology and Frankensteinian kinds of things as examples of science just about to go awry. What is your perspective on all of this?*

HERSCHBACH: I have long been deeply concerned about this. As a matter of fact, I was a young faculty member at Berkeley when C.P. Snow delivered that speech and he had visited Berkeley not long before as a visiting professor and, in fact, even visited my laboratory. He spent a whole afternoon chatting with my graduate students and me. We were all reading his books. So I have these personal recollections of talking with C.P. Snow himself on his themes.

It is sadly true in our society that science is regarded as something just for experts, not part of the mainstream of our culture. I think it has reached the point where it even threatens the viability of democratic institutions as we enter the 21st century. There are just so many things that require some understanding of how science works. I don't mean high-level technical knowledge. We need experts, all right, to advise in that.

But the general notion is that scientists wear white coats and have calculators and know exactly what they are doing and all the rest. Public officials need to understand that that's not all true. Scientists are, most of the time, guessing. They're working on a frontier that's not understood. The way I try to explain it is that nature speaks in many tongues and they're all foreign. What the basic scientist is trying to do is unravel to the extent that is possible some of the vocabulary and grammar of at least one of the dialects. To the extent that the scientist succeeds to define nature's messages, we can learn much to the great benefit of humanity.

We can put enormous human and financial resources, we sometimes have, into pursuing some practical problem and find we don't get anywhere. Why? Because we can't read the answers, we don't know the language. If we send an expedition to a foreign land we ought to have someone to speak with the natives. This is the case, as I see it, for the importance of science as a component of our culture as well as a practical matter.

I would say science is really a central humanity and it's tragic that we don't recognize it. For instance, a millennium from now, it's inconceivable that mankind will not be looking back at the 20th century with awe. In particular, the impact of the Watson/Crick double helix, the DNA structure, is profound. It changes the very way we think about what it means to be human. What can be more (central to humanity) than that? So this is the sort of thing I mean. It's a tragic misunderstanding.

I try to combat it as much as I can in the general chemistry course I've been teaching now the last seven years. For instance, I even require my students to write poems to emphasize that writing a poem is much more like doing science than they might imagine. In the introductory courses, the problem is that the student sees it as just a matter of being able to get the right answer by some sort of manipulations or received wisdom. It's not like that.

COSTA: *So you try to personalize it as much as possible.*

HERSCHBACH: The actual work of science is guessing how nature works, what she is trying to say to you. So it's much more like the poet or the artist. It really is a very humanistic effort in the frontier when you're doing it on the front lines. Sadly, barely a glimmer of this comes across to the general public.

This is why, for instance, the politicians don't understand this. And with any scientific questions there's a long debate back and forth. I mean, it's a heck of a long time to settle anything. They can't comprehend it.

COSTA: *The central irony here, too, is that people who are not scientists are using science more and more in their daily lives. Even when one types on a word processor, many people don't realize that they are manipulating zeroes and ones in a binary code.*

HERSCHBACH: And manipulating electrons.

COSTA: *And manipulating electrons, yes. It's rather tragic in some sense that we can't seem to integrate even a basic sense of the science that so affects our lives.*

HERSCHBACH: It's very peculiar. If you look back, say, at the Renaissance times and so on it's impressive that the great figures, the humanistic figures we're aware of, were very involved in science. For example, if you read in Shakespeare—I think it's Act Five in *The Merchant of Venice*—you will find an admirable summary of what Kepler was thinking about the motion of the heavenly bodies. Shakespeare clearly knew exactly what Kepler was up to. And of course it was the same with Ben Jonson. He was very much interested in science and a lot of his writings show this. But, of course, a schism has developed since then and it's a very sad thing.

COSTA: *Let's talk about something even more cosmic than chemistry: baseball. Why does it appeal to so many thinking people?*

HERSCHBACH: This is an excellent question following the one you asked before about the two cultures. To me, baseball has many interesting aspects, but one important one is that it's all a matter of probability. The fans who follow a game are doing so because they want to see something improbable. Baseball is fascinating because it's all anticipation. Somebody has calculated and timed it: There is actually only between 5 and 10 minutes of action, of things actually happening, in a whole baseball game of two and a half or three hours. All the rest is anticipation!

COSTA: *No wonder I buy so many hot dogs.*

HERSCHBACH: It tells you a lot about this deep yearning of mankind to see a guardian angel or whatever, break the rules, let something improbable happen that they would like to see. So I think baseball is almost a religious ritual in this sense.

COSTA: *When we watch baseball—and I ask this since you won a Nobel Prize concerning molecular collisions—do you see inelastic collisions or does a Roger Clemens fastball describe a kind of conic section or tangent or do you see differential equations happening in real life? Or do you just see what non-scientists see, a great fastball?*

HERSCHBACH: Of course, there are many opportunities to make analogies to sports, baseball in particular. In our studies of molecular collisions we try to do what Roger Clemens does. That is, we try to arrange so that one time the molecule will collide as if it were pitched on the lower inside corner of the plate and the next time the upper left corner of the plate, or whatever, and study what happens in these different situations so we can characterize the interactions of the molecules in somewhat the way the pitcher wants to calibrate the batters that he faces.

We get this variety of outcomes in the molecular collisions just as the fans are anticipating that the batter might ground to third or hit a home run or fly out to center field or whatever. In that sense, there is this congruence in that we are trying to map out the probability of various events and then infer from them something more fundamental. The fans, likewise, are hoping that if the probability is worked out the way that they'd love to see it, it shows that their team must be specially blessed by supernatural powers.

COSTA: *At the risk of offending baseball fans from other parts of the country, tell us why Fenway Park in Boston is still the best park to view the sport.*

HERSCHBACH: Oh, it's charming. Immediately you're transported to another world when you're in Fenway Park. It's so small, it's cozy, there is a certain aura about it.

COSTA: *You're so close to the players, too.*

HERSCHBACH: Yes, indeed. It exemplifies what I think is characteristic of baseball in an earlier era. I can remember as a kid that the same era when I was climbing up the trees to look at the stars, I would turn on my radio by the bed very low so my parents wouldn't know and listen to the Oakland Oaks, as they were called in those days.

I loved the Oakland Oaks' battles in the Pacific Coast League, especially against the San Francisco Seals. The Pacific Coast League had a manager who later became quite celebrated, Casey Stengel. I think both teams have vanished from the scene by now. The Oakland Oaks I liked especially because of these improbable comebacks. You know they'd be five runs behind in the ninth inning, they'd bat around and win by a run. I was always waiting for some magic to occur. Of course it often didn't occur but the times I relished were the times it did. That is the way the mind works.

COSTA: *As the former master of Currier House, you've had an opportunity to be with students at close range outside the classroom and to see them and how they change over the years. We read a lot these days about students' mania for financial success in careers, the so-called careerism-vocationalism. Is this trend true here at Harvard, or is it overstated by the media?*

HERSCHBACH: I think it is somewhat overstated. Most characterizations of trends like that are almost inevitably, vastly oversimplified. But there is something to it and that is of course why these observations come out.

First, I'd like to say that my wife and I in our five years as co-masters of Currier House found it a marvelous adventure. Essentially, you're reincarnated as an undergraduate. Your very metabolism changes—it has to because the lifestyle of undergraduates in this day and age involves starting at 11 p.m. and keeping on until 3 a.m. or so. With the ordinary kind of schedule we had in the other part of our lives, this was strenuous. But it was fascinating. There was so much energy and talent in these young people. It was good to be involved, even vicariously, in many of their activities. Cheering them on was quite a wonderful experience.

I think the concern with money [among students] comes from a feeling of insecurity. They look around and see that to go to college takes a vast amount of money. They are aware that they would like to be in a position to send their kids to college. Right now it looks as if the only way you can be confident about that is to make sure you're well off. There are other aspects that contribute to it. For example, surprisingly large numbers of students, while they are seniors, decide to go to law school for two reasons: one can, as an undergraduate, major in anything and still go to law school, and the other is that law school is three years, period. No if's, and's, or but's. There is a reasonable probability, probably overestimated, that you will automatically do well if you get a law degree.

But many of these students whom we met later find they can't stand law. They do something else. I think the reason that they went to law school is they wanted to do something, but graduate school and the pursuit of a Ph.D. looked forbidding because it's much more long-term and uncertain.

I think we've allowed the Ph.D. to drag out far too long. We ought to make every effort to shorten it to four years. No more than four years.

COSTA: *What is the average length of time for a Ph.D. in chemistry?*

HERSCHBACH: In chemistry it's shorter than in some other areas, but not all that much shorter anymore. It's gotten up between five and six years now, not only at Harvard but at all U.S. institutions. I think it's at least that long in physics. It's not that attractive anymore. I think many students who would prefer to go on and study in these other fields where we have great need for people are dissuaded from doing so because it looks like too long a road.

A conversation with

Gerald Lesser

Gerald Lesser is Charles Bigelow Professor of Education and Developmental Psychology and a founder of the children's television program, Sesame Street. Lesser's work has had a profound impact on a generation of children. He is chairman of the Board of Advisers to the Children's Television Workshop, and currently senior fellow at the Gannett Center for Media Studies at Columbia University.

COSTA: *Years ago, television was characterized as a vast wasteland. Many people think it still is. But one kind of television that has been extremely successful is children's educational TV. The best example of it is* Sesame Street. *As chairman of the board of advisers of the Children's Television Workshop, you helped create* Sesame Street. *It is now watched by more than 14 million American viewers of all ages. More than 6 million 2- to 4-year-olds watch the show at least once a week, and 3 million 6- to 12-year-olds watch it. To what do you attribute such great success in this market?*

LESSER: I think *Sesame Street* was created at a time when there was a very strong interest in helping poor children and poor families. . . . Also, the combination of education and entertainment was something we innovated. I'm sure other people have tried to do it. I think the combination of something that is interesting, amusing, and entertaining yet educational at the same time is probably at the heart of *Sesame Street's* success.

The educational objectives are not muffled in any way. They're right out in the open. A lot of people thought, 'Well, you just can't come at education that straight and be successful with the general audience,' but it seems to have worked.

The 6 million preschoolers is about right. *Sesame Street* is watched daily by about 6 or 7 million 3- to 5-year-olds. Actually, 2-year-olds are a major part of that audience as well. And there are 3 million kids who are between 5 and 12. Most people say that *Sesame Street* is not watched by that intermediate age group, but a lot of them do watch. They watch with their younger brothers and sisters.

I'm especially interested in the 6 million adults because 4 million of those do watch with their preschoolers, which is very nice. It's very important educationally to have the adult, the parent, or grandparent share the young child's viewing experience.

But the most interesting thing to me is that 2 million of those 6 million adult viewers don't have any children at home—they watch all on their own.

COSTA: *How do you determine the formula of how much education and how much entertainment?*

LESSER: There isn't a formula. It isn't that we do 51 percent entertainment and 49 percent education. Actually, the trick is to combine them so that you can't differentiate between them. It's impossible to assign fractions because every segment that we try to produce is maximally entertaining and maximally educational, so there isn't any division there. It's a matter of how can we get the entertainment to complement the education, and how can we get the education to be as entertaining and as enjoyable as possible.

COSTA: *It's amazing how you've changed the culture of the adult world. I've worked in newsrooms where we've actually had people referred to as Bert & Ernie or Oscar the Grouch. But* Sesame Street *is certainly not bound solely to the American culture and, as of last year, more than 75 countries were airing the show around the world. What have been some of the difficulties of producing* Sesame Street *for different cultures?*

LESSER: Let me update the number first of all. It's 84 exactly. Forty-four of those countries carry the program in its English-language version, as it is produced in the states. It is carried in major English-speaking countries such as Great Britain, Australia, Canada, and so forth. In addition, it's carried in a great many smaller countries such as the English-speaking countries in the Caribbean and elsewhere throughout the world.

The 40 other countries produce their own foreign-language adaptations in their own language, culture, and tradition. They generate their own educational goals depending upon what is important to teach preschoolers in their countries. Then they design their own programs.

The usual system is that half of the program is designed and produced abroad and then the countries can borrow from the *Sesame Street* library what they feel is culturally appropriate for them. We've done over 2,500 programs to date in our 20-year history, so each country can dip into our library of material—animation, live-action film, Muppet material, whatever they choose—and incorporate it into their programs.

You asked what the difficulties have been. Of course, there are always problems in getting it right, getting that right combination of entertainment and education that we talked about before. But even across 100 countries, I would say there have been remarkably few problems. I think that is perhaps because the adaptation process is left to that country to decide. They decide on their goals, they decide on their strategy, they decide on their approach. They certainly model a lot of what they do on *Sesame Street*'s history and experience, but they're really producing their own programs reflecting their own vision of what is important for preschoolers and for families in their countries.

COSTA: *Do the Muppet characters translate well in every country?*

LESSER: They translate remarkably well, but keep in mind one reason for that: a country can select from the thousands of Muppet segments that we've produced and take segments that seem most suitable to their country. They do the dubbing and translating of that rather small fraction of all of the Muppets segments that are available to them. Actually, they do travel very well.

COSTA: *With the increase in the numbers of the mothers who work outside the home these days, many children are spending much more time watching television—even with their new childcare providers. How is children's television programming taking this increase in potential audience size into account?*

LESSER: I don't know how television in general is doing it, but I could tell you that what we're trying to do is figure out where the kids are these days. Certainly there are enormous changes, as you've indicated. It's an exceptionally fragmented childcare arrangement that we have in this country. There is family day care—some of it licensed, some of it not licensed. There are people taking care of small groups of children in their homes. There is institutional day care, which is more formal and more organized. There is corporate day care, there are extended school day programs. The kids in families where both parents are working are . . . all over the place.

It is true that television is being used in different ways because of these demographic changes. We're not quite sure yet how we can be most helpful to those children. About two months ago we started a rather detailed study of what goes on in family day care arrangements, and what goes on in institutionalized day-care arrangements or organized day-care arrangements so that we can be most helpful to the children and their parents, or the care providers, in those settings.

It's a very complicated terrain and we're not quite sure yet how we can best get into it, not in terms of marketing *Sesame Street,* because as you know we're a not-for-profit, noncommercial organization. We don't make any money, but we do want to serve these children as well as we can. In order to do that we have to know where they are and under what conditions they are living in these various caregiving kinds of situations. We've embarked on a rather complicated job of tracing those demographic changes. Then once we have a better fix on that, we can try to figure out how we can be most helpful.

COSTA: *One of the ironies is that* Sesame Street *and programs like it—such as* The Electric Company—*have been so successful as models for preschoolers that some of these institutional childcare providers use the very materials from* Sesame Street. *In fact, they are not going to be watching* Sesame Street *because they are having real-life* Sesame Street *in their day-care centers.*

LESSER: I think they do both. I think they have real-life *Sesame Streets* in their day-care centers, as you say. I think a pattern is developing. It's a little early for me to say this . . . but one of the things that is happening rather rapidly is that videocassettes are coming into play very actively in a lot of these childcare settings. I'm working in the Bromley-Heath area here in Boston in a project that runs a health center, and they have their own day-care facility within it. Of course, they have a videocassette playback machine and they'll even tape *Sesame Street* and show it for short periods of time whenever it seems appropriate to the people there.

We've also created 14 half-hour versions of *Sesame Street* on very focused topics like the alphabet and numbers and solving problems without resorting to violence and so forth. They'll very often use those cassettes. We've also developed some material in Spanish for the Spanish-speaking population so that if the day-care providers choose to present material in Spanish, they have the opportunity to do that.

COSTA: *In preparation for this interview I not only read your book* Children and Television *but I also watched* Sesame Street *last night and I saw Oscar the Grouch urging two men to sing together to promote what he called the spirit of cooperation. On the same show I listened to Kermit the Frog sing about young tadpoles. I also saw harmony between people of different races and ethnic groups, talking together to solve problems of common interest. This is how we would all love the world to be, but isn't there some cognitive dissonance for these kids watching this utopian world, when in fact the world in which they live is often violent, impoverished, and bleak?*

LESSER: You're absolutely right. We made a deliberate decision 20 years ago and we think it has worked, so we've stayed with it. It's controversial [but we believe] that there is enough harshness, enough difficulty, and enough problems in the lives of poor, inner-city kids. Maybe we present a rather idealized view of what life can be like, how good life can be in an integrated neighborhood where people treat each other with a certain kindness and consideration and affection, and maybe it doesn't always happen that way in real life. But what we're really trying to present is a vision of what life can be and not necessarily what life really is in its harsher realities for kids in an inner city.

One could argue about that. One could say, 'Well, aren't you faking children out a little bit, aren't you giving them a somewhat distorted view of what the realities are in life?' We do aim for a kinder, gentler community in which these kids can grow up. We try to present a picture of how that can be and what role they can play in it.

You're absolutely right that we run the risk of distorting reality. At the heart of that somewhat rosier view of what life can be is that people from different cultural backgrounds, different ages, and with different personal predispositions can all, if they work at it a bit and give each other a certain amount of respect and generosity, live together in a comfortable, interesting, and pleasant way.

Maybe there are other opportunities for kids to encounter that [harshness] and learn how to cope with it. We even do a certain amount of resolving conflicts without resorting to violence, taking another person's point of view, and cooperation. We're quite deliberate about saying, 'Hey, things can be better, and here is how things can be better for you.'

COSTA: *Let's look at what some of the critics say about television in general and about educational television. They say that television by its very nature remains a passive medium, that television does not engage the mind the way reading does and therefore its use as an educational tool is limited. What do you think of these criticisms?*

LESSER: That one you do hear a lot. My response to it is not to say that several criticisms of television are not warranted. We could talk about violence, we could talk about commercial advertising to children, and I would give you quite a different answer than I will with regard to passivity. I think we do present many, too many, images of violence and aggression on television, maybe even occasionally on educational television, although we vowed 20 years ago that we would never do it, and I don't think we have done it once on *Sesame Street.* Commercial advertising directed to children has become an increasing abomination through the years; it's gotten worse and worse.

On the issue of passivity, I think that criticism comes from people who have never watched children watch television. If you watch children watch television, they are very active both physically and mentally if the material that you show them warrants it. You have to present something that's interesting and stimulating and makes them think and makes them get up and move. When children watch television they don't just sit there and watch, about 60 percent of the time they are up and moving around and doing this and doing that, some of the things provoked by what they see on television, some of the things that they find more interesting at the moment.

I would say there is some passivity occasionally generated by poor programs, by programs that don't induce an active frame of mind in kids, but if you present interesting stuff for kids to respond to, it can be one of the most active experiences that the child can have.

For example, one of the things that we always find is that a simple presentation of stories from books, if they're presented in an interesting way, always causes a run on the libraries. The kids are out looking for those books and trying to find them because they've been exposed to them. They've gotten interested in them and they want to follow up on them.

COSTA: *I know that each* Sesame Street *character has a designated function. Why don't you run down the list. Like Big Bird, for example.*

LESSER: Big Bird is a proxy 5-year-old. He's rather innocent and somewhat naive, makes a lot of mistakes, but even with the mistakes, he learns and is eager to learn and with the mistakes he remains in the affections of the people on the street.

Oscar the Grouch is, I think, one of our most interesting educators.We were told when we began designing *Sesame Street* 20 years ago, that 3- to 5-year-olds were really too young to learn how to take another person's point of view, that is, for me to understand what you're thinking, and for you to understand what I'm thinking or feeling at any particular moment.

Piaget had written that children have to reach the age of about 7 or 8 before they learn this ability to take a differing perspective, to take another person's point of view. But we said, 'Well, it's an experiment. We are going to be doing something different, we might as well try teaching even younger kids, 3- to 5-year-old kids to take another person's point of view.' So Oscar the Grouch was born. Oscar always takes another point of view. Sometimes it's a contrary or different point of view, but he's our differing perspective.

COSTA: *What about Bert & Ernie?*

LESSER: That is friendship. You said you were listening to *Sesame Street* last night, well so was I. I was watching a Bert & Ernie segment in which they're saying that's what friends are for. Their friendship continues and persists despite the fact that they're, as you know, an odd couple. Each brings a different personality to the friendship, but the friendship persists and they remain good friends despite the differences. That again comes back to that sort of integration of differing perspectives: people who live in different ways but respecting those differences, treating each other with kindness and affection. Bert & Ernie play that role. It's a modeling of friendship and the hanging on to friendships with two quite different personalities.

COSTA: *You've reported that a child learns 5 to 10 times as much when he or she views an educational television program with a parent, an older sibling, or a friend, than if the child viewed alone. How do you account for that?*

LESSER: We have just finished a study of all of the research that has accumulated in the various countries that carry either versions of *Sesame Street* or

Sesame Street in its English language. There are something like 400 research studies out there and many of them are on this issue of co-viewing. They do indeed confirm this multiplier effect, that is, that when parents or older siblings watch with young children, it produces 5 to 10 times more learning as when children view alone.

You asked me to explain it. While I know it exists—there are perhaps 10 to 12 replications of it in different countries—it's hard to explain for the following reason: it seems to occur under several different conditions. It occurs when the parent is there being quite active in conversing with the child about what they are viewing together, or following up with play activities based on what they have seen, or anticipating for the child what kinds of things might happen. It's almost tutoring. Engaging the child almost conversationally and almost playing the tutor.

Yet, at the same time, it occurs maybe not at quite the same magnitude but at a very substantial magnitude when the parent just simply sits down and quietly, without any conversation at all, keeps the young child company, shares that viewing experience with the child without being encouraging, without tutoring, without intervening in any way, just sitting and sharing that experience.

When I reflect on that a little bit, I say to myself, well, maybe it's a very unusual experience for a child to have a mother quietly sit down or a father or an older brother or sister just quietly sit down, and without intervening in any way, say, 'Hey, you're doing something that is kind of interesting, that is valuable, valuable enough for me to share the experience with you.'

So this multiplier effect of co-viewing seems to operate both with active tutoring on the part of the older person and also with just the simple sharing of the experience. I think there is a very important lesson in that. Giving the young child credit for doing something that is worth sharing.

A *conversation with*

Florence Ladd

*Florence Ladd is director of the Mary Ingraham Bunting Institute, a
multidisciplinary postdoctoral fellowship program. Ladd was associate
executive director of Oxfam America and liaison to the United Nations.
Her training was in social psychology; her publications address differing
perceptions between generations, socioeconomic classes, races, and cultures.*

COSTA: *Gloria Steinem once said that the women's movement is the only
movement whose members grow more radical as they grow older. Do you
agree with that?*

LADD: Women who are involved in the women's movement have become
more committed with age and, certainly, given the rate of progress with respect
to the advancement of women, we grow more passionate about the movement
and about the importance of the advancement of women, and more irritated as
well as more radical.

COSTA: *How is the movement doing? It seems to have suffered some set-
backs these days with the present Supreme Court and its chilling effect on civil
rights and women's issues.*

LADD: It's difficult to assess the advances and the losses. Overall, I think
[there's] still a healthy, growing awareness of the need for equal opportunities
for women across the board in a society. The movement is healthy.

COSTA: *You are a former dean of Wellesley College. What are the goals of
a single-sex institution?*

LADD: Single-sex institutions, women's colleges, or women's schools offer to their students an opportunity to participate fully in the entire range of offerings of the institution. We will need single-sex colleges, women's colleges, for a long time. We won't have true coeducation in this country until we have equal numbers of women and men on the faculties and in the administrations of colleges and universities. Women students, I think, are perhaps better served by women's institutions at this point in history because they are offered women as models, women in leadership positions in those institutions, women who represent the intellectual distinction on the faculties of those institutions, and they see women in larger numbers on the faculties and in the administrations of the women's colleges than they see in the coeducational institutions.

COSTA: *Studies seem to show that those women who feel less good about themselves often do less well in the work world, and that single-sex institutions help nurture one's self-image. One can't really talk down to the girls or women at a private preparatory school or a college if there are only women in the class. Studies show that the teachers talk more to the boys and the men in the class than the women. Do single-sex institutions help in this respect?*

LADD: All the studies that have examined the classroom climate, that have paid attention to the frequency of recitations, contributions by girls vs. boys or men vs. women, show that boys and men occupy a disproportionate amount of classroom time, and that teachers call on boys and men more frequently. It is essential for women to have a chance to express their ideas, to have their voices heard. We are trying to find ways of making space for women's voices in coeducational classrooms but it will take generations of retraining the society, retraining teachers, and reeducating boys and girls and men and women about interactions in situations in which they have equal status.

COSTA: *What kind of progress has been made for women who want to have a career and a family?*

LADD: It's the question of having it all: can women have it all, accomplish all that they want to accomplish, all that we must accomplish in a single lifetime. We are learning something about timing [our] various activities and [our] professional and personal requirements. Luckily we are living longer and luckily we are learning something about the length of the [re]productive cycle. We are now told that one may safely have a first child in the late thirties, early forties. So that is adding a little more time, or giving us a few more hours on the biological clock.

I think with other changes, too, with an understanding on the part of institutions and corporations about the kind of flextime that will allow women to be involved in child rearing and will allow men also to be involved in child care and child rearing, there will be a more equitable distribution of the time that men and women can give to the development of their professions, their studies, and their careers. It is something that couples, especially dual-career couples, are struggling with and still learning about. But I think they learn from each other and in each decade it seems to be a little less complicated—though never entirely uncomplicated.

COSTA: *Let's talk for a moment about some of your travels and past jobs where you spent some time in societies that really did disenfranchise women. Let's talk about the time you went to South Africa for the Institute of International Education. What was that like, seeing people who have to live under apartheid?*

LADD: I was there for the purpose of tracing former students who had taken university degrees in the U.S. The Institute of International Education administers a program for black South Africans who study at U.S. colleges and universities. Part of the program is an evaluation to learn something about how they fare once they return to South Africa. So my primary contact was with people who were well educated, who had the advantages that one has of very good educational training prior to coming to the U.S., and generally they had been placed in our major colleges and universities. They returned to South Africa to find that nothing had changed, at least at that time and in their situation. They returned to live in shanty-like dwellings, very often in the townships, which always are a dozen or more miles from the cities in which they worked—those who worked in the major cities of South Africa.

Those who were trained in education and who were working in education worked in the townships primarily as teachers in the black schools. Those who worked in the health and human services sector also worked in the townships and had the limiting experience of having their worlds confined and conditioned by apartheid and by an enormous gulf between the high level of living that white South Africans enjoy in very sophisticated, advanced cities.

Those in the corporate sector or those who had received M.B.A.'s from the Wharton School or from Cornell returned to find that they weren't well received by corporate entities in South Africa. Their frustrations, I think, were most acute. It was painful to find gifted, well-educated, eager individuals, people eager to demonstrate what they had learned, eager to make a contribution to the future of South Africa, thwarted and turned away by the authorities—in quotation marks—who very much are threatened by the black majority and its potential.

COSTA: *Did you feel restrained personally?*

LADD: Psychologically, it was very, very oppressive. One cannot get away from the discussions of, the evidence of, and the concern about apartheid. Blacks and whites always ask, what do you think of it, what does it mean, how does it feel to you, does it register with you in the way that it registers with us, what do you hear about it abroad, what do people say about it, apartheid. It was everywhere. It's very pervasive, it's a concern of all the people I encountered, people who were committed to changing the system, the whites and the blacks. And also the occasional white person one would be seated next to on a plane or in transit—they, too, wanted to know. They sometimes wanted me to know that they had their reasons for separation, that South Africa is different from the United States and they claim that South Africa would not have been developed to the extent that it has been if it had not been for the right invaders. 'Invaders' is my term, not their term. They discount the culture that was there, and just have no thought of ways in which the patterns of living of the indigenous people, the people who were there, the people whose land it is, how those patterns were destroyed by their intrusion and their domination of South Africa.

COSTA: *What do you think can be done, other than a violent overthrow, to end apartheid? What do blacks and whites who want change and equal rights say should and can be done?*

LADD: We are all very much encouraged by what is now being done with the De Klerk initiatives, with the release of Nelson Mandela, and with the meetings of the ANC with the South African authorities. There is for the first time the beginning of a dialogue, which may bring about a transformation of that society. I think that's what all thinking, well-meaning people want, and want somehow to occur without violence.

COSTA: *You've also spent some time in another part of the world that is known for gender separation: Turkey.*

LADD: I lived in Turkey for two years.

COSTA: *That must have been quite an experience, too, because it is clearly a male-dominated society and women have so few rights.*

LADD: I had the privilege of teaching at Robert College and the American College for Girls. It was a chance to learn something about the difficulties that women encounter in an Islamic society that is tradition-bound. Certainly, there were many examples of women on the faculty of the American College for Girls, and women in various professions whom I met in my years in Turkey, who had overcome some of the barriers and restrictions, and who are making a contribution to changing the traditions that have inhibited the possibilities for women.

COSTA: *Concerning the mission that you are on now at the Bunting Institute, what would you like to achieve there?*

LADD: Since 1960, when Mary Ingraham Bunting founded the Institute, it has been committed to the advancement of well-prepared women. It has been a place that has given women the opportunity to work on projects that will make a difference in their careers and will also make a contribution in their respective fields. We are a multidisciplinary institute and we have an interesting range of disciplines represented. We have women in the physical sciences, natural sciences, and social sciences, and women in the humanities. We have visual artists, we have novelists, poets, and playwrights. The Institute is unique in that regard and as a center for advanced studies for women. I want to carry on that mission. We feel we make a contribution to increasing the possibilities of equity for women throughout our society. By that I mean it's important to prepare women for leadership positions, for visibility, for visible opportunities across the board in our society, not only in academia, but also in our political institutions and our social institutions and in the arts. When you can open your favorite newspaper one morning and see positive stories, as many about women or with women as spokespersons as you do men, then we'll be getting there. Then, to some extent, our mission will have been accomplished.

COSTA: *You have some wonderful alumnae of the Bunting Institute. Can you tell me about some of them?*

LADD: It is a very interesting group. Among the poets, Anne Sexton was a fellow, as was Denise Levitov, Kathleen Spivack, and our current poet-in-residence Marie Howe, whom I'm sure will stand in that company, too. Alice Walker was' a fellow at the Bunting Institute. In our own University, the Institute has contributed to the careers of Sara Lawrence Lightfoot and Carol Gilligan. Pam Solo was a Peace Fellow at the Institute and she, like Sara Lawrence Lightfoot, both have been MacArthur recipients.

COSTA: *What seems to be students' main concerns these days?*

LADD: At this point in my life I have a son who is a student. He is Michael Ladd, who is nineteen years old and a student at Hampshire College. I use him as a reference figure when I talk with students. I've been doing that through public letters to him, my 'Dear Michael' letters. Recently I spoke to a group of students at Phillips Brooks House and the subject for that group was religion. I try to say to students what I tell Michael. I speak to groups of students with the kind of candor that I bring to our very special exchange, the exchange between this mother and that particular son.

COSTA: *Do you talk about things like the perils of peer pressure?*

LADD: No, I think those messages are conveyed earlier. I talk with him about the importance of peace and justice, and we struggle with our different views of how we are going to contribute to peace and justice in this society, in this world, and in our time. I point out to him that he has certain advantages and he is indeed expected to use his advantages in the interest of improving conditions for his generation. I have made him feel that he must be a peacemaker and refrain from taking sides in some issues—issues black and white, political issues, left and right—but try to present himself as someone who will be a mediator, who will bridge the differences, and who will help us reconcile some of the divisions that have fragmented our troubled society.

I tell other students that, too, and feel that the students we encounter here have to take seriously their moral and social responsibilities for the entire range of people in their generation. They should not only look among themselves as the reference figures of their generation, but should consider the young people they left behind who've dropped out or who have been forced out of their generational cohort, and reach out to them in some ways that will make their generation a healthier society than we have created for them. It's a heavy message that I lay on my boy.

COSTA: *It sounds like it. Quite a mission he has. You've done a lot of work with adolescence and that seems to be the period in one's life when most temptations occur and most good direction can be given to a person. What can you tell adolescents and what do you try to steer them to?*

LADD: Certainly, I encourage people to begin to think about those larger terms and issues, peace and justice, in interpersonal ways, ways in which they play themselves out in their own lives. I'm very concerned about the level of violence to which our young people are exposed, and to which some of them are drawn. The media, the television programs that are offered in this country only serve to reinforce the value and the romance of violence. That children play with toy guns, that this society condones war play and violence, that there aren't the restrictions, that there isn't an official loud condemnation of violence, that our clergy or the moral authorities in this country are not crying out at this point, is something that we all need to be concerned about.

COSTA: *People at this point in their careers usually look back and say, well, there are some things that I've left undone, new areas that I'd like to try. What are those areas for you?*

LADD: At this point, I'd like to continue the work that I have begun at the Bunting Institute, and if in various ways I can make an important contribution to the opportunities and careers of the distinguished women who will pass through the Bunting Institute, that will be a very satisfying part of my work at this point in my life. There is a part of me that would like to continue to advance the cause of the peaceful settlement of disputes and to facilitate ways of enlarging discussions of peace and justice through organizational work, some of which I'm involved in, and through my writing and other work of various kinds.

COSTA: *There appears to be a lessening of the polarization concerning the women's movement. Do you think more coalitions are being built around women's issues now than before, or do I have it wrong? Is there still polarization? Excluding the abortion issue, of course.*

LADD: I think there is a greater understanding of shared agendas on the part of women's groups. I think that there is more unity among the groups that support political candidates, for example, who are promoting women's issues. In the political arena it's reflected to some extent.

It's difficult to assess it from here, but there certainly seems to be more harmony and there are more coalitions of women. I hope they are bringing along some men, too. I do think that there is greater understanding on the part of men [who have the] influence to change opportunities for women, the understanding of the importance of giving women more space and hearing the voices of women.

A conversation with
Charles Maier

Charles Maier is professor of history. A scholar of the social ramifications of political upheaval, Maier received a MacArthur Foundation grant for research on peace and international cooperation concurrent with a Fellowship at the Woodrow Wilson Center. Forthcoming volumes focus on the reconstruction of Western Europe after World War II, and on German reunification.

COSTA: *Recently we marked the 50th anniversary of the beginning of World War II. You are the author of a new book,* The Unmasterable Past: History, Holocaust, and German National Identity *[Harvard University Press]. It used to be that the best historians were for the most part ostensibly neutral. That is, they did not let their personal politics affect their assessments of historical events and people. Now we have avowed Marxist historians, feminist historians, conservative historians—historians who often view history through the lens of political ideology. Have things changed in history, or are we just more astute at identifying historians' political ideologies?*

MAIER: I don't think historians were ever neutral. The most you can ask of a historian is that he or she knows his or her political preferences and states them up front, and then the consumer or the reader can at least be forewarned that there may be bias in the interpretation. It is impossible to be absolutely neutral. On the other hand, I don't believe that a historian should just be an advocate for one side or another. There are certain elementary methodological rules by which you can try to place yourself within the perspective of a historical protagonist and try to see things from that actor's point of view. I think we are more honest, we are also more diverse. It used to be that history was a rather conservative profession; in the last thirty years it has vastly expanded. This is normal and it is a good thing in general.

COSTA: *In fact, hasn't there been a sea change where theoretical historians have advocated things like psychohistory, using science more, using the primary source documents as much as possible, etc.?*

MAIER: We are supposed to use the primary documentation. We're supposed to build history from what is left to us from the past: artifacts, texts, other materials, and sometimes quantitative data. I think what has happened is that the range of available or acceptable data has vastly expanded. People know what to do with numbers in a way they didn't used to know. They know that statements such as, 'Most people thought,' or 'He was likely to do this or that,' are in fact disguised quantitative statements. . . . There are of course different methods that come into vogue; some of them prove fruitful, some of them prove less fruitful. We differ on which ones are going to be fruitful. Psychohistory enjoyed a big boom ten years ago; I'm not sure it's as popular now. On the other hand, no one would want to do without some degree of psychological or even psychoanalytical sophistication. Quantitative history came on like gangbusters about twenty years ago; some historians feel it's been disappointing in what it can answer. Nonetheless, I think we just keep on adding methodologies such as the history of everyday life, and the infusion of anthropological methods of listening to historical subjects—like ethnographers might listen to a primitive tribe; that's now very popular. Generally, I think it has to do with the quality of the researcher who undertakes the work, and less with the particular method that is chosen.

COSTA: *In journalism, we are often told that after a presidential administration leaves office we should not be too judgmental, but to let that president be judged by historians. Perhaps Truman was a great president on hindsight, and maybe Nixon was better than we thought because, his supporters say, he did wonderful things for foreign affairs.*

MAIER: I hear this often. It's a naive statement—history will tell us, history will judge. There is no greater degree of certainty for history writers for historical judgment than there is for political judgments, pure and simple. There is no greater degree of certainty, I believe, for economic history than there is for using a given economic policy. History does not have a capacity for judgment, that is, independent of people's political stances.

What historical judgment can add is more information. We may know more and may uncover more evidence as time goes on, which will let us see what motivations people brought to events, what the background was, and why they behaved in certain ways that we didn't know at that time. It's naive to think that the historian is going to clean up this mess of conflicting judgments and somehow establish certitude. That won't happen. It's a spurious claim; it's not what we should be asking of history.

COSTA: *Who was a better historian in your eyes, Herodotus or Thucydides? I thought Herodotus was more fun to read, although I do admit that I think Thucydides was more accurate.*

MAIER: You know, if you were talking about anthropological approaches they would go back to Herodotus; he loved foreign cultures, he loved travel. Nonetheless, I think Thucydides is the really first great, I would say even modern, analytical historian. He's got a clear sense of establishing causality. He's got a clear sense of the great issues that are involved. The discussion of the origins of the Peloponnesian War is beautifully done in its separation of long-term and short-term causes, and between ostensible grievances and deep-seated grievances. It has a great sense of sophistication about the structure of power relations; the gradual accretion of Athenian hegemony, and the fear of the Spartan coalition. All of this. It really hasn't been improved upon. It can be laid out a little more differently.

What we find problematic in Thucydides is his making up speeches after the fact. But, to my mind, Thucydides is a giant and any historian who deals with war can read him with profit, and any historian that deals with political conflict can read him with profit. He was clearly a favorite of Hobbes, who translated him with good reason.

COSTA: *Does one person create history or do the times make the man? This is the sort of question that I think Tolstoy wrote about in* War and Peace. *Would there have been a world war without Hitler—I ask you because you are a European historian with expertise in that area—or was Hitler just riding the curve of society at the time?*

MAIER: If any war is the creation of one man, World War II was Hitler's creation. Far more than World War I, World War II started with a program for changes in the map of Europe, which could only be achieved by hostilities. That, I think, is clear. Without Hitler's particular charisma, political entrepreneurship, what have you, German society may have never been in that position to try the mad program that it undertook in World War II. Nonetheless, Hitler, while certainly an individual factor, could not have come to power without certain conditions in Germany that we would have to study with far more aggregate methods: voting, the Depression, grievances caused by Versailles. No one man arises *ex nihilo* in a vacuum.

So the question of what the individual is, or the underlying sociopolitical conditions are is really a question of perspectives. This is another one of my pet peeves, if I can digress a little. We're always being told by critics, 'Show us that people count in history.' Well, of course people make history; it's not made by white mice. People are the actors in history. Nonetheless, why people act, and the context within which they act is not always appreciable by focusing on the biography of the leader. We certainly have to know about Hitler and we certainly have to understand that he was instrumental in all this. But why he occupied the place he did or how he came to be there requires a study of a far wider backdrop.

COSTA: *How would you explain the success of the Nazi phenomenon?*

MAIER: What do we mean by the Nazi phenomenon? If we mean how did it take power—it seemed they had about 40 percent of the electorate behind it at the point it took power, which is by far a significant amount in 1932, and yet was not a majority. Hitler's coming to power depended upon a clique and a cabal around the leading circles, President von Hindenburg and others. If we mean the general enthusiasm that the Nazi Party and Hitler generated during the period from 1933 to 1938 or 1940, we would have to look at other factors. Why did it come to power? It came to power building on a widespread sense of grievance about the results of World War I: Versailles, a feeling that the war hadn't been lost but that they had been tricked into a bad treaty, and a depression that made people very desperate, and had lowered the prices for farmers—who were the first major bloc to vote for Hitler. If we then want to explain the post-1933 enthusiasm that Hitler generated, I think we have to deal with the phenomenon that Germans felt that they were really coming into their own again; they weren't getting kicked around. Germany was awakening. Certainly if you had taken the plebiscites after he came to power, he had a much wider degree of support. Anti-Semitism was used instrumentally in that program. I think it was crucial to the cohesion of the party, but less crucial to the role of the party perhaps within German society. If you want to talk about some aspects of the Nazi program, the most terrible being the exterminations, then I think you really have to say these programs were designed by a relatively small group of fanatics, although they were built upon the acquiescence and passivity of much of the population. It's very complicated.

COSTA: *In your recent book* The Unmasterable Past: History, Holocaust, and German National Identity, *you seem to criticize other writers for a kind of relativism of genocide. That is, other writers write that Stalin's purges were responsible for even* more *deaths, 20 to 30 million deaths. The Armenians suffered genocide, and more recently the Khmer Rouge in Cambodia also caused genocide. Somehow you seem to say that this should not temper or ameliorate our horror of the systematic killing of Jews by the Nazis. Can you expound a bit on this?*

MAIER: I think you summarized my argument well. The book arose in the context of a debate that was taking place in Germany from early 1986 and continues to take place, although it has died down somewhat. An argument was being voiced by let's say relatively more conservative German historians on precisely the effect that you have cited. Namely that there are a lot of genocides in the world so why should we Germans have to take the rap for our genocide for ever and ever. It arose after Bitburg. It reflected a certain impatience [on West Germany's part] thinking that it was constantly being bullied about [because of this] terrible historical event, but it was one in which most Germans had not participated, and most of the population had been renewed since then. The consequence was that one had this revisionism. 'Why do we get the rap?' some asked.

My point and the point of many West Germans who reacted quite vigorously against this view, is that this was a very special genocide. Every genocide is probably special, but the commonalities that this one has with others—large body counts, terrible inhumanity—should not obscure what was special: the systematic hunting down of a population group throughout all of Europe, and the designing of facilities just to kill them, for no other purpose. Also, the ideological centrality of the anti-Jewish theme within the Nazi program. I guess my book was, in a sense, to tell Americans about this argument, to weigh in on the side that I thought was the right side in the argument, and then to bring up a whole group of questions about German national identity and recent German history writing that I thought would be of interest.

COSTA: *And yet there still seems to be some denial, not everywhere, but in some very small pockets around the globe, that the Holocaust may never have happened. Some people actually believe that.*

MAIER: There are some people who believe that. It's a hard event to come to terms with and I think this will persist. I cannot fathom the psychological makeup of those who refuse to accept what I think is demonstrated beyond dispute. That fringe to me is less important because I think they are irredeemable in some way, than the larger group of people who said: Well, it took place but really it wasn't so bad after all, or it's a fairly common occurrence. Those who refuse to admit that it had taken place are a different sort of political phenomenon. Ultimately, you can't argue with them, and you just have to outnumber them.

COSTA: *For years Western powers, and certainly European powers could see a war with Germany—I'm talking about World War II—on the horizon and yet there was an unbelievable inertia that had to be overcome before England and the United States could start to do something about the imminent war. How do you explain that inertia?*

MAIER: It's unclear what war was seen as coming. The inertia is very complicated. It used to be that those responsible for the inertia, the appeasers as they were called, were condemned out of hand. First of all not everyone took Hitler seriously. Even if they had read *Mein Kampf*, they thought: Well this was an early statement, the man is surrounded by more moderate colleagues, he will have to behave responsibly. In a certain sense one downplayed the radicalness of what Hitler hoped to achieve.

Secondly, one did not know about grievances concerning Eastern Europe, which the British in fact thought were quite legitimate. They felt that much of Hitler's program was just bringing into the Reich Germans who were living outside of it, or German-speaking peoples who might want to be included in it. If we believe in self-determination, determination of nations and people, why shouldn't these people have been given the right to approve of it. There was the hope that the revisions that Hitler wanted in the Treaty of Versailles could be made peacefully, and there was just a general unwillingness to pay for and to gear up for war. Remember, the First World War was a terrible, catastrophic war; it cost millions and millions of lives, and there was a belief, as one grew away from it, that it had been a mistake among many. Many English liberals thought this had been a mistake and there was no reason to fend its results. In any case there was even more of an isolationist reaction in the U.S. The French also indulged in appeasement, but they felt they just couldn't stand up to this vigorous and large country on their borders, and just hoped to keep the wolf from turning west rather than east.

COSTA: *From a military viewpoint there are some new technologies that change the way people fight wars, that occurred during World War II. First, there was the introduction of the German U-boat submarine, as a powerful new force now making the seas unsafe; American could no longer rely on its two great oceans for safety. Second, there was the use of air power on a nearly global scale, and then we had things like radar to let people know that there were problems in the air. Then, lastly and most dramatically, was the atomic bomb; a technology that virtually guarantees that the next world war will probably be the last one if it occurs. Could you comment about these warfare developments technologically and how it changed the nature of war and the way we look at war?*

MAIER: Let me correct you on one thing. The U-boat was almost a decisive weapon in World War I. Its technologies developed before World War I, and the amount of merchant shipping that it sank made the problem of its uses serious for Britain really in the First World War, or just about as serious as in the Second World War. Air power is clearly a major new technological device. I'm never quite sure how much technologies alter war or make a decision one way or another. We can point to radar, which the British had a few years before the Germans, and show that it gave a great edge in defending Britain during the Nazi bombardments of 1940. Even without it, though, it's unclear that those bombardments would have been decisive. The Germans thought more about using these weapons, thought more intelligently about exploiting the tank especially, and tactical aircraft in the early stages of the war. The results made for the success of the *blitzkrieg*; the quick wars against Poland and France, in the spring of 1940. Then city bombing made a difference; it changes the way death and destruction are dealt out. It probably makes each war more lethal.

As you said, an atomic war certainly would place the others in the shade. Whether the results are altered materially is harder to say. Once America entered the war, the industrial might of this country combined with Britain and Russia really foredoomed the Axis, just by looking at the figures. But it didn't necessarily affect men's will to resist, and it didn't put a time limit on how quickly the war could be ended.

COSTA: *Is it a myth that the German army was a better army, the best one that the earth had seen up until that point?*

MAIER: If it is true, it's probably not what you mean as a myth. I think probably pound-for-pound the German units were the most efficient fighting units of the war. I'm not primarily a historian of war or the military—at least the military side of war—but if you look at the speed at the early stages of the war and the resistance in the last stages of the war, they were remarkably disciplined and cohesive units.

There have been a couple of remarkable studies of strategy that some Israeli historians have produced. They seem to look at the German army as an army—obviously not ideologically, but tactically—to emulate in some ways. They found that the German army, because of it's high degree of self-sufficiency of the combat units, fought very effectively. America maximized its strength in economic force, in technology, and in the use of planes. We could out-produce any country. But I still think that unit-for-unit the German army probably had the best fighting units of the war. They were just overwhelmed at the end.

COSTA: *I'd like to ask you what one lesson you see coming from World War II?*

MAIER: There you have me: I see a lot of lessons. You know it's very hard to know what the lessons are. Don't let someone like Hitler come to power. That's a good lesson. How do we know it's someone like Hitler? Don't appease. Well, sometimes appeasement works and is rational, and sometimes it makes no sense whatsoever. It's easier in retrospect. Pay attention to what people write, even in their ideological tracts? Yes, although some people write excesses.

It's very difficult to give one lesson. I think ultimately World War II was a war, that if it had to be fought, was worth fighting. Studs Terkel called it the last good war; far less morally ambiguous from my point of view than Vietnam. The lesson I'd like to leave is a more historical lesson: What we wanted to achieve with World War II, was the destruction of Nazism, and fascism, and Axis, and expansionism, which we did achieve. Of course, there were tremendous new problems that were created. I'm sorry it's hard for me to leave you with one simple lesson; I could leave you with dozens of them.

COSTA: *Perhaps I should follow up with this. Arthur Schlesinger, the historian, says that history is cyclical, that things repeat, that trends repeat, that eras repeat, and that it is possible that fascism could come to the fore again. Do you think that is possible?*

MAIER: History is not exactly cyclical. It's like the cycles described in chaos theory, which are somewhere in the same neighborhood, but never repeat exactly. There are patterns of let's call them semi-repetition; you won't get exactly the same constellation of events. You can get reactions of agreed nationalism and belief in authoritarian solutions, but you won't get fascism as such.

Looking ahead, a historian always faces a major question and has faced it with a special urgency in the nuclear era. Does the existence of nuclear weapons so transform international relations that a war the scope of World War II is not really feasible? If so, then history in its certain important sense is not repeatable. If that is not the situation or if we eliminate nuclear weapons to a certain extent from our calculations, then maybe we will revert to a more traditional type of conflictual mode in the world. But, it won't be on the basis of relatively small nations. Europe is little; Germany, even a united Germany as I said, would just absolutely get devastated by a war. Any one of these countries, and our country, too. What will happen between some regional blocs a century hence, one would be a fool to predict. I think the one constant thing you could say about history is it's always full of surprises.

A conversation with

Bill Kovach

*Bill Kovach is curator of the Nieman Foundation. He earned
high regard for his work at the* Atlanta Journal and Constitution,
*which won two Pulitzer Prizes while he was editor. He was a
distinguished journalist for two decades at the* New York Times,
and a Nieman Fellow.

COSTA: *As you know, major metropolitan newspapers are becoming an
endangered species. Fewer and fewer cities have financially robust, competing
daily newspapers within their city limits, and most cities are lucky if they have
a single daily newspaper. Worse, for the newspaper world, is the fact that a
majority of Americans today get their news solely from television. Most people
don't read newspapers at all. What do you think is happening to readership?*

KOVACH: I think a good part of that started in the 1950s and '60s as owners of newspapers in America panicked with the advent of television and the
explosion in the sale of television sets and the expansion of the television market. Rather than invest in their newspapers, they began to pull the profit out
and diversify their ownership. The end result of that was as the population
grew, as the demographics changed, as people moved to the suburbs, newspapers weren't able to take advantage of the enormous increase in population as
the post-World War II baby boom began to move through the system. They
had antiquated presses, they couldn't produce enough newspapers, they didn't
take advantage of technology to follow their readers to the suburbs—they

could have used helicopters to move newspapers out there, they could have used the satellite technology that was available then.

They finally woke up in the 1970s and began to strengthen the newspaper. But the decline of the newspaper had less to do with the impact of television than it did the shortsighted investment policies of the owners of America's newspapers. Mostly it was the afternoon newspapers that failed. I think there is a little bit of a brighter future coming now with the new technology—desktop publishing. The cost of producing modest newspapers is almost within the reach of any of us, and as that process develops, I suspect you're going to see a lot of small, independent newspapers—aggressive newspapers—develop in urban areas. I think ten years from now you're likely to see three, four, or five competing newspapers in the large metropolitan areas.

COSTA: *That's similar to what they called 'zoned editions,' which the newspapers of the '30s and '40s used to do so well. That is, to take a couple of pages and dedicate them to an area within the city. Now you are saying that with desktop publishing we might have small local newspapers able to do that for different communities.*

KOVACH: I think that's a very possible future.

COSTA: *The irony is that most theorists and newspaper investors believe that newspapers should imitate television—make it glitzy, put more graphics in, use more color, make it more visual. You're saying that is really not the case, and that newspapers are probably in decline because they didn't think about how they were going to get their newspapers through the rush-hour traffic in the afternoon.*

KOVACH: I think that's the biggest part of it because every serious and in-depth survey of readers and potential readers that I know of concludes the same thing: people want more news, more information. The world is becoming more complex, it's more threatening. They need more information, they know they need the information and now with the internationalization of the economy, the economic questions are decided not necessarily in Washington but maybe in China, maybe, by 1992, in Paris and London. Farmers in Iowa know that. They need the information. They're desperate for information. As I say, every survey I know of—the most recent, which was done at my old newspaper down in Atlanta just in the past six months—shows that the main concern of the consumer is for more information, and for more international and national information.

COSTA: *Let's look at broadcast news. Even the strongest supporters of television as a news medium agree that television news, as it is presently done, can only give its audience the headlines. They agree with the premise that if you want to get information, you have to read about it in newspapers and magazines. And yet television news seems to be abandoning even the surface of news events and routinely now crosses into the entertainment world. I'm thinking of recent examples in which television news shows staged a few events to show the viewers how they imagined an event would be. They seem to have this need for action pictures at all times and they avoid the visually dull, but important, stories like Watergate. They were terrible on Watergate—they couldn't get a handle on it. That was a newspaper story. Does this skew reality since, for most Americans, television is their only window on the world? Is television getting too much like entertainment?*

KOVACH: I think those approaches do skew the consumer's concept of reality and I do think that they're reacting much the same way newspapers reacted to television. Television network owners are reacting to the proliferation of cable in the same way newspapers reacted to television. They're not doing what they do best in terms of news—the kinds of pieces that Edward Murrow did and Walter Cronkite did, which were very popular. *60 Minutes*, in its earliest incarnation, was a really special news show. It's become an entertainment show now, but in the beginning it was a great news show.

I think television is thrashing around and I think their first reaction is the same as newspapers, which is to try to change themselves and to make their news divisions into entertainment divisions and I hope that over time that will work itself out, because when it's properly done, a documentary or an in-depth report on television can be a very powerful information tool.

We're beginning to see enormous changes in the Soviet Union, China, and previously closed societies simply because information is loose in the world. We have to hope that, at this great juncture of the ability to move information and the need for information, the systems that produce it really take advantage of that opportunity to provide the kind of information that people need.

COSTA: *There's a big crossover these days of heretofore newspaper and magazine people going into television, largely because of the huge financial rewards and the chance to be on camera. Some of your friends have done this. They have gone from the* New York Times, *where you were Washington bureau chief, to television and they seem to have added another dimension of real news reporting on camera. Do you think this can help the news programs?*

KOVACH: If it picks up again. That sort of thing has slacked off. It may be starting again but some of the best print journalists who were in television have been squeezed out in this current period of the entertainment focus. I'm thinking of people like Fred Graham, who in effect created the Supreme Court coverage for CBS Television, and who was one of the great legal affairs reporters who had ever worked on television. He was squeezed out by this desire for more entertaining journalists. Fred was not an actor. So a lot of very good people have been moved out.

There are efforts now by people like Mike Gartner, who was a newspaper editor for most of his career. He is now in charge of NBC Television News.

Mike is trying to attract into NBC News journalists not necessarily for on-air work, but to produce reports, to do the reporting. If they can find a format in prime time that's not glitzy showbiz but is a serious news report, I think Mike Gartner might begin to show the way for a real future for television news.

COSTA: *Newspapers are not without guilt these days in looking for controversy for controversy's sake. Critics of the press say that the First Amendment doesn't give the press the right to perform what is a ritualistic assassination of one's character on the altar of the front page. Yet, if you talk to a lot of young journalists, as you certainly do in your travels as curator of the Nieman Foundation, many of them—not the ones who become Nieman Fellows, I'm sure— think the only journalism worth doing is investigative journalism, and investigative journalism as they define it is journalism that exposes personal faults and failures. Nothing is too personal and private not to be reported. What do you think of this trend?*

KOVACH: It's a little bit disturbing, but what worries me most about it is not the fact that it's done, but the way it's done.

I think one of the things that has happened in the last fifteen or twenty years in American journalism is the women's movement has generated a whole new level of concern among citizens about issues we never worried about before— there are women in the workplace, women making decisions, women who are helping set the political agenda—and the sort of behavior that was accepted by a politician when it was a man's world is not accepted any longer. Women want to know a little bit more about the behavior of a male politician or a female politician, in family terms. They're beginning to demand that kind of information. So I don't think the press began to develop that information in a vacuum—it was beginning to be demanded by a changing society.

I think the problem comes when the herd instinct of pack journalism takes over. You get a situation like the story about Barney Frank's personal behavior—which I happen to think is a legitimate area of inquiry for any politician. Once people elect someone to public office, the public has a right to know pretty much everything about that person. I don't personally have a problem with looking into the private life of a political figure, a public figure. What I do have a problem with is when it becomes the only story. Once the story is out, the notion that you have to get something better than your competitor had, that unrestrained competition that builds a story far beyond its intrinsic value is what troubles me and I frankly don't know what to do about it. It will only correct itself when the consumer says to the producers of the information, 'Enough, we don't want any more of that.'

COSTA: *When I was a reporter and then later as an editor, I could never get away with running any story or writing anything in my reports about a person, even a public figure, based on unnamed sources. My editors wouldn't accept it, and when I became an editor, I wouldn't accept it. I had to know one source. There seem to be a lot of unnamed sources stories and many say they represent the worst kind of journalism. What do you think of that?*

KOVACH: I'm astounded at that. When I was an editor, there was one very simple rule: I, at least, had to know who the source was and I had to have the option to share it with my superior, either the executive editor in New York or with the publisher because I had to protect the integrity of the newspaper. The only thing a news organization has to offer is its integrity. The job of the manager is to protect that. I was at a seminar recently with a bunch of young reporters and when I said that, they all gasped. They had been conditioned by editors to accept the notion that they had a right to guarantee anonymity and to not tell the editor. I don't think that's going to continue because as one of the other trends in American journalism, newspapers and news organizations are beginning to behave more and more as businesses rather than organizations in service of an idea. The courts are beginning to react to journalism as a business too and they're beginning to rule on what used to be First Amendment issues as matters of contract and business law. The statement of a reporter to a source that he or she can guarantee anonymity has been ruled in one recent case, as a contract. If the newspaper breaks the contract, it can be sued for violation of the contract. So I think that's going to help discipline that kind of behavior.

COSTA: *You recently wrote an op-ed piece in the* New York Times *about your view that newspapers are depending too much on polling and are doing a lot of opinion news reporting, that is, simply covering the polls. What is your view on that?*

KOVACH: I think the thing that disturbs me is that it has become so commonplace now. So little distinction is made between opinion and demonstrable, objective, provable fact, even by the journalist. Every second of air time, every inch of space that you report on opinion is space or time that is taken away from the kind of fact people need in order to make decisions. It worries me that a news organization will use its resources to ask people, 'Do you think banks discriminate against black people, rather than use the same resources to discover whether or not blacks are being discriminated against?' It's a misuse of resources, and it's certainly an abuse of the consumer's time because the opinion means nothing to them. An opinion is not a position, it's not thought out. It's a response to a question, and just the asking of the question begins to set the priority in the respondent's mind. So it's relatively useless information except to people like political leaders, like salesmen, who want to manipulate opinion or want to move opinion in one direction or another. That's not what journalism is about.

Some of the best use of opinion polling by newspapers is during a political campaign. Some of that is very valid and useful information on issues and how people are responding to issues during a campaign. But they've carried it to the point now where during this last campaign, news organizations were doing tracking polls, which try to judge movement of opinion overnight. For a politician it's useful to have that sense. But the pollster and the politician know that that information is valid only the minute it was taken, and yet journalists have been printing and broadcasting it twenty-four hours later and, in effect, have begun to impact on the system itself.

COSTA: *What do you think about the state of political reporting? I've seen you at the conventions with an army of people from the* Times *who are actually on the convention floor getting facts and not relying on polls. That seems to be changing too. Are political reporters not as aggressive as they should be?*

KOVACH: Again, it's the herd instinct. And the larger the herd becomes, the stronger that instinct is. Maybe it's human nature, maybe it's our history as animals that when we get into large groups we all want to go in the same direction. I think the failure of political reporting now—if you can call it that—is that too much time is spent in service of the campaign itself. The campaign uses the press to work its will on the public, and the press spends far too much time in service of that need. As a consumer of political information, I would feel a lot better about a reporter who went out and talked to people about an issue and explained to me the impact of one position or another on my future and the future of my children and grandchildren, rather than telling me whether or not this candidate believes in the American flag, or that candidate is patriotic. Those issues are irrelevant to my future.

COSTA: *What do you think is the most underreported area in journalism today?*

KOVACH: I guess the thing I would like to have more information about is the way the system now ties itself together. I think I get too little information out of my newspapers and off of my television set about the relationship between local government and state government, state government and federal government, federal government and international issues. I don't quite understand how the system works anymore. I don't see the connections that I used to see. As I was growing up, I think I had a fairly clear view. I know the adults in my life had a fairly clear view of what it was they could do to affect the situation, what it was they could do to have an impact in terms of their own lives. I think we've lost that. I think we've lost a sense of the connection between things, and I wish more stories helped me understand what they are.

COSTA: *Have you also lost a sense of 'crusading journalism,' and by that I mean the kind of journalism you did early on in the 1950s and '60s when you were covering civil rights in the South. There was a story that had to be told, it was painful, but you went wherever the story took you. Nowadays, there doesn't seem to be that kind of continuity and coverage of a major social trend like that.*

KOVACH: I think we don't know what those trends are. Clearly, the environmental movement is one, and the reporting is beginning to pick up on that. I

149

think we're creatures of crisis. One of the problems with journalism is that we have allowed the most potent system of communication and information the world has ever seen to develop without any real control in the development. We still don't know how to report process, we still don't know how to report quiet events. We tend to focus on confusion and rock-throwing and riot and revolution. The countries of the world that are relatively quiet may be having more impact on our future, but we never hear about them because they're quiet. We don't know how to report those stories. The most exciting time of my life was covering the civil rights movement in the South, but that story became the crisis it became because all of us, including the press, had not reported the civil rights problems that had been developing over the previous fifty years that led to that explosion. It was brought home to me on a trip to Central America a few years ago when the leader of the organization for human rights in El Salvador—who was assassinated two weeks after I saw him—asked me, 'What chance do we have to get into your newspapers? The killers can take guns and shoot their way in. But we're trying to solve this peacefully. How do we get into the newspaper?' It's an interesting question because I couldn't answer it. A human rights advocate who sits down and across a table rationally tries to discuss an issue is not going to get into the newspaper and we have yet to learn how to deal with that information. It may be the most important information we can give.

COSTA: *Getting back to the business of journalism and how it may affect the practice of journalism, let's talk about the decline in independently owned newspapers and broadcast outlets, and the rise of group ownership. Does working for a group affect the news business? Are there profit motives that sometimes outweigh journalistic motives? What do think about this controversial area?*

KOVACH: I think it goes both ways. Group ownership can be a very valuable thing for journalism. [There's] concentration of resources. You get a chain like Knight-Ridder, and the quality of journalism in virtually every city in which they have a newspaper is better because of Knight-Ridder. You go to a city like Philadelphia and you have Gene Roberts, one of the best editors I ever knew, who puts out one of the most aggressive and best edited newspapers in the country, and that's because Knight-Ridder encourages that. There are other chains that are more interested in impressing Wall Street and their performance on the market and profit motive, and those chains will draw resources out of newspapers. Chains, per se, are neither good nor bad. It depends on the ownership of chain.

I think the underlying danger is this urge to constantly grow. It's almost a parallel to what our automobile industry got into: this notion that every quarter had to be bigger and better than the last quarter. As you take a newspaper and force growth for growth's sake, what you tend to do is homogenize the newspaper. The larger the circulation of a newspaper becomes, the larger the franchise, the more there is to protect, the more there is to lose, the less willing the ownership is going to be to take a risk, to take a chance, to do an offbeat story, to do an aggressive story. So the growth factor is an inhibiting factor. [It would be good if] owners could content themselves with a steady, reasonable profit rather than—as some now demand—as high as forty percent profit. There are newspapers now whose goal is to keep forty cents of every dollar they make. That is not an institution in service of an idea—the First Amendment—that's an institution in service of a business, in service of profit, and I do not believe the First Amendment was written into the Constitution in order to generate business.

COSTA: *There are good signs. People going into journalism today are much better academically prepared than twenty or thirty years ago. They do have a sense of history, they do know some economics now, and they certainly know more science than anyone else previous to this generation. Do you see that in today's journalists?*

KOVACH: Oh, absolutely. I'm enormously impressed and very heartened about the future, both when I was an editor and I was recruiting staff down in Atlanta, and here at the Nieman program. We had a guest at a seminar recently, David Halberstam, who I consider one of the great reporters of my generation. Dave and I were comparing notes and both of us concluded that it would be very difficult for us to break into the business now, considering the level of competition. The young people who are going into journalism now are not only some of the brightest and best educated, but some of the most highly motivated and most idealistic in the best sense of the word in terms of their commitment to the kind of work they want to do and their sense that the work they want to do has some strong societal benefit. I'm very encouraged about the quality of people in the trade of journalism.

A conversation with

Orlando Patterson

Orlando Patterson is professor of sociology, author of Freedom in the
Making of Western Culture *(Basic Books), and the forthcoming
second volume,* A World of Freedom.

COSTA: *You will be teaching a course next spring on the concept of freedom,
and my first question is: what is it that makes a society free? I ask you this in
light of what is happening in Poland, East Germany, Hungary, and the Soviet
Republics.*

PATTERSON: The question of what makes a society free is one which, as you
rightly point out, is on everybody's, the world's, mind right now. It depends
very much on what you mean by the term freedom. I tend to see it as a tripar-
tite concept, and it was so from the beginning. It involves three notes in a cultural chord, one of which has to do with this notion of personal freedom, that
is, not being constrained by anyone, being able to do as one pleases. That is
the most fundamental meaning of the term.

Secondly, it has to do with power, which is closely related to the first,
because one wants not to be constrained in order to be able to do things. So
there is always this idea that strikes many as paradoxical: the notion of freedom as empowerment, as power, as having the capacity to do and control
things, including, ironically, power over others.

The third note in this cultural chord is the idea of freedom as participation in one's political community; having a say in the way in which one's community is managed. One is free to the degree that one shares in the decisions which influence one's life. These three notions are closely tied, although at first sight, they may not seem to be. My problem has been to explain how this complex idea became such an important social value, and why this happened only in the West. My answer, in a nutshell, is that freedom became a major value in the ancient West because only in the West was a large-scale slavery a major, indeed, constitutive, institution. Christianity, the religion that shaped the Western mind, emerged in the large-scale society of Rome and its central theme is freedom or redemption, which literally means, to be purchased out of slavery. Jesus, by his salvific act of self-sacrifice bought us our spiritual freedom with his blood, out of the spiritual sin of slavery. So the whole ethos of the civilization is suffused with this extraordinary dialectic of slavery-into-freedom. Historically, it is not correct to say that we become slaves when we have lost our freedom, although that is the way we, and the philosophers, are inclined to reinterpret it. The truth is, we are only free when, and because, we are not slaves. Once you see it this way it is easy to understand what is going on in Eastern Europe, and why.

COSTA: *It seems that what you're saying is that there may indeed be levels of freedom, for example, people who suffer poverty may have constitutionally guaranteed rights, but they are not able to live life as freely as, say, those who are economically better off. So, in a sense, there may be levels of freedom even in a free society like our own.*

PATTERSON: I'd rather say there are elements of freedom because people believe that being free in the sense of not being constrained is an important value in itself, which even the man under the proverbial bridge, the poor man, does value. We've all heard the criticism of personal freedom, that it means nothing if you're so desperately poor that you can do nothing with it. But I think that is a misconception. My reading of the history of freedom in the West suggests that people have always valued personal freedom in itself and see it as something to be cherished, even when they are very, very poor, and would not, if presented with the choice of having the capacity to live well, accept that as an alternative to being free in the sense of doing as you please.

It is an easy criticism to make of personal freedom, but the historical sociology of freedom suggests that, whether rightly or wrongly, people throughout the history of the West, have enormously valued this thing, personal freedom. This was true of the ex-slave in ancient Greece and Rome who, in fact be shown to have lost out economically on becoming free. It was true of the ex-serf who became a free man in Medieval Europe and who, in fact, often became more insecure economically. It was true of the ex-slave in the American South who usually was far more insecure politically and economically, who in fact was exposed to every vicious racist in the local community and was often forced to leave the state, but still valued this thing: not being under the personal power of another person.

At the same time, I must emphasize that people in the West have also always conceived of freedom as a power over others; and democracy, when it has existed, has always entailed an exclusive club of voters which usually kept out women and groups that did not belong. There has always been a dark side to freedom. It has been a great and generative value in Western culture, but it has also been, and remains, a scary value. Nazi Germany was a very free state, for the Germans. And we should never forget that Southerners fought the Civil War in passionate and genuine defense of their freedom, including their freedom to enslave blacks. Believe me, it's a wonderfully weird and paradoxical thing, this central value of Western civilization. So while I do not wish to pour cold water on the great transformation taking place in Eastern Europe today, it would be irresponsible of me, as a student of freedom and slavery, not to point out that the situation is fraught with dangers. It is always a dangerous development when societies become impassioned with freedom especially in contexts where there is no institutional support for it, and worse, where there are unrealistic material expectations associated with freedom. I hate to say it, but one quite frightening possible outcome of events in Eastern Europe is that the whole region could go fascist.

COSTA: *You've written extensively about the obverse of freedom—slavery. In preparing for this interview I read something that you wrote eighteen years ago, in which you said that a grossly neglected area of black American history is the nature of the black experience during the period of slavery. Has that changed? Are historians and sociologists dealing with that question now?*

PATTERSON: Oh, definitely. There has been an explosion of studies on blacks during the period of slavery and on slavery generally, but I have found one glaring deficiency in these studies. It's the fact that people very rarely ask, 'What is the nature of this thing, slavery?' That is to say, there are endless numbers of studies of the economics of slavery, culture of blacks during the period of slavery, but very few people have asked what essentially was the nature of the relationship between master and slave? What gives it its special quality? What makes it such a horrible thing, morally, socially, and politically? It is amazing how few studies have addressed that particular problem. My last book was concerned with answering just that question. Once you ask that question, you inevitably find yourself addressing it comparatively because you find that slavery, if only as a minor institution, has existed all over the world, and so my concern was: what is it and why are we so horrified by it, because on the face of it there is really no good reason why we should be. There are other kinds of relationships that are just as debasing and horrendous: the plight of the worker in the 19th-century mines, bondage in Asia, battered wives trapped in marriages they cannot leave, the plight of the untouchables, and so on. Yet we have a peculiar horror of slavery, and it is very interesting to ask why.

COSTA: *Have you come up with an answer?*

PATTERSON: It is the fact that it's a very peculiar form of *personal* domination. First of all, it's personal. It's total, and the master or owner assumes the power of life and death over the slave. The slave is a socially dead person, has no existence apart from the owner and that creates a very peculiar kind of human relationship. And a peculiar kind of social problem: the problem of slave culture. When you have large numbers of persons who are felt not to belong in a society, a predictable set of attitudes emerge to rationalize this strange situation.

But it is the intense, personal possession of another person which most defines the relationship. It resembles some of the more perverse aspects of male/female relationships. It's a peculiar form of dishonoring of the slave and a parasitic ego-enhancement to the master in the very act of degrading the slave. These are the qualities that make it rather different from the relationship, say, between even the most exploitative of capitalists and workers. The capitalist may own the worker's labor but not the *person* of the worker. It is this quality, this personal quality and the totality of it, the dishonor of it, the degradation and the total exclusion from belonging and participation which constitute the relationship. It's those qualities which together make it such a peculiarly evil and destructive relationship and which excites horror in a special way. And rightly so.

Black folks are still recovering from two and a half centuries of it. It is stupid, vicious, and immoral of social analysts to attempt to discount that destructive legacy of this horribly, nightmarish experience for black Americans, to suggest that northern urban blacks were immigrants like all the rest.

COSTA: *How did you become interested in this whole topic of slavery? You grew up in Jamaica. Was that an aspect of your interest?*

PATTERSON: I began simply by trying to understand my own society. Jamaican society, during most of its history, was a slave society, one of the worst slave societies in all of human history, in the sense that it was a total slave society, with no intermediary groups. The few who were free were slave owners or overseers, and the vast majority—over ninety percent—were slaves. It was a brutal plantation system. So to understand that society—its values, its heritage—one had to understand this institution. My original objective was simply to understand the development process in Jamaica, but I became so fascinated with the institution itself that I began to look at other slave societies, including the United States, and wondered whether there were common problems which emerged in postemancipation societies such as those of the U.S. South, Jamaica, and Latin American societies like Brazil, Colombia, and so on. That is what got me into the comparative study of slavery.

COSTA: *What is it about the nature of slavery—is it the fact that it took place over so many centuries, even in the United States—that creates such a long half-life of the effects of slavery? People for generations have been affected by things that happened 200 years ago in their culture and are still being affected by the concept of slavery.*

PATTERSON: What happens is that if you have a large-scale slave society, existing over a long period of time, you have emerging a slave culture which reinforces it, which institutionalizes it. So simply to abolish slavery in the sense of removing the legal controls which legitimize the ownership of the slave by the owner is not to abolish slavery; the institution is still there. People immediately tend to respond and say 'My God, all these socially dead people have been let loose among us. They do not belong. We've got to control them.' So, if anything, what tends to happen after emancipation is that the institutional reinforcements are intensified. This explains an interesting feature of U.S. history, the fact that the most brutal period as far as the history of blacks is concerned was not so much during the period of slavery, but afterwards when the lynchings and so on took place, because then blacks were in the worst of all possible worlds. On the one hand, the owners, who were the well-to-do in the ruling class, no longer had any vested interest in protecting them. The nonslave population felt that these people had no right to be there and felt free to abuse them because they were still operating under the cultural influences of slavery.

So the slave culture, if anything, became more activated after the period of slavery, and this explains compensating developments of the most brutal sort— the massive increase in lynchings, which became almost sacrificial communal events, and then the growth of Jim Crow laws. The same is true of many other slave societies, after slavery was abolished.

COSTA: *You wrote that an irony of pre-Civil War times was that slavery was attacked in places where it did not exist—the West and the Northwest—and it was accepted where it did exist, primarily in the South. This certainly isn't true today in places like South Africa where people are fighting daily to overthrow apartheid.*

PATTERSON: No, that was actually a quote from an anonymous U.S. congressman and it is one of the ironies of the Civil War: the fact that, for many, it was really about keeping slavery out of the Southwest. No, it's not true today, but I do not consider apartheid, however horrible it may be, a form of slavery. I think it is very important to be precise about one's use of terms. South Africa is not a slave society in the sense of personal ownership or possession of one person by another.

COSTA: *They disenfranchise people in South Africa, but they are certainly not sold on the block as it once was done.*

PATTERSON: They lack political freedom, democracy, and in many respects, maybe worse. I mean, there are conditions worse than slavery, for example, the condition of Jews in Nazi Germany. So again, my concern is to be precise about what we are talking about here, and I think people too indiscriminately use the term slavery to refer to other conditions which, while horrible, are not conditions of slavery. Having said that, though, it is important to understand that the slavery-into-freedom idea is so powerfully ingrained in our culture that we often use it as a metaphor for all forms of domination and restraint. So powerful is the metaphor that we can speak of evil empires and mean by it exactly what we mean by slavery.

COSTA: *Supreme Court Justice Thurgood Marshall recently started refer-ring to blacks as Afro-Americans and you've done so much work on where slaves came from—which parts of Africa—to the United States. This term is so loaded now: some people think it should be African Americans, some people think that the word black is sufficient, others say at least it's a progression from the word Negro of the '60s. How do you feel about this label Afro-American?*

PATTERSON: What this illustrates is the fact that the process of social defi-nition is still going on with respect to black Americans. It also reflects how much we're still caught up with the problems which derive from the past, and the peculiar set of problems which black Americans have, which differentiate them from Italian Americans, and so on. The recent tendency among neocon-servatives is to say, 'What's the difference? It's just another ethnic group, it's the same set of problems, why can't they solve it in the same way our ances-tors did?' They can't, because there is a very distinctive set of issues here. One of which, perhaps the most important of which, is the one I mentioned earlier, that black Americans had to put up with, and come to terms with, and strug-gle with, life in a slave culture. That poisoned America's attitude towards them in a way which is not true of the Italians, Jews, Russians or whatever, who came over here. American slaveholders deliberately and systematically destroyed the black family. The immigration experience did not destroy the family of European immigrants to America; if anything it strengthened the institution.

There is a sense in which the civil rights movement can be seen as one stage, perhaps the most important stage, in the abolition movement. It was essentially a struggle against the persisting slave culture. A major part of that movement was the problem of defining black Americans as a group who belonged to this society precisely because one of the central features of being enslaved and of being the victims of a slave culture, which America was, and to some extent, still is, was the insistence that black Americans did not belong, even though as a group they've been here longer than almost any other group except the descendants of the Pilgrim fathers and the Native Americans before them. Yet they've had to struggle with this problem.

So the problem of self-definition became very crucial and it immediately relates to the issue you raise. Now, this is a complex matter and I think it is going to go through several phases. I think it is important, at one stage, for black Americans to define themselves as black, as part of that struggle to negate the way blackness was defined as something wrong and unacceptable to the dominant group. So, you disarm the aggressor and assert your own dignity by embracing his own weapons, you more or less throw it back in the face of the oppressor and simply say, 'I'm going to embrace this notion to let you know that I belong here and I'm proud of this designation.' But I think it's a fighting term, good and necessary for a period. It has perhaps outlived its usefulness. Blackness is a loaded symbolic term in Western culture. It's too heavy a symbolic burden for a group that has more than its share of symbolic problems. I mean, you're not going to change the language.

COSTA: *You mentioned the civil rights movement. Many civil libertarians worry about what they perceive as a lack of momentum in the civil rights movement during the last decade. It appears that the present administration is also not going to take a very proactive approach to civil rights. How do you think this will affect minority groups?*

PATTERSON: There are really two basic problems facing black Americans and non-white minority groups generally. One is the basic structural problem of finding a place within this economy, especially one that is going through tremendous structural changes. This is the thesis of William Julius Wilson: that the fundamental problem of some blacks, especially the black underclass, is not a racial problem primarily, but a structural economic problem. He is not saying that racism doesn't exist, what he is saying is that if you were to remove all the racism in America by waving some magic wand, you'd still have a problem of the underclass, which is true.

We must be careful, however, not to confuse the problem of the underclass with the problem of all black Americans, which Wilson, of course, does not. Some neoconservative analysts, however, are prone to do so. It's a racist way of dishonoring all blacks, and of obscuring the achievements, and the very real, persisting problems of the vast majority of blacks who are law-abiding, working, and middle-class people. There is a sense in which middle-class blacks, like women, face another set of problems, which really do relate to civil rights issues, and which they have to continue struggling with. Because the problem here is not that of preventing people from falling through the floor of poverty but of breaking through a ceiling, and breaking through a set of norms which define what constitutes leadership behavior in this society. They've been so defined as to make it very difficult for women and for some minorities to break through. These are norms having to do with personal behavior, having to do with personal interaction, having to do with the way in which you administer, the way that you manage, and deal with people, and the access you have to information about people and about systems, and so on.

These are the kinds of problems which I think only a vigorous civil rights program is going to tackle. In my favorite way of putting this: if what it takes to become the head of a major corporation in America is the kind of personality which we find exhibited on television by Lee Iacocca, then women and black folks might as well forget it. That kind of peculiar macho style is just not something which some people are going to be able to acquire unless they do violence to the way they are, and there is no reason why they should. I mean the Japanese have shown us that there are other ways of skinning this cat we call capitalism. And so it's these rules which people have attempted to define as universal and unchangeable, and encoded in the case studies of the Harvard Business School, which have to be challenged.

It's to confuse the issue to argue that such challenges amount to an assault on standards. We are not talking about purely technical skills here, about becoming a car mechanic, or doctor or something wholly banausic like that. We are talking about a very subjective, and very culturally defined art—that of managing people. This is the next great battlefront of the civil-rights movement, the agenda for the nineties and beyond. It's going to be a cultural battle. The solution will not be to let more women and blacks and Hispanics into business schools. That is a stop-gap remedy. The long-term solution will be to rewrite the case studies of the business schools, to change our style and art of management.

A *conversation with*

Edwin O. Reischauer

The late Edwin O. Reischauer was former chairman of the E.O. Reischauer Institute of Japanese Studies and former director of the Harvard-Yenching Institute. His last published book was The Japanese Today: Changes and Continuity *(Harvard University Press). His Harvard career spanned more than 50 years, during which he was Ambassador to Japan under the Kennedy and Johnson administrations.*

COSTA: *Even though Americans drive Japanese cars, watch films on VCRs made in Japan, and take photos with Japanese cameras, Americans know very little about Japan. Often what they think they know is really a misperception of the country. For example, most people in America think of Japan as a small nation. As you point out in your book* The Japanese Today, *even though Japan is not a large geographic country, its population of more than 122 million people makes it twice the size of any of the Western European big four; it's bigger than the United Kingdom, France, Germany and Italy. Isn't it true that Japan has been a populous country for hundreds of years and we have a misperception of it as a small nation?*

REISCHAUER: Yes, that is quite correct. The countries of East Asia had large populations from way, way back. You know China has been the largest country in the world for a couple thousand years and more. The Japanese have been one of the very largest for a long time. Back around 1600 Japan had maybe close to 25 million people. That would have made it the largest country in the area. It is equal to the countries of Western Europe, and gone beyond them for hundreds of years.

COSTA: *You were born and raised in Japan and served as the ambassador to Japan from 1961 to 1966. Let's talk for a moment about some of the geographic aspects of Japan. Could you describe the climate? It seems to be, from what I read, similar to the East Coast of America.*

REISCHAUER: It is basically very much like the East Coast of America. It lies a little bit further south than much of our East Coast. It stretches actually from about Montreal to Tallahassee. That is the scope of it, but most of the country falls in the area around North Carolina and Virginia; that's where most of the population is. It's more oceanic than the East Coast is. It's several hundred miles out to sea, which gives it a slightly milder climate both in winter and in summertime.

COSTA: *How do the climatological effects impinge on the growing season and the agriculture of Japan?*

REISCHAUER: It doesn't affect it too much. But agriculture, of course, does not produce many of Japan's products today. Even with a very garden-like agriculture producing more per square foot than anywhere else in the world, the Japanese can't begin to meet their own needs through agriculture.

COSTA: *In your book, you describe the mountains of Japan. It is so mountainous that you say that 20 percent, or one-fifth, of the country is actually level enough to permit agriculture.*

REISCHAUER: Yes, level enough to permit agriculture or habitation, because cities as well as farms have to come out of that leveler part of Japan. You can fly over most of Japan and it's just a sea of small mountains all covered with trees, but not producing anything in agricultural products at all. A good four-fifths of the nation is covered with trees in that way.

COSTA: *The geography seems to be ideally suited for traditional kinds of isolationism and feudal-lord social organization, which Japanese history seems to bear out, but the last 40 years have seen some quite dramatic changes from a decentralized society to a centralized economic force.*

REISCHAUER: It didn't turn in just the last 40 years. That goes right back to the 1860s. From that time on, Japan has been a tremendously centralized country. They did it largely through education. They brought the people back together to be very much the same type of people because they have the same type of education spread through the whole country.

COSTA: *One of the stereotypes that we hold about the Japanese is that they are very group oriented, that the individual who strikes out on his or her own is to be shunned. Is that true?*

REISCHAUER: Basically, that is true. The country is very much oriented toward a group kind of organization, and this you find throughout the society going back many centuries, back to the time of the early villages. These villages were small, compact units that ran their own affairs. The political format for the Middle Ages, late Middle Ages, and early modern times, was that of the feudal estate, which was a rather large centralized little kingdom. The first Europeans who saw these things called the leaders of them 'kings,' because they seemed to be kingdoms. There were just feudal lords under the rule of some other higher feudal lord, and they held very compact groups of fighting men together who then controlled the peasant villages. The peasant villages had a great deal of autonomy, but they were units that worked together. This kind of unit, both in the feudal estate and in the old-fashioned village, has very easily been transmitted into a form of business organization. In fact, by the 1700s, the Japanese were beginning to build up the corporation. They began to have companies throughout the nation and things of that sort, a very advanced kind of economy. These have all become modern institutions very successfully.

COSTA: *Contemporary Japanese are extremely competitive concerning education. In your book, you published a picture of a mother and father in tears who were standing beside their daughter, who was also in tears, as they read the sad news that the daughter failed to be admitted to the college that she wanted to attend. How excessive and obsessive are families in Japan about education?*

REISCHAUER: It is excessive and obsessive because they tend to judge things in terms of passing certain examinations, and getting into a good school. In order to get into a good university you have to get into a good high school, to get into the good high school you have to get into a good junior high, and so on down the list. So you have these entrance examinations that are terribly competitive, which begin way back in kindergarten. This goes all the way through a child's education. It harms the educational system somewhat, because even though it does make the Japanese learn more facts—a great deal more facts than we do in our education, or the Europeans do—at the same time, it makes them prepare for passing examinations, it proves that they know these facts. It does not prove that they have thought about them or really understand what it is all about.

They are not likely to be very good advanced postgraduate students. They often go abroad at that time because the Japanese graduate schools are not that good, but they are lost because they say, 'Tell me what to do.' You tell them what to do and they will go off and do it and work very hard at it but they want to be told what to do. This is a real weakness in education that exists today.

COSTA: *They value, even almost revere, teachers and professors in Japan. Is that true?*

REISCHAUER: This is, of course, an old tradition that goes all the way back to early Confucianism in China, that the teacher, the man of knowledge, is an important person, and is much respected and given a great deal of honor, if not wealth. Now this is gradually being lost, because they don't pay their teachers enough today. Teachers are beginning to move toward a teachers' union and fight the system for their salaries. So there is less respect for teachers than there was, say, forty or fifty years ago, but it would still be a great deal more than we have.

COSTA: *When these graduates enter the work force it is quite likely they will choose a company very much the way they chose the one university they wanted to go to. And they stay with that company perhaps for life. The most important thing, apparently, is loyalty to the company. That is so antithetical here in the U.S. where, if you're on the fast track, you should move every two to four years in order to show some kind of mobility, otherwise you appear to be in a rut. How do you explain this Japanese phenomenon?*

REISCHAUER: Of course, their attitudes fitted in with old society. The feudal class to which you belonged, you belonged to for life. You had no option there, you couldn't move to a different one. Or the village to which you belonged—you were there and there for life. They took that over into modern times and put it into the educational system. In education you got into better schools by getting into the preparatory school for those better schools. So you join that particular school line as early as you could and tried to work your way up in it.

Then you get to the business world and you start in a company at the bottom and if you're a loyal member of the company you would be advanced and eventually reach somewhere near the top. Everybody can't get to the top, but most of the people get to a pretty high level. If you wanted to go from company to company, people would look upon you as being somewhat unstable. People would think that you can't get along with people, obviously, and there is something wrong with you, and you're the one that is wrong, not the company. You get no brownie points for moving from company to company. Now this is all changing a lot. This is moving very rapidly and they're beginning to pick up our practices. Many, many Japanese now are very happy to join Western companies because you can make a more rapid motion upwards, or sideways from one company to another, until they find their way towards the top.

COSTA: *You were ambassador to Japan in the early 1960s, during the Kennedy era. Could you reflect for a moment on what the political conditions of Japan were then and what you think they are now?*

REISCHAUER: Back in the Kennedy era, which was the early '60s, Japan was really just getting on her feet at that time. She was finally proving herself successful, but she wasn't sure of herself at all and nobody else was sure of it, and we didn't pay much attention. It was interesting how little attention even America paid to Japan at that time, let alone the Europeans and others who almost completely ignored Japan.

Well, now, in the intervening thirty years, tremendous changes have taken place. Everybody realizes the Japanese are right up in the front line with everything and even the Japanese have convinced themselves that maybe they are up in the front line. They are worrying about the problems of being a person at the top, because these are very different problems than the problems they've had ever since the 1860s when they started trying to catch up with the West, and then they had to start catching up again after the great defeat in World War II. There is no model for them to follow, but they have to find the new road and they are very good at some aspects of this as we know perfectly well through their various productions, but they aren't as imaginative, as inventive, as one might expect them to be. It took a long time before America was competitive with Europe, let's say, in point of view of creativeness. We like to think of ourselves as all having been Edisons and people like that who worked with our hands and invented things, and we felt ourselves to be catching up there. But it took us a long time, well into the 20th century, that the United States was catching up in science and other things like that with Europe, and it may be that Japan is just in the process of catching up, having started further behind us.

COSTA: *Some of our CEOs in America blame the economic miracle of Japan on people like General MacArthur who helped that nation get on its feet right after the war. I'm wondering what your perspective is on that and also whether the fact that they haven't had to spend large amounts of money on defense has helped Japan economically?*

REISCHAUER: Back in MacArthur's time . . . nobody was worrying about Japan as being competitive, as being dangerous. We wanted to have it [be] a stable country and a democracy because it was on the front lines. . . . Even though she was not a military power, she was of great intense value to us as a base for our military power, and as a strong democratic country that was on our side of the fence. So she was highly valued. Nobody was criticizing Japan in that way at all. Later on as you look back now, you can say, well, we were a little bit overgenerous, perhaps, in letting them go on with their self-protectionism much more than they needed to, and we should have been a little more insistent that they give up protectionism at an earlier date and gotten used to the normal practices of international trade that the rest of us have. That criticism can be made today.

As to whether or not Japan did not pay much for military matters—I would say it's an important point that she did not put four percent, five percent of her gross national product into military buildup and very carefully kept it down to one percent always, or if possible, slightly below that. That was a great asset for them. But it's not the main explanation.

COSTA: *A lot of other people are also bitter because Japan is investing so much in our country. They own some of our movie studios now, and just recently they bought the Rockefeller Center from the Rockefeller family. People are worrying about their incursion in the United States and in our economy. Are we becoming too dominated by the Japanese and their investments?*

REISCHAUER: It is a worrisome thing in some ways because it stirs up a certain amount of racist feeling. There is a good bit of anti-Japanese racism involved in this. Somehow it seems more horrendous for the Japanese to be owning Rockefeller Center than if Canadians owned it or even Dutchmen owned it, and so on. Well, if you look at the actual statistics, you will find that in percentage terms the Dutch own more than the Japanese do in the United States and whoever heard anything about that? We've never been worried about that, and there has been no great outcry. Of course, Canadians are the ones who have the largest percentage of holdings here and, of course, we accept that perfectly well. The Japanese will have to be careful in the way they handle this and they've tried to be careful in not stirring up American feelings on this side. But this is a matter that I think is more our problem, that we cannot get over a feeling of racism involved in this.

COSTA: *Two of the negative things that I have read about are that the Japanese harbor feelings of racism, and also that women in Japan are still held in fairly unequal positions and low esteem.*

REISCHAUER: These are very valid points of criticism. When I spoke of American racism I should add quickly that the Japanese are much more racist than we are. In fact all of the people in East Asia are terribly racist: the Chinese, Koreans, Japanese. Even the way they feel about each other is really terrible. So they've brought a good bit of this down upon themselves.

On the matter of the women, this is a rather crucial moment. We may be witnessing right now the start of the women's revolution in Japan. I think that is the most interesting thing going on in Japan as of today. The Japanese women are tremendously well organized and for a long time of course they ran the families, they run the children and their education, the PTA, which is a big organization in Japan, is purely in their hands, and so on. The local organizations to improve streets and things of that sort are done by women because the men are all at work. The men have to commute for such long hours that they are never around, and their social habits are such as to keep them downtown drinking beer in the late evening rather than coming home and being a member of the community.

So the Japanese woman is pretty well dug in as a power person back home, and now she is beginning to realize that she's got the vote. There are more women voters than anything else, and one of the major parties, the Socialist party—the second largest party—has actually chosen a woman as the leader, which was unthinkable as of a few decades ago. There's this sudden wave of women coming up for positions of considerable influence. I would not be at all surprised to see a tremendous change in the place of women during the next ten or twenty years.

Japanese women have always been felt to be the stronger of the two sexes, having a lot more guts than the men do. The men have their own particular Japanese type of macho that they flaunt, but still the Japanese women are the ones who have the real inner strength. If they make that inner strength partly a political strength, why, you may have a very interesting change in Japanese politics. You find that suddenly it becomes important whether or not a man—a politician—is having a mistress, or how he is treating his mistress. Men are being asked to live up to standards they were never asked to live up to before and they suddenly realize they aren't going to be elected it they don't live up to those standards.

COSTA: *What do you predict will happen to Japan? Is this economic giant going to continue, or will they be like an expanding sun and eventually lose gravity and cave in on themselves? What do you think will happen?*

REISCHAUER: If it is an expanding sun and keeps on going and does not begin to put on the brakes of some sort, the whole world trade is going to get so out of balance that there will be a tremendous collapse and Japan will be the country that gets most hurt. That would be a real fall for Japan. I think they have enough wisdom to see that they just can't do that, that they must not do that, and they are going to find ways to try to avoid that, and there are lots of ways. They need to put a much bigger investment into the nation itself. The superstructure of society, the underpinnings of society need much, much more money than is being used. The Japanese deserve more of the product that they produce. They deserve better wages. They seem to be terribly wealthy but they aren't wealthy. They have all this money but things are so terribly expensive there that they are poor, they can't afford houses. The streets are too small, and so on.

So there is much, much to be spent in Japan itself to improve things there. Then there is a great deal that they are going to have to do for their neighbors. They've earned themselves a very unpleasant position in the world, they are not admired by the people around them basically.

A conversation with

Frederick Schauer

Frederick Schauer is Frank Stanton Professor of the First Amendment at the John F. Kennedy School of Government and author of Playing by the Rules: A Philosophical Examination of Rule-based Decision Making in Everyday Life *(Oxford). He is an authority on the First Amendment.*

COSTA: *The earliest Geneva Convention, held in 1864, provided for the humane treatment of prisoners of war, the wounded, and civilians in a time of war. Later conventions, in 1899, 1907, 1929, and 1949, broadened those agreements to forbid human rights abuses like deportation, the taking of hostages, torture, and reprisals of all kinds. Yet despite these conventions few modern nations at war respect them totally. Why is it that those internationally agreed-upon rules, which seem just to all of us, aren't followed? Also, what is your reaction to some of the press reports that we've been hearing about Saddam Hussein, who has allegedly broken almost every one of the Geneva accords by parading brutalized prisoners of war and gassing his own civilians before the war broke out.*

SCHAUER: Perhaps more than any other issue of current importance, this whole issue of the Geneva Conventions or the laws or rules of war raise a series of related questions about the distinction between rules and the paper that they're written on and the way in which they're enforced.

One of the important things about the very idea of a rule is that rules exist when the people that they're addressed to take them as reasons for action, or take them as reasons for doing something rather than something else. Now, why would they do that just because something is written down on a piece of paper? One reason is enforcement. If we think about the rules of law we think of them as being related to the possibility of enforcement. Once the enforcement drops out as a very strong sanction, as it does with rules like the Geneva Convention or even rules like, 'Don't put your elbows on the table' or 'Make sure you write a thank-you note after you're invited to someone's house,' then it becomes somewhat more difficult to think about why anyone would follow one, especially when we think of rules as frequently imposing on people the obligation to do things that they don't want to do.

In the case of the Geneva Convention, what we have is a bunch of words written on a piece of paper. For example, one of the most talked-about provisions of the Geneva Convention right now is the prohibition on holding prisoners of war up for 'public curiosity.' The issue is, does putting someone on television qualify as holding somebody up for public curiosity? Certainly nobody in 1864 was thinking about television, so part of the question then comes down to what degree of shared understanding is necessary for a rule to operate. Without some degree of shared understanding, rules can't do their work. With complete shared understanding we don't need the rules. What rules generally do is draw on some degree of shared understanding about the meanings of words, shared understandings about practices, and then try to impose those shared understandings on future events that may not have been imagined when the rule first came up. But, ultimately, the rule isn't going to do anything unless the addressee of the rule has a reason for taking it seriously. When there is no elaborate enforcement mechanism as there is not with respect to international law then the world or a society has to think about creating the attitude in people such that they will take conceivably unenforced or unenforceable rules seriously for reasons of international cooperation, coordination, or local cooperation or coordination.

COSTA: *There's no way to enforce these rules. What can we do—bomb Saddam Hussein into submission to the accords? The Nuremberg trials did a lot to raise the world's consciousness concerning accountability for actions. Can the lessons learned at Nuremberg apply here?*

SCHAUER: I think quite a bit, and in two different ways. First of all, the Nuremberg trials issue raises this central point that, just as I said a few minutes ago, you can have things that look like rules written on a piece of paper and not have rules in fact. Nuremberg is just the opposite. You can have no rules written on a piece of paper and still have a degree of internationally accepted norms and impositions of behavior such that people will be punished for violating them even with no words written on a piece of paper.

COSTA: *There's a saying, 'Rules are made to be broken.' Actually, I thought that rules were made to be obeyed. But what does that say about our adherence to rules if many people believe that rules are made to be broken?*

SCHAUER: As with a number of other popular sayings, I think it may identify something philosophically important. It identifies the fact that rules are generalizations and like other generalizations—Swiss cheese has holes, German wine is sweet, philosophers are clever—they're not always correct. Sometimes they get it wrong. We have to recognize that rules—which are crafted at one point in time—confront a changing future, and occasionally they're going to get it wrong. It's built into the idea of a rule that it is crude, it is general, it encompasses a larger category than we might want to deal with, and it cannot fully reflect the detail and richness of human experience. What that means is that on occasion what will be the best thing to do will be different from what the rule says. In some decision-making environments we take rules to be very important and we don't want them broken; in other decision-making environments we take them as mere guidelines, rules of thumb. We expect the person that is the subject of the rules to consider whether this might be the case in which the rule of thumb has gotten it wrong. That's what 'rules are meant to be broken' is trying to get at.

COSTA: *Don't we have a 'rules are meant to be broken' situation on a very cosmic scale in the Gulf, when people say the rule of thumb is, 'America shouldn't use nuclear weapons unless America's existence is threatened.' But perhaps there's an exception here if we're going to lose 50,000 or 60,000 American men and women in a ground warfare action. Some say that tactical nuclear bombing might actually save lives. Here's a rule in conflict.*

SCHAUER: Yes. When we find a rule in conflict with what we now think we want to do and what we now think we have good reasons for doing, our inclinations are to change the rule. But because we think there's something fishy about changing the rule, we use exactly the trivializing language that you just used: We make an exception. Saying we make an exception looks like we're not doing anything very significant, but the power to make an exception to the rule is the power to change the rule. It might, as in a number of morally pressing events, be a good thing to change the rule. But when we say we're making an exception, we *are* changing the rule. We are saying, 'We didn't get it right last time around, we want it more qualified, we want to change the rule.'

But, of course, it's not only a change in the rule, it's a grant of authority to the rule-changer to make the change in the rule. To take the declaration of war example, if we were to accept the argument that the declaration of war power residing in Congress is obsolete with modern warfare, we're not only saying that this is an appropriate exception, we're also saying that the president is the one who will decide when there will be exceptions to the text of the Constitution. When put in that way, it's a much larger and much more pervasive issue.

COSTA: *Couldn't someone like Saddam Hussein say, 'The carpet bombing by B-52s is so extreme that my reaction to it is: since the United States is doing massive bombing and putting my people at risk then the Geneva Convention is out the window.'*

SCHAUER: Again, we commonly want to think of rules as working only when they serve our own best interests. Therefore when we're constrained by rules we want to think of some good reason why they don't apply to us. That's why, as I think about rules, I want to think about the relationship between rules and sanctions, punishment and reward, more than is common certainly in the philosophical literature and to some extent in the legal literature. Because it is precisely at the point at which somebody says, 'I don't want to follow the rule' that it becomes remarkably easy either to come up with a reason for not following it or a reason for saying that it doesn't apply, and if we think from the perspective not of the subject but rather from the perspective of the person who makes the rule or the person who designs some rule system, sanctions may play a larger role than is often appreciated. It's at that point that we want to say to somebody, 'You think in your perfectly good-faith best judgment that this is not the time to obey the rule. But what the rule is all about is that there are times when your perfectly good-faith best judgment is not all that matters.'

COSTA: *I guess there are some historical reasons for following a rule and some even quite eloquent philosophical ones. I'm thinking of Kant's second categorical imperative that says one should act as if one is behaving for all mankind.*

SCHAUER: The kind of rule I find most interesting is by definition not ultimate. It has some justification behind it. 'Speed limit 55' reflects a background justification of safety. 'No vehicles in the park,' to take the classic jurisprudential example, reflects a background justification of peace and quiet in the park.

COSTA: *Yet there are only about seven people in Massachusetts, I think, who obey the 55 miles per hour rule.*

SCHAUER: Which is another interesting question. What is the speed limit in Massachusetts? Is it 55—what it says on the sign—or is it, in fact, the enforcement practices of the Massachusetts State Police? But what all of these rules share in common is that they are instrumental guides to some background principle. Kantian ultimate rules, by definition, are not instrumental guides to anything because nothing is behind them. They're bedrock. They're as far as you can get. I think thinking about them is very different because a Kantian ultimate rule cannot, because it is ultimate, be underinclusive or overinclusive. It can't get the wrong result compared to its background justification. These more instrumental rules can and do all the time.

COSTA: *You, of course, know quite a lot about the First Amendment. To get an idea of the exact language I'm going to ask you to read the First Amendment and then we'll discuss it.*

SCHAUER: The First Amendment actually includes a lot more things than people think. 'Congress shall make no law respecting an establishment of religion, or prohibiting the free exercise thereof; or abridging the freedom of speech or of the press; or of the right of the people peaceably to assemble, and to petition the government for a redress of grievances.'

COSTA: *People who are clearly radical leftists often are in complete agreement with right-wing reactionaries about the words of this amendment. Why is this so?*

SCHAUER: The most interesting social and political development in and around the First Amendment in the United States in the late 1980s and '90s is that it's no longer accurate to assume that free-speech First Amendment arguments are the arguments of the political left, and arguments for restriction are arguments of the political right. Whether it be the issue of pornography from a feminist perspective, or the issue of controls on racist or sexist speech, or the issue of campaign finance regulation, or the issue of cigarette advertising, or TV violence, over and over again, the people that are claiming free speech rights or are making strong free speech arguments are increasingly George Will, Philip Morris, the Michigan Chamber of Commerce, to take a recent Supreme Court case, the various conservative political action committees. Conversely, arguments for restriction are being made increasingly by those who would not want to be called liberals necessarily but certainly either left of liberal, or broadly speaking, on the political left. That, it seems to me, is not a surprising development although it may be surprising that it has happened only so recently.

Speech is, in the language of classical political theory, an other-regarding act. It can cause consequences, it does cause consequences, and it can cause harm. As a result, it may very well be that in modern times those who are concerned about racial harm, those who are concerned about sexual violence—especially in an era of mass media—increasingly see speech not as this ineffectual act but rather as something that very likely is going to contribute to the very kinds of harms that they're worried about.

This, of course, is a central dilemma for why we have the idea of free speech, why we have a First Amendment that, as we all know, protects speech not because it's harmless, but despite the harm it may cause. It's a feature of American constitutional doctrine, at least since the mid-1960s, that it protects a wide array of harm-producing speech and does not impose nearly the limits imposed by every other country on the face of the earth. We do this, traditionally, in this country because we have thought that the harms of doing anything else—empowering a certain group of decision makers to decide what's harmful or not—is even more harmful. That's the very tension that is now under such great discussion academically and in the public arena. It's an interesting time to be thinking about the roots of free speech theory.

COSTA: *Are there any rules about free speech? What about the invidiousness and insidiousness of being politically correct, that only certain politically correct ideas should be allowed? There are charges that the left in universities across America get more free speech than the right. How would you address these criticisms?*

SCHAUER: Free speech—which has also frequently used the 'marketplace-of-ideas' metaphor—has more to do with markets than we commonly think. That is, arguments about political correctness are very rarely about administrative or legal restrictions. They are about the climate that exists in the absence of government restriction, a climate that says that certain things are more appropriate to say than others, certain things are more acceptable than others. Although this has recently been a hot issue, that climate has always existed. There were politically correct ideas in the 1950s, even on those campuses that resisted most strongly any of the pressures of McCarthyism. Certain ideas go down easily and certain ideas don't. That's a sociological question that serious thinking about free speech cannot avoid. Unfortunately, all too much thinking about free speech has assumed that when government is out, everything operates smoothly and all voices are equally heard. But if we think about the marketplace of ideas as a market, we can recognize that even with government out of it, there are economic forces, social forces, psychological forces that determine who talks, who gets heard, and a whole range of other related issues.

COSTA: *Senator Jesse Helms thinks he knows what is obscene and what is not obscene and has been talking about that a lot, and there has been much controversy about it over the Mapplethorpe exhibition. How does one define obscenity in 1991, and what makes something legally obscene?*

SCHAUER: I think you asked the right question because there is a dramatic difference between what is legally obscene and what Senator Helms wants to withhold funding from. The category of legal obscenity that has been developing in the courts for literally 150 years and that now comes from a 1973 definition says that material is legally obscene if it appeals to the prurient interest, which means that it's designed to produce sexual stimulation, *and* if it is patently offensive to contemporary community standards, *and* if it is lacking in serious literary, artistic, political, or scientific value. When you combine all of those together, the short answer is virtually nothing is legally obscene. The Mapplethorpe photographs were not even close. It was not a plausible argument that they did not have artistic value, especially given that the Supreme Court has made it abundantly clear for 12 or 13 years now that the determination of literary, artistic, political, and scientific value is based on national standards and not on local standards. That prosecution was a constitutional loser from the beginning; it had no hope regardless of what the jury did. The category of legal obscenity therefore is almost inconsequential. It is the tiniest category of the hardest of hard-core materials. As a practical matter, there is not very much prosecution.

However, what people think is obscene or what they think shouldn't be funded or what they think shouldn't be in their libraries and so on is a much larger category. The National Endowment for the Arts debate is the much more pervasive debate about what things that clearly cannot be prosecuted by the criminal law are still not entitled to government funding. Here the issues are difficult, in part, because although I have no sympathy whatsoever with the standards that Senator Helms would impose, I fully acknowledge·that deciding what gets funded and what doesn't involves making the kinds of distinctions that are clearly impermissible when the law operates in terms of the criminal law.

I am a photographer myself. I would not plausibly maintain that the National Endowment for the Arts has to give me money just because it gives people money to show the photographs of Robert Mapplethorpe. They are fully entitled to determine that Mapplethorpe's photographs are better than mine, which they are. They are fully entitled to determine that some art is better than others, all determinations that, of course, are impermissible if the government is prohibiting. But once it's the government's money and the government's enterprise, there's this very tricky area about which there is very little law about what kinds of distinctions can be drawn. Is it permissible for a library to decide not to buy *Hustler* magazine or *Soldier of Fortune* even though, of course, they are constitutionally protected? Is everything that is constitutionally protected entitled to the same degree of government support? Of course not. If that's right, then government is drawing the kinds of distinctions that classic free-speech theory says government cannot and should not draw. [This is] another fascinating issue of current free-speech controversy about which there is very little case law.

A conversation with

Mary Karr

Mary Karr is a poet and a 1990-91 fellow at Radcliffe's Bunting Institute. She is professor of poetry at the Syracuse University Graduate Writing Program, author of Abacus *(Wesleyan University Press), and a recipient of fellowships from the National Endowment for the Arts and the Artists Foundation of Massachusetts.*

KARR: This is a poem that I wrote in response to burying too many friends because of the AIDS virus. I think of it as a public poem [so] this is the right format for it. It's called 'Etching of the Plague Years.' It first appeared in *Poetry* magazine.

In the valley of your art history book,
the corpses stack in the back of a cart
drawn by an ox whose rolling shoulder muscles
show its considerable weight.
He does this often. His velvet nostrils
flare to indicate the stench.
It's the smell you catch after class
while descending a urine-soaked
subway stair on a summer night
in a neighborhood where cabs won't drive:
the odor of dead flowers, fear
multiplied a thousand times.
The train door's hiss

seals you inside with a frail boy
swaying from a silver hoop.
He coughs in your direction, his eyes
are burn holes in his face.
Back in the fourteenth-century print
lying in your lap, a hand
white as an orchid has sprouted
from the pyramid of flesh.
It claws the smoky air.
Were it not for that,
the cart might carry green cordwood
(the human body knobby and unplaned).
Wrap your fingers around your neck
and feel the stony glands.
Count the holes in your belt loop
for lost weight.
In the black unfurling glass,
study the hard planes of your face.
Compare it to the prom picture
in your wallet, the orchid
pinned to your chest like a spider.
Think of the flames
at your high school bonfire
licking the black sky, ashes rising,
innumerable stars. The fingers that wove
with your fingers
have somehow turned to bone.
The subway shudders between dark and light. The ox plods across the page.
Think of everyone
you ever loved: the boy
who gets off at your stop
is the faint ideogram for each.
Offer him your hand.
Help him climb the stair.

I was warned by a lot of poets, most of them men, not to write about having a child because, I guess, writing about history or other subjects are
considered—in quotes—larger. I could not really imagine what could be a
larger subject than becoming human. So I have a series of poems and this is
one, 'Baby Studies the Table.' It's about a child learning to walk.

He wants to take this ocean of wood
in his mouth where he can chew it whole.
He pounds and croons: table song, wood song,
song of rising on two legs

only, so the world shrinks from him.
How boldly he stands
in his solid cathedral of bone,
slapping his shadow, which blooms
large across the table's surface
like a black, man-sized suit
he will grow into or like
the hole in the earth he'll someday
fill. Wavering on its edge, he seems
to know that, and twists to look
at two figures in the sofa's flowers.
They point to the shadow's abyss,
extend their arms to call him back.
Instead, he retreats
to the sweet shape of his own mind,
that graceful canoe no one can touch
and into which he joyfully steps.

COSTA: *Some writers I know say that writing for them is something they're driven to do, that it's like a dam bursting. One novelist told me that it was rather like epilepsy: he had collected all these ideas and they just uncontrollably burst out. Is that what poetry is for you?*

KARR: I wish it were. I think it would be easier to write if that were the case. I've heard it talked about that way. I liked the way the poet Ezra Pound described it, that as you get older the machinery of your mind grows so intricate that it takes a larger emotional charge to set it into motion. I think when we're younger that it *is* like a dam bursting. Eliot talked about the difference between poets under 25 and over 25 and I think that's one of the differences. When you start writing it's like that, and then you develop a kind of machinery that's both good and bad for the impulse of the work.

COSTA: *Octavio Paz, who received this year's Nobel Prize for Literature, said that he was proud to be a poet because unlike novelists, who are very famous for 20 or 30 years, the poet is almost immortal and his or her poetry lasts forever. What do you think?*

KARR: I hope it's true for Paz. He's someone whose work as a poet and a critic I admire tremendously. I was pleased to see he'd won that prize. But I would disagree. A poet [once] said that the poet's job is not to become immortal herself, but to immortalize his or her beloveds. And by 'beloveds' I mean not only people, but certain states of being. I would like to think those endure.

COSTA: *How does one know one wants to be a poet? Is it a calling like the ministry? Is it like walking some psychic road to Damascus, a revelation that seizes you and says 'you will be a poet'? And if so, why be a poet, and not, say, a short story writer or a novelist?*

KARR: For me, there was a calling. When I was little I sat on the Riverside edition of Shakespeare and saying this you'll think I grew up in a quite literate home. In fact, I grew up in a sort of crackerbox in southeast Texas and that was one of the only hardcover books there were, and the phonebook was too thin to sit on and get any height. So I read those poems and I read Cummings as a little girl. If you had asked me at the age of five what I wanted to be I would have said that I wanted to be a poet. So for me there was a calling.

I couldn't write short stories. I've done three drafts of a novel I'm working on now as a memoir, but basically every time I ever tried to write a short story everybody was dead by the second page. I also think in poetry—and this is something that you can contradict by looking at all kinds of wonderful lyrical pieces of fiction—your attention to and passion for language is heightened. There's certainly very lyrical, linguistically intricate prose that I enjoy reading. But part of it is, I think, a belief that most of our living takes place transcendentally; it doesn't matter whether I'm here or in Baltimore, it's more my state of mind and how I perceive my world that matters.

COSTA: *Norman Mailer once said he respected poets like Auden and Lowell, but no other, lesser-known poets. Mailer said he thought poetry was easier to fake than to craft a large, big-bicep, muscular novel, as he would call it. What do you think about that?*

KARR: I think that's absolutely right. In fact I just saw him on video introducing Robert Lowell at a Vietnam war conference. Lowell was at Harvard then. Mailer stands up and he says, 'All poets either grapple their way up from the bottom or they descend to us from the top. And this is Robert Lowell. He's descending from the top.' I think he's right. I think it is easier to fake. I think that it's not easier to fake for long, and, because there's so little money in it, if you're faking it there's no reason why you would continue unless you're just a lunatic and have nothing else to do. Unless the work yields up some enormous reward for you, you'll quickly find yourself put out of the poetry business.

I often think that young fiction writers are served better by those writing programs than are young poets, simply because there is so much technique and so much that can be taught in fiction. In most of the writing programs that I know of I don't think the academic rigor is there for poetry or the sense of poetry as an art rather than as a craft. . . . I love Stephen King, I love Dick Francis, I love all kinds of pulp fiction that's well crafted. But there's no parallel. It doesn't hold us as a great poem that is a work of art should.

COSTA: *You jokingly said that when you tried to write a novel your characters died by page two. Why is it that most poems deal with loss or death?*

KARR: Because those are the things from which we get the kind of emotional charge that Pound said was required to set the machinery of our incredibly busy, small minds in motion. Think [of] the quotidian of daily living: I'm inundated, as is everyone. I hold no special position as a poet. I still have to buy dental floss—that's one of the things I did today. I couldn't get the *New York Times*; I had to buy the *Boston Globe*, and I got home from New York and there's Lego all over my house. I'm about to pick up my son from school. There's no gas in my car. I couldn't find a place to park—these are the things that occupy us. There are a seemingly endless number of them. It seems as if you could spend your whole day straightening up the top of your desk and being hygienic and cultivating your social network or sending birthday cards to people that you like. I think in order to stop us and to seize our attention something large has to happen to the writer and, obviously, I think dying is probably the thing that I most don't want to do. It certainly changes the tenor of everything about being alive.

COSTA: *Is there any discrimination today in being a woman who writes poetry? I'm thinking of the remark you quoted, 'Don't write about your children.'*

KARR: I think so. I just started teaching graduate writing students and I'm struck by two things. After the third workshop when the students began signing up a little more aggressively for conferences [with me], all of the women who had signed up—they were second-year students—came into my office and, in various ways, told me that what they were writing about, they feared, was unimportant. One of these was a 35-year-old woman with two children who's lived in France for eleven years, who has just moved back to this country and is a single mother. One is a young woman writing about her relationship to her own mother. One is a young woman writing love poems. They all had a sense that, in some way, their endeavors were small and insignificant. Not one of the men had this sense. Not only that, but I've been teaching for some six or seven years, and I've never had a man come to me and say, 'I want to write this, but I'm really not sure that it's important enough or that it's major enough or that it warrants anyone else's attention.' I think that kind of modesty, for which critics have praised women through the centuries, hurts them.

I also think that many of the subjects that are important to women are taboo. I see writing about having a baby, which is what I'm doing now, as not some domestic little enterprise that I take up because I'm not able to fly over to the Middle East and go into a war, but as observing very closely—I think mothers observe very closely—how we become human, how we perceive the world, how our selves gel and take shape and take form, how we become conscious, how we learn to speak. Those all seem very large to me.

The [other] problems with writing are economic, that it pays no money. Our own social attitudes about ourselves as women I think do as much or more damage. I don't have a statistic but I would guess from looking at the rooms full of these students in writing programs that there are far more women than men, and far more of those men will go on to get jobs or to win the Nobel Prize, for instance.

COSTA: *Why do you think so? Is it because the culture helps men to be more confident?*

KARR: I think that's a lot of it. I see young women—often not young women, often women my age—who have uncertainty about the value of their experience and are nearly convinced that it's in some way small or trivial. I don't think that occurs to most men. Even men with the smallest and most trivial lives manage to believe otherwise.

Also just the sheer grit, the number of hours. I have a husband who does an enormous amount of childcare. And I've also noticed that when he picks our son up at school the teachers slather him with praise. They're so amazed and pleased that he does this. He gets enormous credit for it, and I'm constantly told how lucky and how fortunate I am that I have a man who is *willing* to do this and who has taken some economic beatings of his own in order to be able to spend time with our son. For me, it's expected and, in fact, people wonder, 'You're commuting? You're away from home two nights a week? How old is your son?'

I also think that motherhood in general is still grossly sentimentalized in this country. It's still represented in a very 19th-century fashion. Many of the poems I'm writing now are about wanting to kill my child, and anyone who's a parent knows that experience, and yet it has never been written about. It's always either idyllic or the parents are some horrific monsters enacting traumas on hapless little blank tablets.

COSTA: *For centuries, the greatest praise for women who wrote poetry and novels was that they write like men. Some of that still lingers. There are some retrograde men who say they can look at the writing and know that it is a woman writing. Do you believe that that thinking is prevalent today?*

KARR: Again, I think it is more in the subjects that women choose. I like what the fiction writer Judith Grossman said to me very casually one day. She told me that while she was in school at Oxford the women were all working very hard—and I guess this was in the '60s—to learn the rules and adhere to them. Meanwhile, the men were all out changing the rules and trying to write like James Joyce. Of course, when a poet like Emily Dickinson is perceived as doing the tremendous job of innovation she did with lineation and punctuation, all of those new things were attributed to a kind of ignorance; they could not have been deliberate, this was a woman who never got out of her house and didn't know what the rules were and didn't know how to adhere to them.

I'd noticed in fiction, in memoir, and in nonfiction almost the opposite trend that we're told to expect: that men are very comfortable using the first-person pronoun, and writing about their lives and writing emotionally about their lives. I think Tobias Wolff's *This Boy's Life* is a moving memoir. In *Esquire* they line up Richard Ford and other young [male] fiction writers who are all comfortable writing in that way. There is almost no parallel in women's fiction. Certainly not about women's adolescence. The woman adolescent, as far as I can tell from the current canon, is such an unlovely creature that she does not bear being written about. There are [very few] first-person memoirs. I can think of Rita Mae Brown's *Rubyfruit Jungle*, but most of them are like that— novelized—or there's a third-person narration.

Ironically, I think the authoritative trappings are often more clung to, it seems to me, by women. I'm hoping that that will change. In poetry, I don't know. I have a feeling that because women have a different experience of the world their poems are different. I've read a lot of books about this and I haven't yet found the right set of qualities to isolate to say that this is a female aesthetic, this is a male aesthetic. I do have a feeling that that is true, and yet with all the theories I've read about it, I find myself saying, 'No, that's not right. This is not accurate.' It's sometimes that way, or there are these men who are counterexamples.

COSTA: *A lot of would-be poets think that the most important thing in writing good poetry is a love of the language, a facility with the language, and verbal wit. As they grow older they realize, perhaps, that the most important thing is a way of seeing as a poet. Could you talk about that?*

KARR: I'm reminded of an anecdote which I believe came originally from Samuel Johnson. When some woman asked him how he arrived at the definition for the word 'pastern' in his dictionary as 'the knee of a horse,' his response was 'pure ignorance.' I think pure ignorance is, in many ways, what I look for. I used to want to be smart and then I moved to Cambridge, where everybody is smart, and I realized that being smart was a kind of commodity and that however smart I got to be, there will always be people who will be lots smarter than I.

I think that we have a series of habits in perceiving the world and ourselves in that world and that if we're going to become autonomous and make choices freely that we can live with, that are not accidents, that we somewhat choose with some passion and some conviction, then we have to pay attention, we have to be alert. At least one of poetry's jobs is to wake us up and to shake us out of that slumber of the quotidian in order to be more alive. That's very romantic. I guess it was Shelley who said that poetry humanizes us. I like what the English poet Philip Larkin said: it's a kind of machine made of words that recreates a certain feeling. For me, the emotional or passionate element of the poem is not in the writer, which seems to be all that we've talked about since Wordsworth—people talk about what the writer feels—but in the reader. How the reader feels reading a piece of poetry and how he or she can be stirred out of the quotidian, out of the plodding lives that most of us lead. For me, it's trying to pay attention.

COSTA: *Do you think writing of this supercreative kind can be taught, or is there some little trigger in our DNA that says, 'You, Mary Karr, are going to grow up to be a poet'?*

KARR: I think it can be taught. [Look at] these writing programs: brains and talent are very cheap. Everyone is smart. I went to school with people who were far smarter than I, or far more talented, showed far greater promise. But there are all these things that interfere with one's work. No one wants you to write poetry. No one. Even the people who love you most in the world and respect your work the most do not want you to write poetry. They want you to make dinner, they want you to vote, they want you to do other things that are of perfectly good value but there is no slot carved out in which we write poetry.

I grew up in a town where my father didn't finish the sixth grade and I'm always amazed when something has been published and I'm home and show it to a friend of mine who finished the ninth grade and went to prison, that he or she can tell the quality of the thing. At the sort of muddy level where the poems are wiggly, it's hard to tell. Then there's a certain level of quality where it's all sort of good. But at that highest level of quality, at the level of *The Waste Land* or some of the poems of Elizabeth Bishop or Adrienne Rich, people recognize it. It's not unrecognizable and it seems absolute.

I taught in public schools for a long time and I used to have an exercise where I would have children in second and third grade wad up balls of paper on their desks, then I would read them poems. I would have them throw the paper wads when the poems were bad. I would always mix in something I'd found from a little magazine with Wallace Stevens or William Butler Yeats, and they were unfailingly correct in their choices. Maybe, again, there was something in the timbre of my voice or the look on my face that communicated my sense of value, but I think not. I like to believe that there is such a thing as quality, that however difficult to define in intellectual terms is recognizable to anyone human.

A conversation with

I. Bernard Cohen

I. Bernard Cohen is Victor S. Thomas Professor of the History of Science. His inquiries have focused on Leonardo DaVinci, Sir Isaac Newton, and Copernicus, among others. His books include Benjamin Franklin's Science *(Harvard University Press) and* Revolution in Science *(Belknap Press).*

COSTA: *Science in the 1740s was a cross between magic, explaining the unknown, and some very crude kinds of experimentation. Would you set the scene?*

COHEN: Science wasn't really a great deal more magical than it is today. People liked a good show. We know that a number of lecturers made their fortune by talking about science. Electricity was popular because there were fascinating new demonstrations in Germany in which you made people's hair stand on end by giving them a bit of an electric charge. There were electric shocks to make people feel exhilarated. People wanted to see novelties.

They also went to hear lectures about such subjects as the meaning of Newtonian philosophy, the nature of the universe and the forces that held it together. They wanted to hear about new discoveries in biology, about certain kinds of marine life, for example, a starfish, which could lose one of its arms and then regenerate it. How did that happen? There was very deep concern about generation, human generation, animal generation. Did humans and other animals come from eggs or did they not? And there was a great discussion about whether there were little preformed individuals who would just grow and grow. Some people felt these were little males and some people thought that these were little females. But particularly, they wanted to know about novelties, what was the latest thing. The newspapers had much more accurate science reporting then than they do today.

COSTA: *Franklin was one of the first, as you wrote in your book,* Benjamin Franklin's Science, *to use the words—in the scientific sense—positive and negative charge, electric motor, and electric battery. He also was the first to show that lightning is actually a flow of electricity from the ground, which is charged positively, to the clouds, which are charged negatively. Most people, even to this day, think lightning goes from cloud to ground, but actually it flows from ground to cloud.*

COHEN: Primarily. As to the lightning, Franklin made a series of very important phenomenological discoveries. For example, he found that if you bring a pointed object like a needle near a big charged globe, if that needle is in a wooden handle, which is an insulator, nothing happens. But if you run your finger along, so that you become the grounding part of the circuit, and touch the needle, it will silently draw the charge off this object. Grounding, the action of pointed conductors and other phenomena that he had noticed, led him to think that if the clouds are electrified and if lightning is an electrical phenomenon, then if you could get a point that was connected to a grounding wire and get it up high enough, maybe you could prove that the clouds were electrified by drawing off some of their electricity.

COSTA: *Tell us about the famous kite experiment.*

COHEN: First, the original experiment Franklin devised was to have a long rod erected in a sentry box. He had hoped to put this on the top of Christ Church in Philadelphia. He was waiting for that spire to be finished and in the meanwhile he published an account of his proposed experiment. The book was translated into French, the experiments had been shown to the King of France and applauded, and the King of France said, well, why don't we do that lightning experiment? They did it successfully. In the meanwhile Franklin, not having heard about these experiments, suddenly had the idea—how it came to him we just don't know—that maybe a way of getting that rod up in the air would be to send up a kite. If the kite had a thread that was made of the right kind of cord it would become damp and conduct electricity. A point of metal would be put at the top of the kite so that it would draw off some of the charge in that silent way that I mentioned earlier and then the key at the bottom was the place where the charge would be drawn off. The key was attached to a silk thread, which is a nonconductor, so the charge would not go through the string and through you and give you an enormous electric shock.

COSTA: *So that's why he didn't die during the experiment. If he had used a conductor as the kite string we wouldn't have heard about the experiment.*

COHEN: Exactly. There are many people who write in an unhistorical, uncritical, and rather ignorant way that the most interesting thing about that experiment is that Franklin wasn't killed. I found that there are dozens of records of that experiment having been done in the 18th century, so it obviously was a pretty safe one. Only one person who did the experiment was killed, in St. Petersburg. He didn't understand how to ground himself and he did it through a rod that was projecting up through the chimney. If he had followed the instructions, he probably would have been all right too.

COSTA: *Churches throughout Europe rang their church bells when a thunderstorm was overhead in the mistaken belief that the pealing of the bells would drive off the devilish spirits in the thunderclouds. Actually what happened, you report, is that many bellringers were killed by lightning, and the bell towers in which they were standing were also demolished.*

COHEN: Franklin himself collected the statistics on that. Many people were very, very concerned about lightning rods. They were concerned, I think, primarily because of a fear, which many people have, of interfering with the natural course of the big forces that are in the world around us. People objected to inoculation in the early days because they thought this might give you the smallpox. You really shouldn't interfere with whatever divine will or force of nature was producing the kind of effects that it does.

Franklin lived in the age of reason and many people thought that one of his greatest contributions was to show that the lightning discharge is not the act of an angry god telling sinful man to change his ways, or else.

In Boston there was a clergyman by the name of Prince. He thought that there was no way of circumventing God's wrath. If you set up lightning rods, which would have the effect of preventing destruction by lightning, then this lightning would accumulate in the bowels of the Earth and produce an earthquake. That would be the way that nature would get even with you for trying to stop the lightning. There is a long tradition of that kind of thinking.

There was also a great fear, which we know from certain novelists of the nineteenth century in America, that if you put up a lightning rod maybe it would *attract* the lightning. This is the same as the fear that inoculation might *give* you the smallpox, and so on. We find it hard to believe that today. But I can only tell you that I did a little study not too long ago in preparing for my book and I discovered that destruction by lightning, particularly of agricultural buildings, is the fifth or sixth largest cause of fire and it destroys millions of dollars of property and livestock every year. So we really must not say that the people in the 18th century weren't quick enough to accept the lightning rod.

COSTA: *I recently walked across Harvard Yard looking at the buildings and spotted no lightning rods.*

COHEN: The only lightning rod near the Harvard College Yard is on the Roman Catholic church on the top of the large tower, and I am happy to report that it has never had any damage from lightning as a result.

COSTA: *In fact, religion did play a factor in the non-use of lightning rods. Many of the Catholic churches during Franklin's time refused to put lightning rods on their church steeples.*

COHEN: That is true. On the other hand, it is also true that when a famous Franciscan church in Italy was destroyed by lightning, the Pope gave them money to reconstruct the chapel, but the condition was that—and there's a tablet that says so in Latin on the wall—'electrical Franklin rods' be erected to prevent similar damage in the future.

But the populace worried about things like that. In Vienna, for example, the ordinary people were very worried that perhaps there would be a drought as a result, and insisted that the lightning rods be taken down. In France, a man who had set up lightning rods received such a reaction to them that a big lawsuit resulted. He had a very good lawyer just starting his career by the name of Robespierre and Robespierre won and it started him on his reputation. There is a case where a little science comes into ordinary history.

COSTA: *You say in your book that perhaps Franklin's success as an ambassador and as a political person was guaranteed because he was internationally known as a scientist. Is that true?*

COHEN: There are some people, American historians I'm sorry to say, who think that perhaps we aggrandize Franklin's importance as a scientist because he was so significant in American political history. My thesis is just the reverse. My reasons go something as follows: when Franklin went to France as the representative of the colonies, he wasn't really in any full sense an ambassador—he didn't have the status yet because we weren't a country. But he was not just another American who had written some books like John Adams or many of the others who went there, but was a man whose name was known from one end of France to the other. As a scientist of world renown, his book on electricity had been published in five editions in English, it had been translated into Latin, German, and Italian, there had been three editions in France. People knew about lightning rods and called them Franklin rods. Particularly in that age in France, during which Voltaire was a popular figure and where people had an enormous admiration for science and rationalism, Franklin was not only the symbol of a bold, new world and new ways of thinking about science like electricity, but he had shown that this terrible force of lightning could be reduced to reason, and he removed, therefore, a certain amount of superstition. And as if that were not enough, he had then gone on to show how to protect ourselves from the lightning. So he was a hero of enormous importance.

Accordingly, he was treated with a measure of respect that one wouldn't find for anyone else. For instance, while Franklin was in Paris there arose the great episode of Mesmer. Mesmer was a man who had mesmeric cures. He was onto the beginnings of psychosomatic problems and the relation of the mind to the body and all of that. But everybody was disturbed because he was attacking not only the medical establishment but the political establishment as well. They set up a commission to look into this. Lavoisier, the famous chemist, was a member of it. But who was the most outstanding member appointed first? Visiting American Benjamin Franklin. Now *there* was a person of real importance. When he said something you had to listen.

COSTA: *And yet he was a very practical inventor. He invented bifocals, the Franklin stove. He did a study about people in the tropics and why they should wear white clothing—because it reflects sunlight and is cooler. He is credited for that wonderful line about the worth of basic science. When he was in Paris watching the first balloon ascent he overheard someone say, 'yes, but what good is this ascent?' And he responded, 'what good is a newborn babe?'*

COHEN: Exactly. That's my favorite quotation as well. Franklin was, like all people in his age, a practical man. There is no question of it. He was a printer, a tradesman, an artisan. He thought that the highest position that a man could have was by his own skill and his hands to earn his own living. The plowman on his knees, he wrote, is better than the lord in fancy clothes sitting on his exalted chair.

Franklin made many improvements in casting type, he invented the rocking chair, he invented the long arm with which we take things down from shelves in grocery stores or in our homes, and many other practical inventions. These were inventions that didn't require any science, but simply mechanical skill. These have to be contrasted, I think, to his invention of the lightning rod. The invention of the lightning rod was not something that you could have produced by simply saying, I would like to have some way of helping us be safe from lightning. What step would you take? You wouldn't know. When Franklin began his work on electricity, it had no practical use. The only use that anyone thought of was to help people with paralysis. If you gave them a shock, you'd make their limbs move and maybe that would get them started. Franklin tried. He didn't really believe that it helped very much. He said, it's the will of the patient to get better that makes the difference.

He went into electricity because it appealed to him; it was a new subject. He had leisure, he had been reading deeply in the sciences, he was well educated and ready for a career of a scientific investigator, and this subject interested him. No practical use whatever, except that believing in the precepts of Bacon, he felt that anyone who really explored nature would eventually learn, to some degree, to control the environment. But how, he had no idea.

Franklin believed that all the experiments you do with small models in a laboratory are telling you something about this enormous force of nature outside. What Franklin showed, therefore, was that any physics, or natural philosophy as they called it, that did not include the science of electricity was incomplete.

COSTA: *You also mention that it was perhaps serendipitous on his part that he read Newton's book on optics because it contained very little advanced mathematics. He wasn't schooled in mathematics, and he probably could not have read the* Principia, *which was a very advanced book that used difficult mathematics from start to finish. So, in a way, reading the optics book gave Franklin a view of scientific method.*

COHEN: Newton's book on optics was an extraordinary book in that, for the 18th century, the century after Newton's death, it set forth a program of experimental investigation. It set forth the idea that knowledge could be obtained not merely through mathematical deduction from first principles, but by firsthand asking questions directly of nature, experiment. At the end of the book, Newton set forth a series of so-called queries, questions, things to be explored by experiment. They ranged from pure optics to physiology, the analysis of sensation, how does the brain transmit commands to the muscles, how do sensations go from the extremities to the brain, questions of heat, conduction of heat, radiation of heat, electricity—which Newton had just seen—and so on.

Franklin, like many other great scientists of his time, read these very, very carefully, and from them adopted not only a method of doing experiments, but the concept that one should explain all the phenomena of nature by what were then thought to be mechanical ideas. By that I mean that for Franklin, as the basic element of his theory, the rubbing of a piece of amber with silk or wool and the rubbing of a glass tube doesn't produce electricity, it merely transfers it; it's not an act of creation. Indeed, some people hold that Franklin's greatest contribution was the statement as a theoretical principal and the proof by experiment of what we call the conservation of charge. That is, that equal amounts of plus and minus charges are always created simultaneously or disappear simultaneously and this is in that great tradition of the Newtonian natural philosophy.

COSTA: *What about the controversy concerning other scientists who claimed that they did the first kite experiment?*

COHEN: Great discoveries and lesser discoveries tend to be multiples rather than singletons. For a long time, people thought that discoveries that were made independently but at the same time was a rare thing and not worth study. But a study by Robert K. Merton showed us how often this happens and that, from the point of view of the history of science, is extremely interesting because it raises a very important question of why that should occur. We know today that it occurs because knowledge reaches a certain stage that produces a kind of intellectual and environmental pressure and a number of very bright people reacting to that produce something creative. The simultaneous independent discoveries, which are multiples, are often not exactly identical, but similar, and would lead us in something of the same direction.

It raises then the question, what is the role of the individual genius? In part, it's that his appearance accelerates this development, that one man may . . . determine the next direction of science. Many times we see that a certain discovery should have been made but there just wasn't anyone with a creative genius working in that area sufficiently well prepared.

Now, in the case of the lightning rod, many people discovered afterwards that Franklin wasn't the first person to guess that lightning might be electrical. After all, if you make sparks in the laboratory and they produce burning, make holes in paper, and things of that sort, it does look like lightning on a small scale. Simply to observe that is nothing. What is important is the next step, namely, how would you go about proving it? Having proved it, then what do you do about it? Clearly, when Franklin had discovered the action of pointed conductors, when he had found out about insulation and conduction, and other facts of electricity became generally known, the notion that you might have an experiment on lightning occurred to several people. There are at least two, whether they really had known of Franklin isn't entirely clear. I think the man in France, De Romas, probably didn't know about Franklin's experiments, but it's hard to say.

COSTA: *Franklin made one career sacrifice, as you point out in your book, and that is that he spent a lot of time, energy, and imagination in conducting scientific experiments, writing about them, and documenting them. But he let his love of printing slide, and the quality of his book publishing company really declined when he got more involved in science.*

COHEN: That's true. Franklin delighted in having been an artisan. The fact that he was a printer who could make something with his own hands was a very important part of his makeup. I think it's what attracted him to experimental science: that you could really do something. And although Franklin was a great writer, a great wit, and a very profound thinker on many different levels, all of which we don't give him credit for, it remains true that for himself what he loved were things that he could make and do, and printing was his great love.

A *conversation with*

Jerome Kagan

Jerome Kagan is Daniel and Amy Starch Professor of Psychology and a member of the Faculty of Education. A Phi Beta Kappa Traveling Scholar and author of Unstable Ideas *(Harvard University Press), Kagan's 30 years of research determined not only the biological inherited basis of shyness, but resulted in a test to detect this trait in 4-month-old infants.*

COSTA: *Many parents over the last 20 years have reared their children with Dr. Spock's book at their side. Today they are taking the blame for years of problems that the kids themselves may have developed. Do you think parents are being too hard on themselves? Some scientists and psychologists say that often a child brings his or her own set of problems locked in their own DNA codes, so to speak, and the parents aren't responsible for everything that is wrong with the child. What do you think about that?*

KAGAN: The modern West, that means Europe and North America, are relatively unique. All cultures over history [do not agree] that parents should assume the primary responsibility for the outcome of their children. The Mayan Indians that we studied in Northwest Guatemala ten or twelve years ago and their parents and grandparents didn't assume that. The Romans didn't assume that. If we looked at all cultures, we would see that most cultures don't believe that at all. As a matter of fact, they believe that it is the qualities of the child—the qualities today we call temperamental—that they might attribute to sorcery or witchcraft. Remember the line you must have learned as a child: Monday's child is fair of face, Wednesday's child is full of woe. That was their way of saying, 'Look, this child has qualities.' So, the modern view is unique and it begins somewhere in the 18th century after Rousseau.

It's not clear why we believe that what the parents do, primarily the mother, essentially controls all the child's development. We will not go off into that, that would be a two-hour discussion. Your readers should understand that this is a very unusual belief . . . . Since it is believed, it will vary in the degree that some actions are assumed good or bad. For example, whether the parent should be permissive or restrictive will go in cycles. How restrictive a parent should be cycles every forty or fifty years. We just passed through a period of permissiveness, and now we're starting a period of restrictiveness. When I'm gone and you're gone there will be another period of permissiveness. So the general answer to your question is yes, American and European parents assume a lot of responsibility. It's not that they have *no* influence, but their influence is far less than they believe.

COSTA: *As we both know, parenting and the roles of parents, and the make-up of the nuclear family have changed with the high divorce rate and the tension in the urban environment. I'm curious to know whether these changes in family structure are reflected in the ways we bring up our children?*

KAGAN: Let's deal first with the divorce rate. Yes, the divorce rate is very high. Unfortunately, we can't say what the consequences are of the high divorce rate, because it has been correlated with other things; drugs on the streets, violence, economic situations. You can't pull out the thread that says this is the divorce rate, what does it cause. My own belief is that no single factor in a culture—whether it's what's on TV or the nature of the family— has its own set of causes, independent of what else is going on in the culture. The divorce rate is going to go down, because each generation of adults feels anxious and—in our culture—blames its own childhood for why it feels anxious. This generation of parents, as they assume maturity, because so many of them have experienced divorce, are going to say, 'Oh, I know why I'm anxious. It's because my parents got divorced. I'm not going to visit that evil on my child.' So you will see the divorce rate decrease now. It will not decrease to what it was in the 19th century, but it will go down.

We're in the middle of a hurricane; when society is changing, the divorce rate will change. It's very hard for me to answer your question, I'm not being evasive, but it's hard to say what the divorce rate is.

COSTA: *I remember in the fifties when I was seated in junior high school classrooms, there were perhaps only 2 out of a class of 35 who had moms and dads who had gotten divorced. Now kids look around and they say, 'Hey, Billy's like me. His mom and dad are divorced too.'*

KAGAN: Precisely, and that leads me to my next point. One of the serious consequences for children of divorce is whether or not the child feels deviant. When Billy is the only child of divorced parents, that is more stressful, more generative of anxiety, then if half the class is divorced. So that, I know this sounds paradoxical and I'm not meaning to sound callous, but the more children there are divorced the less toxic it is for the child, because then the child doesn't feel different. It doesn't mean there aren't stresses associated with the fact that you have a single parent.

COSTA: *With more and more women working outside the home and more fathers sharing child-raising responsibilities, are there any sex-determined differences in the way men or women do their parenting? Traditionalists talk about women being more able to do nurturing, and men are just now learning about nurturing. Are there any sex differences in your view?*

KAGAN: I can only give my opinion, there is no good science. There is no technical piece of science that I can quote that says we have compared men and women giving nurture and these are the differences. I don't know. My opinion is that in terms of the capacity for concern, no difference. In terms of the ability to diaper a child, feed a child, read to a child, talk to a child, love a child, probably not. In the practice of being a parent, the pragmatics, probably not.

So where is the difference? The difference is in the minds of people in the society. Our society, like most incidentally, believes deeply that somehow mothers are naturally more devoted parents than fathers. Both fathers and mothers then believe that. The difference is in your head. It's in the belief that males and females hold about whether God or nature intended them to be parents. In the day-to-day practices, no I don't think there are any differences. If there are, they are probably very subtle.

COSTA: *We hear and read a lot these days about so-called 'quality time.' We're told as parents that it is not so much the amount of time one spends with one's children, but the kind of time it is. A lot of this has been debunked. Some believe a lot of time is necessary, even if it isn't quality time. Where do you come out on this issue?*

KAGAN: There is not a fixed amount of time that a parent must be with a child. The idealistic youth that all of us have praised, the ones who stood in Tiananmen Square against the tanks—90 percent of them were in day-care centers from 6:30 or 7 a.m. to 6 at night, because they were brought up in Mao's time. Maybe it's the same today. Their parents worked six days a week, twelve hours a day. Much less time than American parents have, yet there's no evidence that these youth are more aggressive, more delinquent, or more prone to psychosis. Their behavior was very idealistic. That experiment should be proof enough that there isn't a certain amount of time you have to be with your child. It is in the mind of the child.

Suppose your father is president of the U.S. and you say to yourself, 'I know my father can't be with me because he's doing an important job.' That's all the child needs. It's the child's perception of what the parent is doing when the parent is not with them. If the parent is doing something that the child views as important, then the parent doesn't have to be around. If the parent is out doing selfish activity, then the child concludes, 'Well, wait a minute. Why is my parent playing cards or bowling and not with me? Apparently that gives him more pleasure.' So it's not in the amount of time, *ever*. It's in the child's perception of why and what the parent is doing.

COSTA: *What about parents who seem a little obsessive about making every moment quality time?*

KAGAN: I find American parents, and I mean this positively, are very conscientious. The middle class is taking its children very seriously. I might add one reason is that this generation really had a choice. Because of contraceptives, the average mother and father could really decide if they wanted the child. It's not like it was in our grandparents' generation.

When you have a choice there is a very important principle in psychology called cognitive dissonance. When you decide to do A or B and you choose B, then you take B very seriously. Secondly, they are having fewer children, like the Chinese. If you choose to have a child and you are only having one or two, then it makes sense that you would treat this child with a great deal of care. You want it to be the best possible child it can be. That is understandable, and I think it should be celebrated. But then like a shiny new car or a new pair of skis, you devote every moment to it, and I believe some parents are overly anxious, overly zealous. We must say that with a smile. Their intentions are all positive; it's out of love and care for the child. We should perhaps say to them, those who are overzealous, relax a little. It seems to me it's inappropriate to be overly hostile or critical or sarcastic of them because their intentions are positive and to be admired.

COSTA: *You've written extensively about the brain and how it affects development. You seem to say that brain growth during childhood is characterized somewhat by the elimination of synapses that were laid down during the month before and after birth, and that a kind of pruning of cells takes place. You gave this example: if the right hand is used more than the left, then the neural connections that serve the right are expanded. Tell us what implications for maturation this pruning theory has.*

KAGAN: Let me say first that these data are not mine. These are the elegant data of many scientists including Professor [David] Hubel, who's here at the Medical School. During the growth of the brain in the embryo fetus in the early months of life, what happens in nature is exactly the opposite of what you and I would have thought. In the 1800s no one would have thought that as you grow and learn more words and skills you are eliminating synapses rather than adding ones; it's so counterintuitive. That is why I like Richard Feynman's expression. 'Let's face it, nature's absurd so accept nature as she is.'

One of the implications of the fact that synapses are being eliminated is that you start with a large number of synapses. Nature doesn't know what experiences this young child is going to have, and so it generates a large number of possible connections and then it lets experience determine which connections will be used. A poor analogy would be you're going on a holiday but your friend doesn't tell you where you're going to go. So you pack clothes for all seasons and then if you end up in the tropics you get rid of the winter clothes. That is essentially what is going on here. I don't think it has any more implication than the fact that it is an interesting counterintuitive finding.

Now one speculation is that if you did use one area more than another, suppose in a very odd way you were in an environment in which you used vision and rarely used hearing, then of course those areas would be enhanced compared with hearing. But I think as far as the average parent is concerned and their children who live in a varied environment, it probably does not have any important implications.

COSTA: *What about the folklore that says that people who are very verbal aren't good with their hands?*

KAGAN: Of course, both hemispheres can do both verbal and nonverbal tasks, however a respectable group of scientists believe, and they might be right, that the left hemisphere elaborates verbal skills more than the right, while the right hemisphere elaborates manual skills, music, art. Let's suppose that they are correct. Then it might be true that some people inherit a stronger right relative to left, while others inherit a stronger left relative to right. If that were true then it's not beyond belief to say OK, here is a great writer William Faulkner, those verbal skills must be the result of a very strong left hemisphere. For that reason perhaps right hemisphere skills, like fixing lawn mowers and carburetors, were less advanced. Although we've caricatured it here, I think you can see that it is certainly possible. For example, why should Albert Einstein, who was so good in right hemisphere skills and clearly intelligent, have had a difficult time learning a foreign language. Cases like that tend to say maybe there is something to this.

COSTA: *Studies have shown that birth order may be an important factor in the child's development. Could you comment on this?*

KAGAN: First it's important to inject this caveat. The results I'm going to describe only hold for Western culture, because all the science was done on European and American children. Now, these generalizations might hold true in Uganda, Argentina, Sumatra, we don't know.

In general, among the middle-class population, first borns tend to be more responsible, get better grades, go on to better universities, and choose establishment vocation. Later borns, in the same family, get slightly poorer grades even though they are just as bright—that means motivation. They also tend to pick vocations other than the established ones—law, medicine, business—and tend to be a bit more rebellious. Now why might that be. The explanation that my colleagues and I like, goes something like this.

First assume a stable family with good parents. In that setting a first born has only his or her parents to compare with. They appear to the child to be just, competent, kind, loving, so that as representatives of the adult world they are seen in a very positive light. So the child idealizes adults as he or she leaves the parents to go out into the adult world. The child says, well this is a pretty fair, kind, just, adult world. If they are treated that way and enter school, essentially the first born says to the world, 'Very good, what is it you want me to do? I'll do it,' and off they go. If you want me to get good grades, I'll get good grades. If you want me to be an outstanding trial lawyer I'll be an outstanding trial lawyer. First borns behave that way, they are high achievers.

For example, there are more first borns at Harvard than later borns, more than there would be by chance. Someone actually went through the concentrations at Harvard for two years and found that compared with later borns, first borns are more likely to choose vocations that have high status and high income—law, medicine, business, and so on—compared with later borns.

Now let's enter the mind of the later born. You are two years old and you have a brother five years old. Well, your five year old brother teases you and takes your toys . . .

COSTA: *I know mine did.*

KAGAN: Exactly. The world seems less fair and just. He or she gets to stay up later. A later born therefore sees the world more realistically and therefore is less apt to idealize authority. Well now you enter the adult world and you see authority more as if they have clay feet, therefore why work so hard for them. You are much more receptive to having a rebellious attitude. Now the best proof of this comes from an unpublished work of a former junior fellow at Harvard who is about to publish a book with an extraordinary finding. He took a large number of revolutions in science where the populous cared about the results, like Copernicus or Freud or Darwin. Those ideas that challenged what most people in this society believed. Sure enough, [of those surveyed], the first borns were more likely to disagree with the theory and the later borns were more likely to agree with it. That is fantastic. That says that later borns mentally are more receptive to saying yes, what established authority believes isn't necessarily true.

COSTA: *The so-called yuppie movement is roundly criticized for creating what some think is a shallow and acquisitive society. Has the yuppification of the nuclear family affected the children of that family?*

KAGAN: I don't know. My suspicion is, and I'm going back to my first answer, it will cycle, because who are the parents of this generation. They were the idealistic, less selfish people who marched on Cambridge Common, who marched in Chicago. So it may very well may be that the children of this generation, looking back on their parents will say, they were too selfish, I'm not going to live that kind of life, and we will see a cycle again.

One thing we learn from history is that children do not replicate their parents. Some of the most liberal youth in the South today had parents who were very prejudiced. Remember that in our society one of the implicit goals of children is to differentiate themselves from their parents, not to be a clone of their parents. You can count on every generation trying to adopt a different mode, and my own suspicion is pure intuition, that the children of this so-called selfish generation will be far less selfish.

COSTA: *Psychologically speaking, are boys different from girls?*

KAGAN: Are boys different from girls; I'm sure you mean are boys biologically different from girls. Well, the research of the last decade or so would probably say yes because the differences we see across all cultures happen to match the same differences you see in male and female chimpanzees, male and female baboons, and male and female rhesus monkeys. The human male child is more active, more prone to rough and tumble play, and seems to be less anxious. I suspect that when neuroscientists and neurophysiologists, probably in the next half-century, have the evidence it will probably be the case that there will be fundamental differences in the propensity toward aggression and toward anxiety between the sexes. However, I want to add something very important, and this is not meant in any way to minimize the science, but those data have no ethical or legal implications whatsoever. Society, in my opinion, is basing too much of its ethical conclusions and legal decisions on what science says. Science is a wonderful thing to be celebrated, but the society need not act on that. For example, we now know with much more credibility than 50 years ago that schizophrenia has a partially inherited basis. Is anyone in our society suggesting that we pass a law to sterilize schizophrenics. No, why not? Because our ethics need not follow our science.

If I were a playwright I would write a play, sort of a modern version of *Inherit the Wind*. A woman was certain she was going to be the next chief executive officer of General Motors, and she was passed over and a male was appointed. It gets to the Supreme Court and here is the argument. The defense for General Motors says, 'Look, this is a tough job, a lot of stressful decisions have to be made. We know from science that women are more prone to anxiety, therefore we better have a man in there.' But Spencer Tracy's grandson, who plays the lawyer for the woman, and gives an elegant speech in which he gives us this example about schizophrenia and says, 'The ethics of our society do not have to accommodate to what is true in nature.' And, of course, she wins the case.

COSTA: *If you were to give advice about parenting, what would that advice be?*

KAGAN: Three simple maxims that every grandparent knows. One, communicate to your child—in whatever way is natural to you—that you value your him or her. That need not involve a lot of physical affection; it depends on what is natural to you. Just communicate in your eyes that your child is valuable. Second, worry less about what you reward and punish. Now I'm mouthing John Locke, 'In your everyday behavior display the characteristics you want your child to adopt.' If you want your child to care about intellectual inquiry, then be that way. You want your child to be idealistic, be that way. You want your child to be against war, you don't have to worry about buying toy soldiers, that is quite irrelevant. In your behavior behave as though you are against war, and you'll get the child you want. Finally, be consistent. I think if you follow these three rules you stand a better chance of attaining the qualities that you wish for in your growing child.

A conversation with

Abraham Zaleznik

Abraham Zaleznik is Konosuke Matsushita Professor of Leadership Emeritus at *Harvard Business School. A certified clinical psychoanalyst, Zaleznik is known for his research as well as for teaching courses such as Social Psychology of Management. He has written* Executive's Guide to Motivating People *(Bonus Books) and* The Managerial Mystique: Rediscovering Leadership in Business *(Harper & Row).*

COSTA: *In your new book,* The Managerial Mystique, *you state that the problem is not that we need more managers but that we need real leaders, people who have vision. Can you explain this thesis a bit further?*

ZALEZNIK: With industrialization and the rise of large organizations, people became aware of the need to coordinate the activities of a lot of people who were massed together under one roof in the factory. They discovered that it was also important to plan how people work, not simply to let each person do as he or she sees fit. This was called management—the planning and coordination of human activity to achieve a goal or a purpose. Of course, it was a very important idea: witness the incredible productivity that our factories were able to achieve during World War II. When we came out of World War II we were a nation full of pride, we were the arsenal of democracy, we demonstrated a capacity to produce what was unimaginable in an earlier period. This was—and rightly—attributable to management, the coordination and planning of human activity. But as with all good things, when carried to their logical extreme, distortions creep in. This is precisely what's happened to American enterprise, and I think what accounts for our failure to be competitive and to maintain our position in world markets. It's as though the tension had turned inward to making an organization work better and better, more and more smoothly, reaching accommodations, for example, with labor unions and attempting to improve coordination, working on the thesis that if you can manage one thing you can manage anything, therefore encouraging the conglomeration of corporations.

COSTA: *You've written that 'Managers perceive life as a steady progression of positive events resulting in security at home and school and in the community and at work, but leaders are twice-born individuals who endure major events that lead to a sense of separateness or perhaps estrangement from their environments. As a result, they turn inward in order to reemerge with a creative rather than an inherited sense of identity.' Are these essentially the key differences that you see in the two?*

ZALEZNIK: Yes, it's the difference between looking inward to an organization to try to perfect it—as though it were an instrument that is capable of perfectibility—as compared with leaders who look outward. These leaders have a vision that's related to what people do in the world at large, consumers, customers of one kind or another, how to make things better for them, how to give them value.

COSTA: *Can you give contemporary examples of both, managers and leaders?*

ZALEZNIK: Sure. I think the epitome of management was Harold Geneen of I.T.T. who perfected or thought he could perfect instruments of control through numbers. They would enable him to fine-tune and control an enterprise and what managers did, through getting numbers on performance, setting up budget systems, providing compensation programs, rewarding people for meeting expectations. That proved to be incorrect. His successors almost immediately began to undo what he had done. A good example of business leaders are people like Sam Walton who developed the Wal-Mart retail chain. People like Leslie Wexner who founded The Limited chain. I think in his time Dr. An Wang was a real leader. The company has fallen on hard times, unfortunately, but that doesn't take away from his great accomplishments as a visionary business leader who saw the potential in a technology and made it work for a market, and that's the key: having a sense of what people need and how to serve their needs and provide them with value. That is an important difference. Those are some of the illustrations of it.

COSTA: *One of the most visible managers of a company today is Lee Iacocca. Would you say he is a manager, or a leader?*

ZALEZNIK: I think he is a leader, without a doubt. Of course, we were all intrigued reading his book because we all love gossip and we were terribly keen to know how many bottles of champagne Henry Ford the Younger drank, but nevertheless there is a real human story. I mean the man basically loved the product—the automobile—and loved the industry and loved the people in it and it was a crushing blow for him to be fired out of the presidency. It's a poignant story of how he was suddenly cast out without a role, and then into his lap, as though the gods were smiling on him, came the Chrysler Corporation with its terrible problems. Now there is no question that in times of crisis it is easier for leadership to make itself felt because people are aware that it's a life-and-death struggle, much like wartime. But he was able to definitively plan a strategy for reviving the company and he did it by recognizing that the company had to break even at a million units a year rather than three. He also recognized that he didn't have the time to refurbish the product line immediately so he adapted the old Seventh Avenue knockoff concept: find out who the great designers are and imitate them at a lower price. He did it and did it successfully. I would call him a fine American leader of an American enterprise.

COSTA: *He also had the kind of vision that you mention in your book: He helped bring about the creation and manufacture of the Ford Mustang.*

ZALEZNIK: Yes, although he's not a well-loved figure at Ford Motor Company, as you can imagine. There has been a lot of badmouthing of Iacocca about who invented the Mustang. Well, it was his baby. He got the engineers and the designers working on it, it was a great success, and he deserves the credit for it. He was the guy in charge.

COSTA: *Do leaders have to suffer some kind of personal stress? Is there a kind of Saul-on-the-road-to-Damascus approach, that they have to have a vision or endure some sort of setback?*

ZALEZNIK: Those whose lives are ever onward and upward we think of as highly adaptive people. Whatever the environment demands they seem to be able to change and go for it. I call them chameleons. They live from the outside, and I think that is a typical manager. He wants to know what his constituents expect of him and how can he perform, rather than how can he change his constituents to meet whatever situation is arising. Leaders are forged out of conflict. They experience deeply at some point in their life disappointments or frustrations, and it causes them to think about themselves. When they emerge from this period of introspection—which may incidentally be accompanied by some depression—and assuming that they have one important ingredient called talent—we tend to ignore the importance of talent, but it is an extremely important ingredient in the characteristics of leadership—then they emerge with a conviction, they emerge with a purpose, a vision. They become very energetic and active in bringing their vision into reality and this is why they inspire people. They tend to evoke awe in others not only because of their performance but because of the awareness that this individual has been through some kind of fire, a personal torment, and has mastered it and is now moving into life with new energy. We admire this.

COSTA: *There are several paradoxes in your book that trouble me. For example, you say that times of crisis bring about leaders and leadership. What has happened in America? We're certainly in a crisis now, we're almost a Third World nation, in the manufacturing sense.*

ZALEZNIK: Right. I think that America has undergone a massive repression, a repression of the responsibilities as a world leader and also the repression of the notion that there are limits to what you can do in world leadership. We're also in a state of repressing the fact that our society is split between those who are in it and those who are out of it. The people who are out of it are the people in urban centers, minority groups who, psychologically, because of the way they have been brought up and live, are totally unfit for work, work of any kind. They can't do the most basic thing, which is delay gratification, and it's not their fault although it is in the sense that they are responsible ultimately. But now we have a whole underclass. While groups of us are getting more affluent, there are other groups that are living outside of society. You can't have this kind of layering effect in society and expect it to be vibrant. Our leadership has wanted us to ignore this. In my own opinion, history will not treat Ronald Reagan very favorably because he colluded with us to engage in this massive repression. As a result, there is no coming to terms with what is the basic problem of productivity in this nation and that is the inability to rally around any kind of authority that we view as beneficent and compassionate and serving the common best interests of all of us. Without that identification with authority you cannot have successful factory systems, you cannot have successful productive enterprises. This is where we have failed, and we now need leadership that will wake us out of our sleep and point to a path. We've got to solve the drug problem, that is absolutely crucial. We have to begin educating people and get them retrained so that they can get into the workforce, and we have to make work and the craftsmanship and the lure of work meaningful to people once again, and this we have not done.

COSTA: *Another paradox seems to be that the people who are trained for management, those who come out of the business schools—and you criticize business schools soundly for this—perpetuate what you call the managerial mystique. They have the skills, but not as much talent. Can you talk a little bit about that?*

ZALEZNIK: I *am* very critical of the business schools including my own at Harvard. I've been here a long time and I feel as though I know the place very well so I think I'm in a good position to criticize not just our place but also the M.B.A. culture and higher education, which is producing enormous numbers—60,000 M.B.A.'s a year. What a phenomenal number and pouring of resources into that sector. A *New York Times* book reviewer said that I seem to be willing to bite the hand that feeds and I guess I am because I am critical. Well, why am I critical? It's basically because we are ignoring talent. At the outset we are. I think it goes back to our admissions procedure. We look for people who can fit in and work within a kind of interactive educational system rather than people who are good thinkers and who have some extraordinary talent that needs honing and development. That's our first mistake. The second mistake is that we have emphasized 'process,' even in our educational program, at the expense of substance and I think that is the crucial distinction between managing and leading. There has to be a balance between form and function, process and substance, and I think we've lost that balance. I am keenly aware of this because I meet people in all walks of life, and those who are outside the culture which I call the managerial mystique are absolutely amused and also bewildered. For example, they will note the way the managers dress. In one instance, the factory supervisors and the factory workers who were seeing them called the managers 'the suits' as in 'Here come the suits.' In another instance, they were referred to as the 'cuffs' because they tended to wear shirts with French cuffs and cuff links. For those who are doing real work, it is hard to take them seriously, yet one must take them seriously for the managers have real clout. We're again in a place where there is a split between those who are doing and those who are supposed to be planning and organizing and coordinating. We don't have this solidity, this identification. The Japanese have it and that is why I think they are successful.

COSTA: *Could Steve Jobs, founder of Apple Computer, have been admitted to one of the better business schools?*

ZALEZNIK: I would seriously doubt it because he would have been considered the kind of person who doesn't fit in. When such a premium is put on interaction, on social skills, that somebody who is a thinker and who values solitude and who is somewhat shy and diffident probably wouldn't get in. The worst thing that somebody who writes a recommendation for an incoming candidate can say is that so-and-so tends to be thoughtful and quiet. That sets off alarms. That person will not get in.

COSTA: *Tell us how Japanese leadership differs from ours. We are under the impression that the Japanese regard their leaders highly and that the Japanese workers are more involved in their work and in the decision-making process. It's much more of a team spirit, and very successful.*

ZALEZNIK: A very successful one, and the historians will certainly be spending hours figuring out how and why it all works. I think there are some very elementary, simple differences that account for their success and our relative decline. One, they tend to work hard. We don't. We are more interested in being consumers than we are workers. I think it makes a huge difference in the rate of productivity if the sole purpose of work is to put in your time and get whatever your pay is, sometimes a lot, sometimes not so much, and then be a consumer. Then nothing much is going to happen.

COSTA: *But the rewards for the Japanese are not always monetary.*

ZALEZNIK: They have a strong belief in their authority. I still think it's basically an authoritarian culture and society. They have identified with authority and they also believe it's their duty and responsibility to work hard because that is what authority wants them to do. Now it doesn't have to be authoritarian to get people to identify. You can identify with a vision, with a purpose, and you can be compensated well for doing it, but you still want to work hard to make that enterprise succeed. I think what we've lost in America and what they maintain in Japan is a sense of the relation between part and whole. Somebody who is working on an assembly line or attending a bunch of semiconductor machines making chips must have a consciousness and awareness of what his or her purpose is and what their activity means in relation to the whole. That sense of the whole. I mean you can be sweeping floors, but you know that the floors must be kept swept because if dust accumulates you're going to turn out faulty products. It's that kind of consciousness that makes for successful productivity and enterprise. Another aspect of it is that we were once great as a society of tinkerers, fixers. Youngsters would buy cars and they would get under the hood and learn how that engine worked. It's the capacity to tinker and fix that I think is extremely important in making an organization work. If every time you have a problem you have to call in a specialist, you're taking on the specialist's problems. I mean he wants to know who his constituents will be and what kind of political clout he can get, but if you know how to fix it yourself, in other words, if a supervisor and some other workers can go over to a machine and figure out what is wrong and fix it so it works right, you don't have to call in a specialist. It's a psychology of tinkering. What is that psychology? You have to know what you're doing. You also have to have a sense of responsibility: I want to make this thing work, we want to make it work. Without that spirit and attitude, work becomes a horrendous conflict, boredom.

COSTA: *What about the loyalty concept and culture in Japan? People who graduate from college in Japan usually choose a firm and stay with it for years and years and years. Here in America we reward people for change and, in fact, look askance at someone who is a 'lifer' at a company.*

ZALEZNIK: We have people in our universities who say that the important thing is to track your own career, and to know exactly when to jump ship and leave one company to join another . . . . What people learn is adroitness, how to jump off the horse just before it's shot out from under you, rather than staying at a company and doing a piece of work. I think what the Japanese engender is this feeling of accountability and responsibility for what goes on, and this must exist at every level of an organization or the [organizations] will not work. That is what we are missing in this country.

COSTA: *How difficult is it for women, who are increasingly employed as managers, to crash through those glass ceilings and actually become business leaders?*

ZALEZNIK: Very difficult. Women work most successfully in businesses where they have a clear-cut specialty. This is why you will see them succeeding in financial jobs on Wall Street or as attorneys and in professions that are well-established like medicine. But when it comes to hierarchical relationships, women have a difficult time because they are not accepted. Also I think that there is a certain anxiety level for them as they go to the top. I'm unfortunately observing too many cases in which women try to imitate men and become politically adept, or try to be. With women it's not such a gracious or graceful thing. I don't think it is for men either, but nevertheless, it doesn't appear right. So they will have a tough time in particular types of industries, and in consumer marketing and things of that sort. Women *should* do very, very well because there are many talents that they bring. In the financial field they do very well. I haven't seen successful heads of manufacturing among women. They haven't broken through that ceiling. I haven't seen too many successful chief executive officers appointed although there will probably be more coming down the way. I think that very often women are manipulated and they become the point men, so to speak, who get blown up when somebody steps on a grenade. That is unfortunate, that is misusing people, women in particular. I think they'll have a long, hard road ahead of them before they achieve substantial power in organizational life. That is not the way it should be; I'm describing the way it is.

A conversation with

Myra Mayman

Myra Mayman is director of the Office for the Arts at Radcliffe and Harvard. Believing that the arts are integral to civic life, Mayman serves on the board of trustees for both Bryn Mawr College and the Massachusetts Cultural Alliance, as well as committees at Boston's Museum of Fine Arts and the New England Holocaust Memorial.

COSTA: *The stereotype of a college student today is one who is preparing to enter one of the professions and amass as much wealth as quickly as possible. That's probably not true. I'm sure there are others who are interested in the humanities and who enter lower-paying professions. My question is: how do you get students of all kinds to participate in the arts?*

MAYMAN: It's not hard. At Harvard there are about 3,000 students involved with the arts. It's not something you have to get people to do necessarily. They come [to Harvard] and they're selected in part because they have a lot of broad interests, and this particular student body is extremely talented.

One of the ideas that I've developed, which is hardly revolutionary nor is it terribly insightful, is that when people are talented they tend to be talented horizontally. That is, you can be a very clear thinker in chemistry and a brilliant musician at the same time, and those two things often go hand-in-hand. Or people who are interested in words may want to go to law school and often are very attracted to theater and the use of words and the use of your body in space and how you project an argument or an idea.

I think people have gotten so used to the idea that things are compartmentalized. I think that the educational system has been geared to lead young people to specialize so that they think they're only good in one thing. In fact, human beings are multi-faceted. They've got a lot of abilities and a lot of talents. To me, it's a very natural thing that students are involved with the arts. Also I think the whole role of the arts in America has changed drastically over the past 20 years despite all the Proposition 2 and 1/2, and the music programs being dropped and so on. Being involved with the arts is part of being a human being. It's not something that's special to special people, although that's the way our society has led people to think.

COSTA: *There used to be an old argument that real talent is something that one is born with, that you really can't teach somebody to draw or to have perfect pitch or to dance. What's your view on that?*

MAYMAN: Genius may be something one is born with, but certainly just about anybody can be taught the things that you've mentioned. Taught to dance or to move? We can all do that. You just have to learn to do it, and you have to learn to hone your skills, and I think hone your vision in a way.

I was involved in a very interesting conversation once with Claire Mallardi, a woman who teaches dance at Radcliffe. We were interested in involving a different kind of student in the dance program, and expanding its impact. If students learn [to dance] well, it's not just learning to move you hands and feet, or learning to tap dance. People have these odd ideas about what dance is. It's really a spatial form and you learn to sculpt with space in time. Anyway, one of the ideas we had was to involve more athletes in the dance program. We had a meeting with a number of the athletics coaches and it was very interesting because [Claire] said, for example, 'I can teach your players, whether they're men or women, to increase their peripheral vision.' The tennis coach and the hockey coach said, 'I don't believe it, I don't believe it.' She said, 'Well, all I can tell you is that it's true. You can teach people to see broader. You can also teach them, for example, if you're on a football field and there is a mass of flesh moving at you at a very rapid rate, you can learn to see the holes in that mass of flesh. You can learn to see the space there and then you can orient your body so that you can swivel your shoulders to the side and dip and move through it. You can learn to do that.'

I thought that was a very interesting example of how you can teach anybody in almost any field how to use what they have better, and what we have is our bodies, our physical set-up, our chemistry, our brain power, all of that. All of that can be developed. As it can be developed in a history course or in a chemistry course, it can be developed in a dance class, in a different way. To expand your perceptions and expand your way of thinking is what I think the value of this sort of program is. That's what so exciting about it.

COSTA: *So there's a practical aspect to the arts?*

MAYMAN: Yes. I don't like to emphasize that and it's not really what I'm into, but, yes, there is a huge practical aspect. If business in this country wants to move ahead, they should have people studying the arts, and learning to think up creative solutions to problems. You've got to learn that you don't have to do things in the old way. You have the power as an individual to create new ideas and new solutions. There's a tremendous practical impact.

COSTA: *Does teaching dance require the most difficult administration? You need space and music and you need people to do things in ways that they probably have never done them before.*

MAYMAN: Administratively, dealing with the arts is fairly complex because you need very specific physical requirements, and not just in dance. But certainly in dance you need a special kind of floor; you can't have people dancing over concrete because they will get shin splints. You need to have light and air because, as I say, it's a sculptural endeavor, not just a movement endeavor, although most people think you can put a dance studio in a basement. It's very hard to create dance without light and air and space.

But the same is true for music; you need certain acoustics. If you want to rehearse a symphonic work you need a place for 106 people to sit with a lot of equipment. In visual arts you need to have, again, light, air, space, water, depending on what you are doing. You need fireproofing if you're doing welding. In theater, you need to have lighting, you need space to move around in. All of these things exist in space and time.

COSTA: *Why are the arts the first to be cut in public schools?*

MAYMAN: Beats the hell out of me. To me, it's a mystery because I think it's such a basic part of human life. Maybe the fact that this country was founded not all that long ago by Puritans, who thought it not nice—at the very least—to dance, or to do things in the arts. Maybe it's a part of that legacy, I don't know. But in this country the arts are considered by many people to be a frill, an extra. I don't think that's true in other countries. Look at the European countries: the arts are funded as a central part of life and culture, something that's important. Somebody selling oranges on the street in Milan is listening to opera. It's a part of their life. You go to church and a part of what you see is these beautiful paintings. The people who founded this country were revolting against that. They didn't want to look at pictures on the wall in their church. There's an argument for that, but at any rate, the legacy of that is that the arts are the first to go in this country.

COSTA: *I want to ask about the salutary effect your Learning from Performers Series had on jazz veteran Illinois Jacquet. Wasn't he inspired after spending time with the students here at Harvard to go out and do some new things in music?*

MAYMAN: That's right. We brought him here first in a course that we sponsored on the history of jazz and after that we brought him in for a longer residency. We've brought in a lot of jazz artists over the years because I think it's a very important kind of music in this country and it has been one of the great cultural contributions of this country to the world. Illinois came for an extended residency and I was delighted and amazed that on a recent record album, called *Illinois Jacquet and His Big Band* that came out in 1987 on Atlantic Records, he attributed the formation of his big band to his Harvard experience. It said that inspiration from his Harvard students led him to form his first big band in almost 30 years. I think he was inspired by the fact that these young people could get excited about the music. Jazz musicians have such a hard time, they have such ups and downs, but I think the fact that there were so many kids interested in this music and were able to play it and appreciate it in a real way, in a thoughtful way, led him to think that he could really get somewhere with this big band. And he did. He had a new album and it was bit of a turn in his career.

COSTA: *There is something that Walter Pater wrote that I'd like to get your opinion of: 'Art comes to you proposing, frankly, to give nothing but the highest quality to your moments as they pass.'*

MAYMAN: It's very beautiful. I think that's probably true. I think one of the reasons people are interested in the arts is because it does give you high moments and it allows you to get up and out of daily life. I think people have always been eager for that. I think it's one of the reasons that there have been so many museums built in this country and people are flocking to them. (They used to flock to churches and religion, which was very involved with the arts, certainly in the medieval period and in the Renaissance.) I think people are always looking for some experience that transcends everyday life. You know, sometimes everyday life isn't so great. We're all looking for some greater good or higher form of thought.

I think that's why people climb mountains or why they go to church or, now, why they go to museums. I think that's one of the reasons why people get so mad about the arts [situation] now. I think that people are looking to artists, whether they realize it or not, if not as soothsayers, then as some kind of truth-sayers. When they don't like what they hear and when they don't like what they see, it's very threatening. It's like having a priest in your town do something that threatens you or something that you don't approve of. I think it has that similar kind of quality.

COSTA: *One political arts event that happened here in Boston is the Mapplethorpe exhibit. It's imbued with all kinds of politics and outrage. What do you tell students about the politicization of art?*

MAYMAN: They have to look for what they think. They have to be educated enough to be able to make their own decisions about things. As I said earlier, I think one of the reasons the arts are so powerful and people get so upset about them, for example, the Mapplethorpe show—even though most people, as I understand it, who are upset about the show have never seen it—is that these images are very, very strong and very moving, either moving in a positive way or a negative way, but they're absolutely visceral. I have seen some of Mapplethorpe's work . . . and it's absolutely shocking, some of it. It's wild in a way, because he takes the same classical approach to the male genitals as he does to an absolutely perfect calla lily. Beautifully lit, laid out in the most extraordinary way—that's a very shocking thing. I don't know quite why it is. I thought I was experienced enough or jaded enough not to be shocked, but I was shocked.

I was talking to my husband and I said, 'You would be interested in seeing these pictures.' He found the whole notion a bit abhorrent, and I said, 'Well, if you saw a female nude beautifully lit against a beautiful background, would that be offensive to you?' 'Oh, absolutely not, absolutely not, that's art.' And I said, 'Well, what's the difference?' And part of it is that you're not used to seeing male nudes. I think there is a male/female double standard inherent there that has gone on for centuries.

COSTA: *It forces us to think about things we don't normally think about. That's a real function of art.*

MAYMAN: [Yes.] Again, it leads you to think about bigger things. What's the difference between a nude—I assume that means a work of art—or someone that's stripped, or someone that's naked? I'm not clear myself on what the qualities are, but I know that there are different kinds of impact from different sorts of images that really get to people.

COSTA: *There is another wonderful quote about art from Aldous Huxley: 'Art is one of the means whereby man seeks to redeem a life which is experienced as chaotic, senseless, and largely evil.'*

MAYMAN: So much for Huxley's happy life. [Laughs.] I think that's true. I think it's that whole notion again of lifting you into another realm, or trying to put some order into what is otherwise chaos. I think that's why people turn to the arts. I think that's why people get very upset these days when artists are not necessarily putting order onto chaos, but they're adding to the chaos sometimes or pointing out the chaos or saying that chaos is life.

A lot of times, because I think the arts mirror life and what's going on and are part of life—it's not something separate—people don't want to see life as chaos, they don't like that. They want to see art as some beautiful object, like the beautiful photograph you have on your wall of the setting sun over the river. That's what people want to see in a work of art. A lot of people don't want to see the ugliness of life. Well, artists are a part of the ugliness of life; they see that, too. I think a lot of artists feel that their job these days is not to make nice, and not to necessarily make lovely objects that people can purchase and put on their walls to beautify their living rooms, but that their role is to confront the problems in society. I think a number of artists are developing a different role in American society now, and that is to be social commentators and political commentators. Since the second world war a lot of people feel, certainly in Germany, that that's what artists should be doing. They shouldn't just be making beautiful pictures. They should be part of political life in the country.

People aren't used to that role of artists and I think that upsets a lot of people these days. Of course, what's interesting about artists is the way they think, by which I mean the way they see or the way they hear and how they express that back to us. That's what's so fascinating about it all.

COSTA: *Let's talk about theater, which is a big part of your program in the arts at Harvard and Radcliffe. A businessman I know in New York City said the reason he liked the theater is because it taught him, as he got older, how to derive some meaning from his own life. What do you think the role of theater can and should be?*

MAYMAN: It can be a variety of things, of course. It can be just entertaining; there's nothing wrong with that. And it can expose these truths about life. It's verbal and you're in the room where it takes place. As a result, somehow the words that are spoken—I think theater is largely about text, although there are artists now who would not go along with that—make you think about things in your own life, if it works well. They expose issues in an emotional way.

COSTA: *What are some of the themes that student playwrights in your programs have written about?*

MAYMAN: Anxieties of all kinds, a lot of anxieties: fitting in, not fitting in, feeling stupid, feeling unaccepted—all the same anxieties we all have. At any age.

COSTA: *What about the actual process of playwriting? What does your program do for people who want to write plays?*

MAYMAN: We run a lovely theater called the Agassiz Theatre, which is owned by Radcliffe, and it was opened in 1905. It was used in the early part of the century by a Harvard professor named George Pierce Baker and he taught playwriting at Harvard and at Radcliffe. (At that time, the Harvard faculty taught twice a day, once at Harvard and once at Radcliffe.) He felt that the test of any play that was written by a student or by any playwright is to have it performed so that you can see where the audience falls asleep or where they wake up or how they react. Then you go and do the cuts that you have to do and make the changes. With playwriting, as with any work of art, the thing doesn't just flow out of you. It's a series of critical judgments and very hard work at honing down what exactly is your final product. So the test of the play was to have it produced.

Well, Baker wasn't allowed to actually have the plays performed as a part of the Harvard curriculum because the faculty thought that it wasn't gentlemanly, scholarly, or intellectual. For some reason, and I don't know why, the Radcliffe dean said, 'This is a terrific part of the playwriting course.' And Baker, in the development of his playwriting course, called English 47, developed something called the Workshop 47, and he became *the* national figure in theater and he attracted remarkable young playwrights. This is in 1912, 1914. For example, there was Eugene O'Neill, who wrote to Baker and asked to come as a special student to study playwriting, or Philip Barry who went on to write *The Philadelphia Story* and other plays. Baker attracted all of these people and out of the classes he would take the best plays, either into Boston or occasionally to New York, to have tryouts. So Agassiz Theatre has a tremendous history of being a wonderful tryout house for young playwrights.

Arthur Kopit, who graduated, I think, in 1958, wrote, *Oh, Dad, Poor Dad, Mama's Hung You in the Closet and I'm Feelin' So Sad*, when he was a senior at Dunster House and that had its first tryout at Agassiz. The late Timothy Mayer, who graduated in '68 and was a playwright and director, did some of his best work at Agassiz. Tom Babe, who is a playwright in New York. Peter Sellars, who is a director from the Class of 1980, did some of his tryout work in Agassiz.

So one of the things that we try to do for students, which I think is a very luxurious thing, is to give them this small, but wonderful theater to try out their work. I think that's a very unusual opportunity and I don't know if they appreciate it while they're here but, boy, it's hard to do when you get out into the real world, for somebody to say, 'Listen, Mickey Rooney and Judy Garland, here's the barn, do the show.'

A conversation with

Edward O. Wilson

*Edward O. Wilson is Frank B. Baird Jr. Professor of Science and
curator in entomology in the Museum of Comparative Zoology. The Ants
(Harvard University Press), coauthored with Bert Hölldobler, was
awarded the 1991 Pulitzer Prize for general nonfiction. The Royal
Swedish Academy of Sciences gave Wilson a Crafood Prize, an award
established to recognize areas not honored by the Nobel Prize.*

COSTA: *The tropical rain forests are diminishing all over the world. Would
you define what a tropical rain forest is and tell me where they are located.*

WILSON: Tropical rain forests are closed, moist evergreen forests found in
the tropical regions with rainfall of 200 centimeters or more annually, allowing the trees, which occur in three layers or more, to have broadleaf, evergreen
form. The tropical rain forests cover about six percent of the land surface of
the world and the largest concentrations are found in the Amazon and Orinoco
basins of South America, the Congo basin of Africa, and the large islands and
Malaysian peninsula of tropical Asia. At the present time, they have been
reduced to about fifty-five percent of their original cover, by human activity.

COSTA: *The interesting thing about the rain forests is that even though they
cover only six percent of the entire Earth they contain more than half the
world's biota [the animals, plants, and fungi of a region].*

WILSON: That's right. It's probably considerably more than half the world's
biota. We don't know the exact figure and in fact have no good idea of what

it is except that it is very large. The number of species of insects in the canopy alone has been recently estimated to fall somewhere between ten million and eighty million. The total number of organisms—plants, animals, and microorganisms—thus far known to science, that is, given a scientific name, is only 1.4 million. So those figures will give you an idea of how little we know about life on this planet, and especially in the tropical rain forests.

COSTA: *I was interested to read in the book you edited,* Biodiversity *[National Academic Press], that from a single tree in Peru, where you were doing some fieldwork, you uncovered forty-three species of ants belonging to twenty-six classes, which is about equal to the entire ant fauna of the British Isles. Also you wrote that Peter Ashton [a Harvard professor of dendrology] found seven hundred species of trees in ten acres in Borneo, the same number of species as in all of North America. We are talking about a real density of species diversity in these rain forests.*

WILSON: That's right. Even biologists find it mind-boggling. The reasons why it's so great is one of the abiding unsolved problems of ecology and evolution.

COSTA: *Isn't it true that one really doesn't know the total number of species that exists in the rain forest because they haven't been studied thoroughly? Isn't there a rule of thumb that scientists use to calculate the number of species estimated to exist on a given area of land?*

WILSON: The rule of thumb that biogeographers use—that is, the biologist who studies the distribution of animals—is that in comparing islands and also in comparing patches of habitat such as scattered patches of rain forest, a tenfold increase in the area of an island or a patch results eventually in a doubling of the number of species at equilibrium, that is, the condition in which new species colonizing the area is equaled by the number of species going extinct there. Then, of course, the reverse is as we reduce the area, for example, of a rain forest, to ten percent of its original cover, we eventually will bring the number of species that can live there down to about one half. We find that in the Brazilian Atlantic forest, which once had one of the richest floras and faunas in the world, the original cover has been reduced to less than one percent and there is plenty of evidence that we are indeed going to lose more than half, possibly three quarters, of the numbers of species that once existed there.

COSTA: *You've written that if present levels of the forest removal continue, within a hundred years, twelve percent of the seven hundred and four bird species in the Amazon basin will be lost, and fifteen percent of the ninety-two thousand plant species will be destroyed in South and Central America. These are compelling figures. But for people who live in the temperate zones and for whom the rain forest is a remote concept, a lot of people would say, 'Well, how terrible is that? How will it affect us here in North America?'*

WILSON: This problem of mass extinction of species, including a great many that we haven't even yet discovered but have only inferred their existence, is one of the four great environmental problems of the present time along with toxic pollution, the greenhouse effect, and depletion of the ozone layer. And it is the one that so far has caused the least concern. I hope that changes. I find that the loss of species—our figures and the ones you site are based on very conservative models; the rate may be much higher than the ones you just sited—is not disputed. This is not one of the controversial areas of environmental projections. Rather, the problem is trying to convey why these species matter. I have two [arguments] that I give and I think they are well substantiated. First of all, diversity of life on Earth has got to be regarded as one of humanity's great heritages. The species that are now going extinct are in most cases hundreds of thousands or millions of years old. The average species is believed to live between one million and ten million years and here we are destroying up to a quarter or more of them within a few decades. The second reason that people might be able to identify more readily, though, is that these species represent a form of wealth that we haven't even begun to utilize. For example, we depend largely on only about twenty species of plants for most of our food. These are the species that were put into use in the early days of the agricultural revolution and the ones that people happen to encounter for the most part in the Fertile Crescent and Mesoamerica and a few other places where agriculture began. But it has been estimated that as many as fifty-thousand species of plants have edible parts and some of the species of plants that are still unutilized or very little utilized, including ones in the tropical forest, are demonstrably superior to the crops now in use. The species of plants and animals that exist in this threatened biota of the world are a veritable 'far-mucopia' of natural products that can be used in medicine. They are also sources of new crops, as I just said, and new fibers, petroleum substitutes, soil-restoring plants, and the like. We've only examined—including the animal species—fewer than a tenth of one percent in terms of their potential.

COSTA: *There is an interesting intersection between science and politics in this area, and that is that most of the tropical rain forests are in what could be classified as Third World nations. For those nations to have a good standard of living and to be a part of the developing world, they need to grow economically. Unfortunately some of that growth is taking the form of slash-and-burn denuding of the forests. What do you think scientists can do to help with that intersection of politics and growth and yet uphold preservation?*

WILSON: The cruel dilemma of the biological diversity crisis is that the countries that own the largest part of the diversity are also the poorest and the least prepared to save it and use it. The bright side of the picture, if there is one, is that development of these countries and the preservation of their own biological diversity are not in opposition. The old model of conservationists poised against economic developers is obsolete, especially in the tropical countries. The new international conservation movement is now completely committed to the idea of linking the preservation and use of biological diversity, country by country, with economic development. That is made possible by the potentially great value of the wild species that live in many of these countries, which offer to them—with just a small amount of research, market planning, and regional planning—very substantial sources of income. Recent studies in the Peruvian Amazon rain forest, one of the most species-rich areas of the world, show that even with our present limited knowledge and very restricted markets it is possible to make more money by extracting natural products such as latex and fruits from the forest as it exists than it would be to clear-cut the forest for timber and then use [the area] for agriculture and cattle. By creating extractive reserves, as Brazil for example is beginning to do, the economy of many regions of the world with the richest biodiversity will actually be better off. Another spectacular example involves a threatened species, the giant river turtle of the Amazon, which is said to have delicious flesh; I've never eaten it, but it has a reputation for that. It can be grown so rapidly in ponds set up along the banks of the Amazon that the yield in meat is approximately 300 times that of cattle grown in cleared forests in the same areas. There are so many opportunities to save biological diversity while at the same time making use of it that I'm optimistic that a greater effort in research and development of particularly tropical biodiversity is going to yield results.

COSTA: *Why did you become a biologist?*

WILSON: Yes, it's an interesting case history, at least to me, and it might be of some use to others. How to use your handicaps. I was blinded in one eye by accident when I was a little boy and I've always been a bit hard of hearing, particularly in the upper registers. When I started out as an amateur naturalist in the woods like so many kids, and turned to bird watching, I was lousy at it. So I discovered, at the same time, that I have unusually sharp closeup vision in my one good eye. As a result, I narrowed down my focus and started paying more attention to insects. I found them so interesting and profitable to study that I became a dedicated entomologist.

COSTA: *Everyone who writes about you in the popular press describes your office with its hundreds of thousands of ant-colony residents. You explained how you became interested in insects, but why ants? Why the social organization of ants and then the extrapolation of that into social biology?*

WILSON: I would say that it was National Geographic, an article on ants published in 1934. Unlike so many of those good golden oldies articles in the National Geographic, the illustrations and the things that were said about the animals were compelling to a boy. But I also had the good fortune for a couple years of living near the National Zoological Park, the national zoo in Washington, D.C., within walking distance of it, and the nearby Rock Creek

Park and the national museum on the mall. Exposure to these grand institutions, along with a little piece of woodland, was all so compelling. It gave me a feeling as a kid that the study of natural history was something grand. It was grand at the national level, and there was a ready access to real wonders in the world. So this, in a way, is a plug for museums and zoos. I think that my experience has been repeated many times over by scientists now in their mature years.

COSTA: *Let's revisit the controversial, decade-long sociobiology conflict. In your autobiography you said that there was a time that you really couldn't even speak out publicly. One day when you were giving a lecture, someone even poured water on you to protest what you were saying. Could you describe that period and what you were trying to say and if you have changed your views?*

WILSON: From time to time, the nature/nurture controversy resurfaces in discussions of human beings. The nature side has never been very popular, especially in the United States, because it is part of the national ethos that mankind is perfectible, and our opportunities for personal development are unlimited. The argument that I built out of comparisons with the social organizations of other animals and from very substantial evidence, which has grown since that time, is that . . . a large part of human nature is inherited. This isn't to say that human potential isn't great, that free will, as we generally understand it, doesn't exist, and that in a free society human beings can't reach very high levels of achievement and fulfillment. It's merely to say that what makes us essentially human does have a biological foundation. I think that's true, I think it's been well substantiated by the accumulated evidence in developmental psychology and human genetics since that time, but I said it at the wrong time. In the '70s there was still a very considerable malaise about American society, about ideology, about our self-image, and any description of human behavior that appeared to be determinist, that appeared to place constraints on what we are and what we might become, wasn't welcomed. But I think even during the height of the controversy, the great majority of scientists, especially biologists, agreed with this view. The number of the most outspoken critics was always very small, but it made for some lively discussion.

COSTA: *You have a new book on ants. Could you describe its central themes?*

WILSON: A resoundingly noncontroversial book, *The Ants* is by my colleague Bert Hölldobler, who worked with me at Harvard for twenty years and then went to the University of Würzburg to take a chair in zoology there last year. It's an encyclopedic account, the first since 1910 of ant lore and it covers every aspect of the biology of ants from the classification of the approximately nine thousand known species through communication, through ecology, to economic importance, anatomy, physiology and the like. It is very well illustrated. I can say that without being immodest because it is due largely to Bert Hölldobler's splendid talents as photographer and artist. It's meant to promote the study of ants, which are, after all, among the most ecologically important organisms on the land, but also to show the richness of the life and biology of a seemingly humble group of organisms that ordinarily we wouldn't pay attention to almost entirely because of their small size.

COSTA: *Does it bother you as an entomologist when you read stories about killer bees coming up to the U.S. mile by mile? What do you think of that sensationalization of the insect world?*

WILSON: It doesn't bother me too much. After all, they are killer bees; there have been a number of cases of fatalities. One of the most recent was a student in a course cosponsored by Harvard University in Costa Rica who got caught on a path near a colony and was stung to death before he could be rescued. But, generally speaking, these bees aren't going to be killing large numbers of people. They just have to be handled more carefully and precautions have to be taken with them that one wouldn't ordinarily take with domesticated bees.

COSTA: *What makes them killer bees? Are they bigger, or is the sting more virulent?*

WILSON: Essentially they are more aggressive. They will come at you much more quickly and they are more persistent in their attempts to sting. That can be gotten around by beekeepers with the right equipment and techniques. If handled right, as experience in Brazil shows, they can actually increase the productivity of the industry because they do tend to be more active and productive and they build high densities of populations where they occur.

COSTA: *You teach an undergraduate Core course here in biology and it's very popular. Do you have a mission in that course to bring biology to young folks, or are you trying to explain the concept of evolutionary biology, that things are still evolving, which a lot of people don't realize these days.*

WILSON: It tries to do all of those things, and I do have a sense of mission for the following reason: It's been said that the three great transforming ideas of the nineteenth century are Marxism, Freudian psychoanalytic theory, which of course is more early 20th century, and Darwinism. Most adults, at least intuitively, understand Marxism and Freudian thinking very well. It has seeped so thoroughly into our culture. But very few people, including college-educated people, really understand Darwinism, the most revolutionary of all scientific ideas, and what it means for our self-conception. Indeed, sociobiology is a thoroughly Darwinian view of human nature, and it was that way of thinking that contributed to the sociobiology controversy more than any particular inference out of sociobiology as a particular body of theory. So I come into the course with the knowledge that I'm facing a bunch of very bright young people, most of whom have not been exposed to this way of thinking.

It's always very exciting to get them to think about many aspects of their lives as well as the whole science of biology through the lens of natural selection theory. Many of them do find it a transforming experience, especially when they begin to see that they can rethink issues such as abortion, genetic engineering, the meaning of ecosystems, the process of aging, the significance of sex, in both a biological and a historical manner.

A *conversation with*

Jan Ziolkowski

*Jan Ziolkowski is professor of Medieval Latin and comparative
literature and is active in developing a curriculum in ethics.
His books include translations and editions of medieval poetry and
songs, as well as a volume of essays,* On Philology
(Pennsylvania State Press).

COSTA: *You will be teaching a course called The Ethics of Friendship. I
assume your students will read about friendship as defined and described by
Aristotle, Shakespeare, and others. How did you get the idea for such a course?*

ZIOLKOWSKI: A few years ago I was casting about for ideas for another large
course to teach. My courses tend to fall into two categories: very small depart-
mental courses and then the large Core course that I teach on beast literature.
I was looking for something human, and this was the idea that came to me. It
came to me mainly, I suppose, because I was looking for a topic that would
enable me to present some very fine pieces by a number of different classical
and medieval authors and a topic that would allow me to work the stretch
between antiquity and Shakespeare. I should also confess, though, that friendship was a topic that was on my mind because of my personal life at the time.
I found in my mid- and late-twenties that I was forming friendships less readily
than I had in my college years. There were other relationships that interfered
with or competed with friendships, so for those personal reasons, the issue was
on my mind.

COSTA: *To take a line from Aristotle, somewhat similar to your experiences, he wrote, 'He has no friends who has many friends.' Isn't that true?*

ZIOLKOWSKI: That is true. There was certainly a sentiment in antiquity and in the Middle Ages that the person who formed friendships very readily and who had a large number of them at any one time was not a person who was deep enough to sustain a true friendship. There was a feeling that you should behave politely toward everyone but that your time was finite and that you had to give a great deal to your true friends. Therefore, the limit of true friendships was bounded by the amount of time that you had at your disposal.

COSTA: *Before we get further into friendship, I'd like to know more about your course on beasts in literature.*

ZIOLKOWSKI: That's one that I've taught for several years and it's one that I continue to enjoy. Once again, I was seeking a means of presenting a broad spectrum of great works by a number of different authors. The theme around which I decided to organize the course was the appearance of animals. This enabled me to put together a course that runs from the Aesopic fables and antiquity up through George Orwell's *Animal Farm* at the other end, stopping along the way at works like Gulliver's travels with its horses, Kipling's jungle books, *Call of the Wild*, and other works of that sort.

COSTA: *To return to the theme of friendship, psychologists, sociologists, and the media today tell us that things have changed in the last 10 years. We have had the 'Me Generation' with people turning inward and going for themselves, the so-called 'yuppification of America,' and the competitiveness of Wall Street, all of which do not lead to friendships. Has the concept of friendship changed because our society has changed?*

ZIOLKOWSKI: Yes, I think that if you look back over time, what friendship has meant has varied a great deal from one period to another and that in classical antiquity having good friendships was an important constituent of having a city-state that operated properly. In the Middle Ages, friendship was seen as a means of practicing toward proper friendship with God or love of God. When you come into our period—I'm not as much an expert on our period as I am on the Middle Ages, so I'm talking off the top of my head now—but as you come into our period, the tension between friendship and finances, and friendship and politics becomes ever greater.

COSTA: *In medieval times, certainly in Arthurian legend, there was a different kind of friendship such as that of the Knights of the Round Table. There was a real devotion to each other, a laying down of one's life for a friend, if necessary. Could you expand on that concept?*

ZIOLKOWSKI: People were often raised, not at the home of their parents, but were sent off to be raised—I'm speaking of noblemen here—with near-relatives, aunts and uncles who were noble. Forging close friendships with other young noblemen during that stage was considered a vital part of growing up because that is how you learned how to behave properly, to earn the loyalty of people around you, and how to retain that loyalty. On the other hand, during that same period, you also find, for the first time, strong conflicts between romantic love and marriage on the one hand, and friendship on the other, In antiquity, that was never seen as a conflict. Marriage played a very secondary role to friendship. But in the Middle Ages, that became more and more of a dilemma.

COSTA: *I'm reminded of a more modern writer, Henrik Ibsen, who wrote, 'A friend married is a friend lost.'*

ZIOLKOWSKI: That's definitely been a dilemma. I would say people now continue to have very close friendships but the idea that romantic love is paramount has squeezed friendship out of many sorts of popular discussions. You will find that people will continue to have close friendships but the advice columns usually have to do with the problems of romantic love, with sex, with family, and much less often with friendships, even though people are forging them and are having problems that they are having to work out in them.

COSTA: *Interestingly, though, one thing in our society that has come about, is that it is now easier for a man to be a friend with a woman and a woman to be a friend of a man. Those barriers are gone. Just 30 years ago, one was looked upon with real suspicion if one had a close friend who was of the opposite sex.*

ZIOLKOWSKI: Yes. That has changed. In the Middle Ages, it was very difficult for people of opposite sexes to be close friends with each other. That dilemma comes out in one of the readings that I plan to include in the course. It's the letters between Abelard and Heloise. After his castration, after they both entered religious communities—he into a monastic community and she into a convent—they had to work out new conditions for their relationship. She was reluctant to deny the previous dimension, to brand it as wrong, and he, on the contrary, was ready to condemn it.

COSTA: *How interchangeable were friends in medieval times? Now people seem to make and lose friends quickly.*

ZIOLKOWSKI: I think that that's truest of our country in the modern world. Because we're such a very mobile society and because we're a very open people, I think that we're used to developing friendships almost overnight, but we're also very ready to shed them when we move on. I think that in other countries, this would be in Europe as well as elsewhere, friendship is still taken very seriously, and if you make a friend, that friend is yours for life.

COSTA: *As a classicist and with your expertise in Latin, you are familiar with the works of Ovid and others who wrote extensively about friendship. One does not see whole tracts devoted to friendship these days in literature.*

ZIOLKOWSKI: No. You don't see treatises being written in the way that you did in the past. In ancient literature, you can look to Plato and Aristotle and

Cicero and Seneca and others, and in the Renaissance you can look to people like Montaigne and Bacon and you can find either whole treatises or else large parts of dialogues or essays that deal with the theme. I don't know of a recent philosopher who's devoted a whole book to the topic, certainly not a book that has caught the public eye.

COSTA: *Why do you think that is true? What has changed that makes it no longer an appropriate philosophical topic?*

ZIOLKOWSKI: I suppose that it's probably partly the result of the turning inward that has come about in the West, the kind of solipsism, the tendency to retreat into yourself and to be skeptical about the reliability of anything outside yourself. You touched upon that earlier when you referred to the Me Generation. I think that that focusing upon oneself and one's own needs are definitely a part of it. And it may also, speaking completely off the cuff, be a consequence of the materialism of our culture because we define people very much by their economic status and by the possessions that they use to establish their identities. It's difficult to possess other people fully enough to make them part of your wardrobe of different designer labels.

COSTA: *In ancient and medieval times, were there any differences between the sexes as far as length of friendships? Did women keep women friends longer than men kept men friends?*

ZIOLKOWSKI: There is a problem of evidence since we have much more evidence of the men than we do of the women for many periods. Literacy tended to be in the hands of men. And it was in the hands of a fairly narrow cross-section of men. So what we're really talking about in many periods is clerics, those people who were in some kind of religious order, or men who were aristocrats. They don't represent a cross-section of society. And we have less evidence about women. The feelings in Christianity during the Middle Ages toward friendship were, from my point of view, fairly schizophrenic because one's relationship with God was put highest in any sort of hierarchy. Relationships with other people, especially friendships, could be seen as distracting or detracting from that relationship with God. People perhaps viewed friendships as being a kind of training for that relationship with God. In other words, you behaved kindly toward children and animals to start out with, that's easy and simple. Then you move on to being good friends with a small group of people and then you move from that coterie to God.

COSTA: *There's an old toast that goes something like this: 'When you ascend the hill of prosperity, may you not meet a friend.' So there are some who think there is a downside to having friends, too.*

ZIOLKOWSKI: That's discussed in some of the treatises. In antiquity, there was seen to be an almost insurmountable problem in parities in friendships. If both weren't from the same class there was likely to be so much conflict between them that the relationship would break up. In the Middle Ages, I suppose the treatise writers didn't worry about that quite as much since they were writing for people who were in the same religious class . . . . Both the classical and the medieval manuals do provide information on how to test your friendships under those circumstances, how to make sure that people aren't remaining friends with you simply for their own advantage or how to break off friendships if you find out that a person is not a true friend.

COSTA: *So there were manuals on how to behave with friends.*

ZIOLKOWSKI: One that I hope to use in this course is by a person named Aelred of Rievaulx, a saint from the 11th century. He wrote a treatise that was modeled closely upon Cicero's 'On Friendship.' It's called 'On Spiritual Friendship.' In it he gives you tips on how to test the virtues of your friend, how to give them confidences and to see whether or not they hold onto those confidences. Then later, if the person breaches those confidences, how to distance yourself from the person. In both the classical and the medieval treatises the writers emphasized that you shouldn't end the friendship abruptly, that it's the job of the offended party to continue to treat the person with the outward manifestations of friendship but to draw back gradually. This is after you have taken the direct approach. Both of them urge that, at the beginning, if you see something that you don't like, to have it out openly with the person, that you owe it to that person to try to teach them to correct their flaws. Then if that doesn't work, draw back gradually because it was considered shameful to have a close relationship with a person and then to cease it overnight.

COSTA: *How ethical is it to plant little confidences—as it was done in medieval times—and test to see if your friend is going to break those confidences? Would we regard that as ethical today?*

ZIOLKOWSKI: No, I don't think that we would. In fact, as we read these sections of the treatises, they upset people and I empathized with them because I find it distasteful too. On the other hand, what we do now in friendships is to accumulate that same data about the reliability of people, but we accumulate it in a random fashion. We often have a dilemma that comes up and a great need for a friend that we couldn't have predicted. We find out only then that the person isn't reliable, that they won't come through for us when we really need them. I think that the way people handled it in earlier times might have made more sense because if you played these little games you would know before the crunch if you could count on a person. For us, it's left to happenstance.

COSTA: *Latin is supposed to be a dead language and here we are talking about Latin literature on friendship that is reinvigorating our talk today. I assume that's what you're hoping will happen in this course, that your students will see the history of the past and try to relive it and rethink the present.*

ZIOLKOWSKI: Very much. I want in this course to bring as much of antiquity and the Middle Ages to people's eyes as I can show them that these were flesh-and-blood people with very real problems like ours. They didn't always handle it in our way, but the lessons that they learned may well be of use to us now. Since you mentioned Latin, it is a particular goal of mine to brush aside some of the cobwebs that build up around Latin. Those who take Latin tend to be taught it very much as a dead language and often associate it with the agonies of learning paradigms in classrooms in high school or in college, and very rarely do they get to the point where they have such ease in reading that they can feel it as a living language. I hope that by using some of these materials in translation that people will get a sense of it as a living language and a language with a very long and rich history.

COSTA: *A lot of people tend to forget that many of the phrases that we use every day, like 'The die is cast,' come from Latin. These phrases, which are part of our collective consciousness, actually were very vital phrases coming out of Rome.*

ZIOLKOWSKI: Yes. We have phrases that have been translated, we have the words connected with law and liturgy that remain in Latin, and then we have all of the words that are derived from Latin either directly or through French. And then to move beyond the words, we also have the ways of organizing material, the stories, the cultural remnants of that civilization. By that 'civilization' I mean not just ancient Rome but also the Latin Middle Ages because it was really in the crucible of the Latin Middle Ages . . . that our own culture came into being.

COSTA: *There is quite a controversy that you've hinted at—that perhaps the Western tradition needs to be amplified with the philosophy and writings of people of different colors and different gender and different sexual orientations, and perhaps we can all profit from reading that material. But I think all of us would agree that the bottom, the bedrock, is that we should know the classics.*

ZIOLKOWSKI: How large a component of education the classics should be is really the question. In earlier centuries, the classics *were* education. Now they've become one small piece of a mosaic that makes up education. They're part of the literature, they're part of the philosophy, the art, and they're not as much a part of, let's say, the social sciences or the natural sciences. But I do feel that they should remain there, that they always must be a piece as long as they're a part of our culture and I think they will be a part of our culture for a long, long time.

COSTA: *Let's talk about perhaps the greatest storyteller in the English language: William Shakespeare. Tell me what you want to transmit to your students about his thoughts on friendship.*

ZIOLKOWSKI: What's fascinating about friendship in Shakespeare is the extent to which it pervades his plays. The plays in which it comes out the most are an early play that's not very highly regarded, *The Two Gentlemen of Verona*, and a somewhat later play that's more highly regarded, *The Merchant of Venice*. You could just as well select almost any of Shakespeare's other plays and find moments where friendship loomed very large. I think that it plays a larger role in his dramas than it does in plays that have been written subsequently. Why, is an interesting question.

COSTA: *He also told us a lot about the negatives of friendship, people like Iago.*

ZIOLKOWSKI: Yes. And the competition that friendship had with money and with power, and the ways in which people could attempt to feign friendship, and the conflicts between friendships and love. As the course now stands in my mind, I plan to end with *The Merchant of Venice*, which I look at as crystalizing some of the conflicts that were becoming larger in the Renaissance between friendship, on the one hand, and money and religion on the other.

COSTA: *I'd like to ask you about the concept of ethics. This university, as you know, is trying to instill in our students a concept of and an appreciation for ethics as a living concept. I wonder if you could tell us what you hope to transmit to your students about ethics.*

ZIOLKOWSKI: I've thought long and hard about this question and I used to believe that the best way of teaching ethics was simply by living and performing ethically in the profession. I'm not certain that that's enough now. I think that people used to come to college having had a fairly sound ethical grounding simply from the models of their families. I don't know if that's true any longer. I don't know if people are spending enough time with each other in their families to discuss these issues or to impart them by example. So I think there is a need now to discuss them openly. Although I have the disadvantage of not having special training as a sociologist or a psychologist, I have the advantage of having wonderful, engaging materials about which I feel very affectionate and that I would like to offer to as wide an audience as possible. I think that by putting on display works in which great thinkers and writers of the past have dealt with these issues that inevitably people will give serious thought to it. I'm not coming into the course with any one party line that I would like to communicate. What I'm hoping, though, is that with pleasure and with seriousness—in other words, back to the old idea of entertainment and edification—people will look at three different texts and will come out of it with a better idea of the problems they're likely to encounter in their friendships after college when, as you mentioned, their friendships which they forged in college will come into conflict with their desire for good jobs, their desire for professional advancement, their desire for money, their desire to be good husbands, good fathers, good wives, good mothers, all of that.

A conversation with

Ronald Thiemann

Ronald Thiemann is dean of the Divinity School and an ordained Lutheran minister. Theimann's mission is to forge a new critical theology that includes education of both ministers and scholars.

COSTA: *Studies have shown that there is a new spirituality alive in America today. Surveys here among our own students indicate that there is a greater interest in religion. This is shown not just in increased church attendance but also in the thriving of religious groups that span virtually every denomination and religious belief. This seems like a paradox when other studies show a concomitant rise in careerism in students who are more and more frequently choosing courses geared to preparing them for the high paying professions of law, business and medicine. How do you reconcile the two—the increased career-oriented education and the interest in things spiritual?*

THIEMANN: I'm not sure I can reconcile the two, but I think the two are related in an interesting way. I'm now seeing—and I think I already saw while I was at Haverford College before I came to Harvard—a growing ambivalence on the part of students who . . . recognize that these are economically perilous times, and know that they have to take steps to provide for themselves.

That's one of the major incentives for people entering professions, particularly the ones that have a high degree of status and of economic security. Yet they're bringing values to those professions which often work against the monetary motivation that might have brought them into the profession in the first place. Often, after five or six years of experience in the profession, they begin to become very restless and they realize they have not been well prepared by their own professional education to deal with the moral issues that they face on a day-to-day basis. So I think they're beginning to look for resources and an orientation that will help them to deal with the moral challenges they face.

Now, many of these people might have been religiously or spiritually motivated in their private lives for a long time. Others might be what I would call children of second-generation secular parents. That is, people whose parents probably thought through religious questions and rejected it. So these children might have been raised in homes where there was no religious practice or no attendance at religious services. They often discover, certainly in college, a kind of intellectual interest in religion that they choose not to, at first, pursue professionally. But there's an aspect of their understanding of human affairs that has been influenced by that.

You have a situation where, on the one hand, people are seeking some degree of economic security, and on the other hand, have values that cut against that economic motivation. It remains to be seen how it will balance out.

I think there is another aspect to it. [We recently had] the first space shuttle launch since the Challenger tragedy. In many ways I think the Challenger accident is a symbol of the end of our love affair with technology. We recognize the importance of technology, we know that our society still depends on it, but it no longer has quite the attractiveness. We're much more realistic. We know the limits as well as the benefits of technology. The fact that Chernobyl happened close to the time of the Challenger tragedy has given us, as a culture and as a society, a much more realistic assessment of technology. There's a sense in which the gods of technology have failed us, and now there's a kind of searching and yearning for other sources of life and vitalization and a sense of moral orientation other than that which the professions and technology can give us.

COSTA: *How about the high visibility of failures in ethics that we see and read about in the media constantly? The problems on Wall Street with insider trading scandals, the failures of people in business, industry, and medicine to do the right ethical thing. Is this also affecting young people?*

THIEMANN: I think it is. I think probably the strongest reaction is: 'That's not me,' when they see these people in high places who are involved in unethical and even illegal activities. That is the very ambivalence that I was talking about before: There's a side of those people that is attracted to the status, the power, the wealth that goes along with the professional positions. And yet there's a side that's horrified by the ethical failure. I think that has allowed the raising—both publicly and personally—of a series of questions about the moral orientation of professions that would have been much more difficult to raise.

Nonetheless, I think I see the trends I described earlier to be sufficiently profound that I think we would have been seeing this spiritual revival even if we hadn't had these almost symbolic public embarrassments. But I think the public embarrassments have helped move the process along a little more quickly.

COSTA: *A few years ago when you were inaugurated as dean of the Harvard Divinity School you said that theological discourse had become 'the language of the elites,' having little relevance either for the congregations of practicing religious people or for the broader secular society. You also said that women and people of color seem to have been excluded from participating in what you call 'the religious conversation' that serves to define the nature and goals of the theological community. Does the recent naming of a black woman as an Episcopal bishop indicate a turning of the corner or change in this exclusionary process? Is it finally changing or do we have a long way to go?*

THIEMANN: Both probably. That is, there have been real changes, but we have a very long way to go. Clearly, it would have been inconceivable a decade ago, for a woman—particularly a black woman—to be elected bishop anywhere in the Anglican community. But, now, the fact that it is not only possible, but a reality, is an indication that there is genuine progress. But we have to remember that it was just two decades ago when ordination was not open to women in virtually any denomination. We're still at the beginning of what is a major, perhaps even revolutionary, movement in the development of religious communities. . . . To think of Christianity as being a religion that's almost two millennia old, and it's only been in the last 20 years that women have been accepted into positions of ministerial leadership, and in some denominations they are still not. . . . That happens now at a time when theological education is experiencing an influx of women. Virtually 50 percent of the student body of the Divinity School is female, so there are pressures built into the system to have more than just symbolic elections or symbolic opportunities for women to move into positions of major leadership. The pressure is continuing to build in the system. That's a good thing in my estimation and I think we can expect to see more of these kinds of events taking place in the future, but there is still a long way to go.

COSTA: *How has the movement for inclusive language helped the degenderizing of biblical text?*

THIEMANN: It has created a context of controversy, and whenever you have a context of controversy, it can both help and hinder. I think we'll be seeing forces and counterforces at work right now in many religious communities. But in the long run, the issue of inclusive language is an important one, because it signals the commitment or lack of commitment on the part of communities of faith to include fully those people who constitute at least half, and in many cases, as much as 60 percent of the membership of those communities.

So it's not just a matter of language. It's a matter of a whole set of patterns of social structures, distribution of power, and political realities that have to change along with the struggle over language. The inclusive language issue is a very important one, but it's one among many that needs to be addressed.

COSTA: *This brings me to a question concerning a term that is much in vogue these days, so-called liberation theology. I'm told it started in Latin America and was aimed at the poor and the disenfranchised and sought to empower them in their culture, not only theologically, but politically and economically and culturally. Is this a role you'd like to see new ministers who graduate from the Divinity School fulfill—entering into so-called liberation theology? I know it's a very controversial area as to how far does one go into a community, and when does the religious aspect become partisan politically. . . .*

THIEMANN: Let me take a little time to describe the development of liberation theology, what some of the principles of it are, and talk about it in the context of North America, because I think it's important to see that it will emphasize different themes depending on its actual social and political context.

When one reads the Gospels, it's clear that the ministry of Jesus is directed primarily toward those who are at the margins of society. These people are variously described in the New Testament text. But one of the categories to describe them is 'the poor.' It's a major theme in all of the Gospels and yet it has not until quite recently been seen as a major theme in theology. So, clearly there has been a failure, for whatever reasons—and one of the things liberation theology does is to try to give us those reasons—a failure in much of theology in the history of the Christian Church to attend to this central theme in the ministry of Jesus. That is, a ministry on behalf of those at the margins, those who are suffering, those who are poor.

There are early stirrings of the importance of that notion in some of the writings that Dietrich Bonhoeffer was engaged in toward the very end of his life in the 1940s in Nazi Germany. Bonhoeffer was hanged by the Nazis in April of 1945 for his involvement in the conspiracy against Hitler in the July 1944 attempt on Hitler's life. And Bonhoeffer was thinking and writing shortly before he went to prison, and while he was in prison, about theology for those on the margins, those who suffer for a just cause. That was really one of the first stirrings.

Liberation theology really developed in Latin America where you have the vast disproportion of wealth: where the distribution of wealth and of property and of land has kept the peasant population in many of those countries radically poor. And it was in that context that—and particularly first in the Roman

Catholic Church—people working in local communities rediscovered and reappropriated that Gospel message of ministry on behalf of the poor, and they saw the notion of the poor not just as a spiritual concept, but as an economic one as well. So they structured both theological thinking and programs to enable people, to empower people, to change that status. They were involved in agrarian programs for agrarian reform, they were involved in political activity, they invoked the message of the prophets of Hebrew scripture, the prophetic denunciation of the misuse of power and the abuse of the poor, which is a theme that runs all through the history of Israel and the message of the Hebrew scripture. It has now become a theological movement and many people in North America have been influenced by it as well. It is, and will be, a continuing part of the kind of theological training that students who attend seminaries and divinity schools in the United States and Canada will continue to get. Particularly for people who find themselves in, let's say, urban situations where their ministry is precisely to those persons. Liberation theology is, I'm convinced, an appropriate way of thinking about Christian ministry in the Gospel to those persons. I think we still have more work to do, particularly at the academic level, to fine-tune some of those themes, and to apply them to a North American situation . . . there are vast disproportionate pockets of wealth and poverty in our own nation so I think some of the analysis can apply quite easily. But I think there is also a much greater middle class in the United States and exactly how these liberation themes will apply, and ought to apply on behalf of those persons I think is a more complicated issue. We have to take seriously the particular political context within which most of our ministries take place. That is a liberal, democratic system . . . in contrast to a military dictatorship.

COSTA: *What kinds of skills is this new ministry going to require? What kinds of things can the Divinity School give to people preparing for this work that they're doing? It's clearly a different role than the traditional ministry where people did sacramental work and weren't involved as much in the community as they seem to be today.*

THIEMANN: I think that's the biggest challenge, but also the most exciting thing about being in theological education at this moment in our history. I think it should be emphasized that for many people who've been involved in congregational ministry, work on behalf of the poor has been a constant. It's not new. The way of thinking about it theologically in terms of liberation theology categories is somewhat newer, but I think it would be a misunderstanding of the history of Christian activity all over the world if we didn't recognize that there has always been concern for, and work on behalf of, the poor. I think we now have a more sophisticated way of thinking about that work. What is different is preparing people in precisely the kind of professional world that I was describing in answer to your earlier question. . . . Preparing people to understand the way in which public policy, for example, is created in this kind of a society, to begin helping them to gain the skills to integrate the theological and ethical resources that they can get from the training we can give them, with the kind of policy-oriented experience they might bring to us.

Let me try to answer your question by talking a little bit about the kinds of students we're seeing coming to the Divinity School now. We see increasing numbers of students who represent that kind of restless young professional group I described in my earlier comments: people who have been trained professionally and who have become restless with the lack of preparation in dealing with moral issues. Many of them are religiously motivated and are now looking to theological education, not to give them the professional skills that they already have in law or public health or other fields, but to give them the theological and moral orientation that they can combine with those other skills.

Costa: *So these are more mature people who have had previous careers?*

Thiemann: Well, we do not call them second-career people. I'd like to talk about them as people who have always had a vocation to public or human service. They might have, in the first stage of their professional lives, thought of working that vocation out professionally in law or business or public health or the human services. They continue to have that same vocation and now they are looking to ministry, in many cases, as an alternative professional outlet for that single vocation. The reason I go to such lengths to make those distinctions is that these are not people who are uncertain about what they want to do. They know what they want to do. What they're looking for is the right professional setting to allow them to do it. And oftentimes, people who are trained in those non-theological professions find themselves not adequately prepared. The problem with traditional preparation for ministry is that we have often not done a good job of preparing them to be realistic about influencing the development of public policy. So I think the great challenge to our Divinity School is to go out and try to identify such people, to get the message out that Harvard is a good place for them to do this kind of integrative work, and to begin reshaping our own curricular efforts, and to bring in new faculty who will help them do that integration.

Costa: *Earlier you mentioned the kind of public life and public issues approach that you'd like the school to take. I have to bring up the question of the failed televangelists for a moment. There still seems to be lingering fallout from that. Has this affected any of your new students, this sort of fall from grace? Again, we're talking about the ethical issues.*

Thiemann: I don't think it's had a particularly major effect on the kind of student I've just been describing—and that's not to say that we don't have students who have commitment to evangelical communities, or even Pentecostal communities. We do. But I think our students, even those who come out of those communities, did not look primarily to the Jim and Tammy Bakkers or to the Jimmy Swaggarts as the role models for their ministry. And I think it's important, as the media gives such attention to these dramatic cases, to remember that Pentecostal, evangelical and even fundamentalist communities continue to play an important and positive role in many ways in our culture, and that we shouldn't dismiss the whole movement because of these rather dramatic public failures. So our students are quite sophisticated when it comes to both understanding their own religious motivations and in the models they set for themselves in terms of their own ministry. I don't think they've really been much affected by it, but I think that it is an opportunity for religious communities across the board—no matter how we would identify them or try to put them in compartments—to recognize the complicated challenge that faces a religious community and individuals in it when one begins to participate in the power and the glamour and the wealth that characterizes our society. In some ways, I think we can see the failure of the televangelists as temptations that await any religious community that begins to accumulate for itself a certain degree of power and influence. . . . I am hoping that it will serve as a good warning to us all about the difficulties and the challenges that lie in wait for those who—as I want us to—become more involved in the public sphere. That's one of the things to be learned by all of us, by the failure of the televangelists.

COSTA: *It may be apocryphal, but there used to be a concept of religious leaders who had a 'calling to God.' They had a call to serve. Do you see this in some of your people, or in your own life? Was there a time when you were walking the road to Damascus when you had a revelation, a calling that persuaded you to become a minister and serve?*

THIEMANN: It's interesting that you understand the calling to somehow be . . . a specific event. You used the term 'revelation' as a virtual equivalent of it. The word 'calling,' in its Latin form, is *vocatio*, and my talk about vocation earlier in our conversation is, for me, the best way to understand the calling. That is, I have a particular vocation that I seek to work out in my life in a variety of ways. I also talk about my vocation to ministries. These are notions that are very comfortable to me. But they're not about dramatic changes in my life. They're not about walking down the road to Damascus and then suddenly moving down some other road in another way. For me, it has been somewhat of a constant in my life, even as it has had various ways of working itself out. Vocation can be understood very broadly, and I think there are many people who would be comfortable with—particularly in the divinity-school context—thinking of themselves as being called to a vocation of ministry. That includes a calling to a sense of social responsibility, a calling to care and empowerment on behalf of those who are on the margins.

COSTA: *Soon we're going to have a new president. If there were a cabinet level post for spirituality or religion, what would you tell him? What would you advise him as a new era begins?*

THIEMANN: It's important to remember that the role of 'prophet' in Israelite religion was not an official governmental role, so the mistake would be to take the Cabinet post at all. Independence and freedom is one thing that people who seek to have something to say to government ought to value. Obviously there's no one thing that I could define as the message that I think ought to be delivered to any president. But if it were possible for us to once again begin thinking in a serious fashion about questions like justice, and their relationship in the development of public policy, I think there is no more important issue.

I was struck, again, in hearing the recent presidential debates, that while there was a great deal of talk about values, there was virtually no specification of those values, or the relationship between those values and questions of justice.

There is a real danger right now that the language of value is being used for its rhetorical effects without being linked to any particular policy initiative that will give us an idea of what values we're talking about. Because right now it's just a very general appeal to 'American values.' So what my hope is both for the remainder of this campaign and certainly for any future office of the president is that we might be much more concrete, honest, and straightforward about what values we think we do want to represent as a people, and more importantly, how those values are to be worked out in the development of public policy. A year ago in October, the Divinity School sponsored a conference on the black church's responsibility to the underclass, and the keynote speaker for the conference that started it off on a Saturday morning was Congressman William Gray from Philadelphia who is pastor of the Bright Hope Baptist Church in Philadelphia. He's also the chairman of the House Budget Committee and in his address he exemplified what I think is lacking in the current presidential debate and discussions. He talked about the issue of the balancing of the budget as one of the most important economic issues that we have to face, but that if we do not raise it as a question of justice, we will not be raising the issue at all; we will, in fact, be avoiding it. That's the kind of conversation we need more of and we need places in our culture that encourage serious conversation about values and about the policy which will carry those values in our culture and society. It's a fairly long answer to the one thing you asked me to reflect on, but I think there's no more important issue for our public life than that one.

A conversation with

Dr. J. Allan Hobson

Dr. J. Allan Hobson is professor of psychiatry. His work focuses on neurophysiology, the mind, and behavior. His publications include The Dreaming Brain *(Basic Books) and* Sleep *(Scientific American Library).*

COSTA: *Ever since Ovid's time, when he wrote about falling into the arms of the god of sleep, Morpheus, we've been reading about the restorative powers of sleep as well as the nightmare of not getting enough sleep. When I'm driving to work after a less-than-good night I think of rewriting that credit card commercial to say something like, 'Sleep—don't leave home without it.' You've just written a book appropriately entitled* Sleep. *In it you define the various stages in the sleep cycle. Could you define the stages?*

HOBSON: During sleep, the brain and all of the body undergoes a regular, sequential change in state throughout the night. The clock in the brain that controls this process times it at about 90 to 100 minutes. There is a cycle.

Sleep is composed of a set of 90-minute segments. Each of those segments consists of an alternation between what is called non-REM, or slow-wave sleep, to indicate the fact that there are fewer or no eye movements recordable and that the EEG activity shows slow waves, high-voltage activity. That phase of sleep is associated with less dramatic mental activity. But still mental activity persists. People have thought-like experiences but they tend to be fairly nonprogressive. You don't get anywhere. You're mulling over something that bothered you during the day.

But then after 40 or 50 minutes the whole process shifts and the brain looks like you are going to wake up. The EEG becomes activated, and then, lo and behold, appear these incredible eye movements, although the eyes are closed and are not responsive to visual stimuli. The movements are, in fact, the readout of activation of motor centers in the brain.

COSTA: *What are these rapid eye movements? Are they one's eyes moving rapidly under the closed lids?*

HOBSON: Yes, you can see them as movements of the lid. In babies, especially, these movements are very easy to observe because they have a lot more of it than adults.

You can observe it in pets. You can observe it in cats and dogs very easily. In fact, in dogs you can see the paw movements which, most people assume, indicate that the dog is dreaming of chasing rabbits.

In any case, in our sleep this rapid-eye-movement or REM phase occurs as the second part of each of these 90-minute cycles and lasts from a few to many, many minutes. Later in the night, the REM periods may be 40 or 50 of the 90 minutes. If we awaken subjects from this phase of sleep, they report vivid dreams with a lot of visual activity and all the usual stuff that makes dreams so fascinating.

COSTA: *Many people think the rapid-eye-movement stage is an important one: if we don't experience that stage then somehow we'll feel more tired in the morning, or our mind hasn't had a healthy release of our thoughts. Is that off the mark?*

HOBSON: The sleep deprivation studies yield a fairly confusing picture, but one thing is clear and that is that sleep is crucial not only to health but to life.

Recent studies from the University of Chicago, using rats as subjects, have shown that deprivation of sleep generally is invariably fatal to these animals. You can achieve the same results by selectively depriving them of REM, but it takes longer. The point is that sleep is absolutely critical to psychological and physical well-being, and now it appears to be critical to sustaining life.

It's interesting that the functions that are deranged in deprivation are very fundamental ones. They have to do with energy regulation and temperature regulation.

It's still impossible to clearly discriminate between the different effects of depriving animals or humans of REM versus non-REM sleep. That doesn't mean that a functional differentiation isn't there, but the deprivation studies haven't brought it out yet. It seems reasonable to assume that REM sleep may have more critically to do with cerebral functioning, with higher brain functioning, with thinking, and with attention than the rest of sleep. I think we're on the threshold of a new set of studies that will ask those questions in a more penetrating way. I would predict that we will find that REM sleep is clearly in the service of higher brain functioning.

COSTA: *Why is it that as people grow older they not only get less sleep but actually start to omit a deep-sleep stage?*

HOBSON: The bad news about sleep is that like many other bodily functions it peaks at about age 25 to 30 and begins a prolonged downhill course at that point. We lose most of the deepest stage of non-REM sleep, called stage four, between the ages of 30 and 40. The rest of the process is a kind of continuous downhill process and the easiest way for us to explain that now is that this tracks the trajectory of the general decay of the brain.

Unfortunately we lose neurons at the rate of about 50,000 a day, spontaneously. Now that sounds like a lot but if you've got a hundred billion in there and you do the multiplication, you lose about 3 or 4 percent normally over a lifetime.

We really aren't exactly sure what the process is that results in the decay of sleep. Surely it will turn out to have to do with changes in the brain.

COSTA: *We've all had older relatives who slept less and less as they grew older but who still seemed to function at a high level. My wife's grandmother used to get up in her eighties at 4 a.m. and do her finest needlepoint and crewel.*

HOBSON: In another sense you can't necessarily conclude that shortening of sleep will lead to detrimental results. I think it's important to point out that at any age there are long and short sleepers. There is a vast distribution of sleep-need across people. It's sort of silly to assume that something like sleep would differ from something like height and weight.

But our behavior is based on the premise that everyone needs eight hours of sleep a night. That is not the case. There are highly productive, even enviably productive people who sleep only four hours. Other people who are in no way impaired need 10.

Whether or not the amount of sleep shortens is not really the point. The point is whether you feel like you haven't gotten enough. In monitoring our sleep, that has to be the critical criteria.

COSTA: *As a professor of psychiatry do you deal with people who ask, 'Do I have a sleep disorder?' What are the hallmarks of a sleep disorder? Is it having trouble getting to sleep, or is it awakening during the night?*

HOBSON: Most of the sleep disorders are of too little sleep. These are the ones we all know. It's normal to have 'white nights,' nights in which you can't sleep. They can be either difficulty falling asleep or difficulty maintaining sleep. The pattern that is associated with stress and anxiety is primarily sleep-onset insomnia. The pattern that is associated with depression and may warrant more serious consideration is early morning awakening. Both are unwelcome and both are now fairly well understood physiologically. We can understand why these things happen.

What we can't do yet is treat them in a physiological way. That's too bad. All of the drugs that are used to treat insomnia are not physiological and have problems associated with them. We know that exercise helps sleep. We know that relaxation training helps sleep. One of the things that I emphasize in the book is that physiology at least teaches us that there are natural ways that we can go about reducing the probability of losing sleep and suffering from the loss.

COSTA: *Folk medicine advises us to have a warm glass of milk before retiring to promote sleep or to take a hot bath or to count sheep or to listen to white noise—those high-tech machines that generate sounds like the surf. What do you recommend for people who can't get to sleep?*

HOBSON: All of those approaches are not irrational; they make some sense. I think relaxation is a critical aspect of falling asleep. [It's important to do what] you can to increase your chances of relaxing your brain. That's what the counting sheep thing does—it occupies the brain circuits with information that is trivial. It therefore replaces the obsessive concerns of the day.

COSTA: *Although mathematicians probably shouldn't count sheep.*

HOBSON: I had a patient who controlled her hallucinations by counting. You can substitute for the pathological, or unwanted, process a different process that isn't negative. That's what counting sheep does.

Now, relaxing the muscles is just as important, so you work on the somatic musculature and the muscles of your body by systematically concentrating on them and letting the tension flow out of them. The reason that that helps is that the brain is responding to stimuli not only coming from the parts of it that deal with thinking, but the parts of it that deal with maintaining muscle tone. They both converge in this interesting part of the brain called the brainstem, where the sleep centers reside and if they're being bombarded by excitatory stimuli from above and below, they just can't turn off. You can't go to sleep.

Warm milk, I'm not so sure about. It probably produces a so-called placebo result, but placebo results are very powerful. People shouldn't discount them. To say that warm milk probably does not promote sleep via some chemical means doesn't mean it isn't useful. If you've got something that works for you, stick with it. Especially if it's harmless.

COSTA: *In your book you also did a lot of research about circadian rhythms. You studied people who were deprived of a sense of time by not having clocks to look at and found out that they were not sleeping well. We do need some cues, some visual cues and light cues. Can you say more about that?*

HOBSON: The sleep cycle we talked about earlier, the non-REM cycle, is itself contained within the trough of a much larger wave which is called the circadian rhythm. 'Circa' means about, 'dia' means a day. This rhythm is about 24 hours long and, interestingly, not precisely 24 hours. The brain has another clock which times this rhythm and it is in turn synchronized or set each day in humans by social cues, by clocks, by alarm clocks. In most other animals it is either lights-on or lights-off which triggers the cycle, and that makes sense. That enables the internal rhythm to come into synchrony with the varying day length.

You have to change your sleep pattern over the year. Many people notice that their sleep gets either better or worse especially at the times of the year when day length is changing dramatically. That is a time when people will typically tell you that they feel as if they aren't getting enough and they could sleep for 12 hours or they can't get to sleep or the sun's coming up too soon and is waking them up.

These are ways, then, in which the brain coordinates its own rhythms with those of the cosmos, with the availability of light and temperature.

COSTA: *There have been many things written about jet lag. What causes jet lag and what do you recommend to fight it?*

HOBSON: Jet lag, properly speaking, is the effect of importing your brain clock across time zones such that it is out of synchrony with local time. This is a clock that can't be reset like your digital alarm. This is a wet clock. It takes several days for the chemical processes that regulate the clock to come into synchrony with a new local time.

Many of the eastbound flyers, that is, those on flights going from Boston to Europe, are not so much plagued by jet lag as they are by sleep deprivation. That is an important distinction to make. When you go to Europe, you only make a six-hour time adjustment. That can fairly easily be made within a day or two. What you can't do is enjoy your first day in Europe, not because of jet lag, but because you really haven't gotten enough sleep on the airplane.

The most effective way to combat that problem is to have your dinner before you get on that plane, refuse the dinner on the plane, get up earlier that day so you can be tired when you get on the plane and be able to use the available seven hours for sleep. Most people get fewer than three. So that effect is mainly sleep deprivation.

It's a horrible feeling on your first day in Europe when you're just absolutely bombed. Usually, if it's one of 10 days, it's a fairly valuable day.

COSTA: *Let's get the Freudians angry with you. Talk about your theory that dreams are not what Freud said they were; they are not unconscious wishes, but rather, I think you wrote in your book, simply transparent, automatically generated brain data.*

HOBSON: It's fun to twist the tiger's tail, but let's back off just a bit and say that whether dreams contain wishes and whether those wishes are or not unconscious isn't so much the issue. I think my dreams contain lots of wishes, some of them less clearly evident to me in my daytime life as in my dream life, so there is some part of the Freudian story that I think is correct.

What's not correct, in my opinion, is the real center of his theory, which was that these unconscious wishes could not be admitted into consciousness or they would wake us up and therefore they had to be decoded and translated via what he called the 'dreamwork' into bizarre images. That's his way of explaining the bizarreness of dreams—why you have characters that are combined, why scenes change, and all this wonderful stuff that really makes dreams so entertaining.

That is the part of the theory that I think he has wrong, not so much as to whether there are wishes in there. I don't think wishes cause dreams. I think dreams are caused by brain activation in sleep, but the content of dreams can be wishful. What we differ with Freud most emphatically on is this issue of how the bizarreness arises. We think it's simply a direct readout of the organic state of the brain. The brain is operating differently. It's not like waking. It may look *electrically* like waking if you recall what we said about the EEG. The EEG is activated just as it is in waking. But the chemistry of the brain is completely different. It's deprived of external inputs and it operates actually much more similarly to the brain of patients with organic mental illness than with any of the so-called functional illnesses . . .

COSTA: *So that is why we have crazy dreams?*

HOBSON: The brain is essentially *normally* impaired during sleep and we think this impairment is probably accruing some benefit. It's a kind of downtime in which certain neuronal systems that are essential to attention, learning, and memory are turned off, and that is why the dreams are so wacky. It's really as simple and as interesting as that.

You've got the visual hallucinations, you've got this sort of strange confabulatory story-building quality, you've got lots of cognitive disturbances, and you have a very poor memory. I think that is crucial to understanding this. You've got two hours a night of dreaming of which I dare say even the best of us recalls less than 1 percent. You've got a complete amnesia and here Freud attributed this to repression: There is an active mechanism by which this stuff was stuffed back down under the rug of the unconscious. I think not. I think it's a simple amnesia of the same kind that a patient with Alzheimer's would have. We wouldn't accuse our grandmother of repressing her memories. She just may not have them. I think that's the case with dreamers as well.

COSTA: *What about some of the folklore that we hear, such as that few people dream in color. Is that true?*

HOBSON: All dream reports that come from home-based journals or laboratory journals that are greater than five lines in length have color descriptives in them. The most likely explanation of the myth that dreams occur in black and white is poor recall, because when recall is adequate enough, color is reported.

The use of the fuzzy-focus, faded shots in movie representations of dreams is another indication I think of the evanescence of dreams and the difficulty of capturing them, and not of their true quality.

COSTA: *Why do people report having the same recurring nightmare?*

HOBSON: I think that that bears on the issue of how dream plots or mental activity plots are chosen. There are a number of factors that obviously influence the choice of a plot. One is recency. Most dreams have got something from the recent past in them.

Another is persistent concern. I don't know what your recurrent dreams are like, but mine have to do with what I call incomplete arrangements. They have to do with missed buses, missed trains, not having my passport on me. This, in a sense, is a kind of persistent concern of mine. I'm a busy person, I travel a lot. I think recurrent dreams are not surprising given the ubiquity and persistence of concerns that we have.

Perhaps the most flagrant and striking examples are the so-called posttraumatic stress disorder dreams in which the individual actually relives the traumatic experience over and over again. Not surprising, since they've had very powerful, one-shot learning experiences. It completely changed their view of the world—in an unacceptable way. There is no way in which you can really work through trauma of the sort that Holocaust victims experienced or that Vietnam veterans experienced. I mean that stuff cannot be accommodated into a civilized frame of mind. It sits there like a kind of psychological abscess, draining forever. Those experiences have the same power to take over when plot selection is needed. You call for something that bothers you.

COSTA: *Not long ago there was a whole industry that wanted to do teaching subliminally, sleep-teaching so to speak. How effective is listening to tape recordings of foreign languages under your pillow at night?*

HOBSON: If it doesn't keep you awake, it probably won't hurt you. But it's certainly not the way to learn French. The way to learn French is to go to France.

I think it's a cultural phenomenon, interestingly enough. The two countries in the world that are most bent upon reducing the need for sleep are the two most competitive countries: the Soviet Union and the United States. In cultures that are less ambitious, less powerful, this isn't so much an issue. People regard sleep as natural, even welcome, in Latin countries. Even with their usual gusto for everything . . . they regard sleep as a pleasure.

We who are kind of mechanical, very controlling of nature, would like to get rid of [sleep]. Thomas Edison was, of course, the classic example. He prided himself on four hours sleep, he only did it under the stairs at Menlo Park, and Edison invented the lightbulb. He's a guy who destroyed the night! It's not surprising that all these things go together.

If only we could take advantage of less sleep. But, listen, the brain has been working these things out for billions of years in evolution. It's certainly not just wasted time.

What we sleep scientists have to do now is further specify the functions of sleep. That's the agenda of the next 10 or 20 years. It will be very exciting. I think we're going to find that far from being downtime or wasted time, the brain is doing very important things during this state.

A conversation with

Stephen Williams

*Stephen Williams is Peabody Professor of American Archaeology and
Ethnology and curator of North American Archaeology in the
Peabody Museum of Archaeology and Ethnology. His specialty is
the prehistory of the Mississippi Valley from the Ohio River to the
Gulf of Mexico.*

COSTA: *You teach a course here at Harvard called Fantastic Archaeology in
which you debunk certain claims, one of which for example is that exotic races
of superior astronauts landed here 450,000 years ago. As a starting point for
this topic debunking speculative claims, tell us about these alleged space trav-
elers whom their proponents call 'astronauts from the unseen 12th planet' and
how you got involved with debunking this claim.*

WILLIAMS: There is a worldwide society of people who believe in the
ancient astronauts, so it's not a minor phenomenon. It's part of a much larger
network of people who are deeply involved with trying to get what I call 'fantastic messages from the past.' As an archaeologist, this is of course what we
are looking for. We're trying to find out what the past was like.

What these people do, and particularly those who use extraterrestrials, is
suggest that there are things on Earth that we can't understand, the archaeologists or anyone else. These people like to reach out to some other area, in this
case another planet, and bring people in who have greater forces or greater
knowledge than anyone on Earth.

This was certainly given its greatest impetus by Erich von Däniken who nearly 20 years ago began writing about it in *Chariots of the Gods.*

COSTA: *But it's become such a popular mythology, and there are even some fairly well-educated laypersons who think, 'Well, maybe there is an explanation for some of these things that we can't explain.' I'm wondering why everyone seems to look heavenward for those explanations.*

WILLIAMS: The notion that there must be an explanation is a rational one: we all want to know what causes various things. But there is a sense that if the professionals say, 'We don't know,' or if they give a rather hedged answer, that isn't always satisfactory. So people will leap in and exercise what I call the 'uncertainty principle.' They're not satisfied with the first answer, so they want a real answer. Who did erect the stone monuments on Easter Island or who did really build the pyramids? *You don't think that the Egyptians really built the pyramids?* Von Däniken was one of the first to say 'there may have been forces from outer space that came in and helped the Egyptians with this task.'

COSTA: *As a scientist you have your work cut out for you trying to debunk all of this. These theorists and popularizers seem to get a lot of press. You have to compete with the Shirley MacLaines out there. What's the latest on 'channeling'?*

WILLIAMS: Channeling is a sense that one can get in contact with people who lived on this Earth at one time. You get in touch with these people via mediums or sometimes other individuals who are able to turn themselves into channels, or receptors, for these messages coming in and then they will give you this information.

One of the most famous psychics of the 1920s and '30s, Edgar Cayce, was in touch that way. He was called the 'sleeping prophet.' He went into a kind of trance and would get this information. He told us a lot about Atlantis, for example.

Shirley MacLaine has been in touch via friends of hers in Peru and elsewhere. When you look at what she is writing about it, it is just rehashed von Däniken. Many times, people who serve as mediums are thought to be not very well educated. But when you see what they're talking about, they're really telling you things that a number of other books have already said ahead of them. They're probably much better read than they want to admit.

COSTA: *Yet there are some physical phenomena that archaeological findings have not really seemed to explain fully, for example, Stonehenge.*

WILLIAMS: I would say that is the simplest one to explain. There is nothing very extraordinary about Stonehenge. There are megalithic monuments all over northern Europe and all over the British Isles, and Stonehenge happens to be the best known. It's nowhere near the biggest or in some ways the most elaborate, although it is indeed the most famous archaeological site in all of Britain today, no question about it.

It is a monument that is over 3,000 years old, closer to 4,000. It is complex, but it has been quite thoroughly excavated. We do understand its building stages. We understand where the materials came from and we can even give a very good answer as to how they did it.

COSTA: *Could you explain that?*

WILLIAMS: It was built over a period of about 1,500 years. Stonehenge was changed, renovated, reoriented at least three or four major times during this 1,500 year-period. There are two different kinds of stone. We know the sources for that material. One of them is very distant: the blue stones, way across in Wales.

COSTA: *How many miles would that be?*

WILLIAMS: Over 150 miles. In fact they probably put them on rafts and rafted them along the seacoast and then up some rivers and then finally over land. It looks to some people as if this were something that no one could do. Yet a group of Boy Scouts with rollers and some rope were able to pull these stones across the countryside very easily.

One of the reasons for this is that we don't understand what our own ancestors could do. We know we can't lift a rock of a ton or two tons or three tons but with the proper leverage and the proper knowledge these things can be moved and were moved all over the world.

COSTA: *Was Stonehenge meant to be used as an astronomical observing sight?*

WILLIAMS: Certainly on the very simplest level I think no one would question that it has certain basic astronomical alignments. Now whether one can take it further as Gerald Hawkins did and say that it's some sort of ancient computer and that it was able to forecast eclipses and the like, most scholars feel that that's going much beyond the evidence.

Yes, it was an alignment to the summer and winter solstices, and, again, there are plenty of other models around the world of similar kinds of alignment. No archaeologist is saying that these ancient people of 3,000 or 4,000 years ago didn't have very good heads on their shoulders, didn't understand mechanics, physics and some very basic astronomy. They did. There is no question about it.

COSTA: *But what you're not willing to say is that these megalithic structures were erected with extraterrestrial help.*

WILLIAMS: There is no need for extra help, any more than there is need for extra help in building the pyramids. We look at the pyramids and say, 'My god. No group of human beings could do it.' Yet we have done the basic time-motion studies of cutting rock with the tools that were very close to those that were used in ancient times and have figured out how long it would take.

Those studies suggest there is nothing impossible about completing the construction in the time given to do it.

Costa: *Since we're talking about megalithic structures, let's talk about the Maya constructions, which were gigantic. Also there are some huge structures in South America that can only be seen from high altitudes.*

Williams: The Nazca lines.

Costa: *Yes. Say something about those.*

Williams: First, let's take the Maya. The Maya were an extraordinary people. They are much later in time than most people realize, really beginning their ascent to civilization not much before the beginning of the Christian era, and culminating in the sixth, seventh and eighth centuries A.D. Yes, their structures are large, but again it's interesting to look at archaeologists in the 1920s. They projected a lot of time into those constructions and they made some very interesting, very egocentric comments. They made what they thought was the best analogy they could. [They just thought] 'they're like our own ancestors in Europe who spent so much time building the cathedrals. Isn't it wonderful? The Maya are like those people.' Well, nonsense. Number one, we've done time-motion studies to try to figure out how much time it really would take to cut this rock, and with better dating than we had in the 1920s, we know these structures were actually built quite quickly.

Again, there is nothing in the evidence to suggest that it's anything but a good Maya workman. It was not working every day for a hundred years either. Instead it was more like completing these constructions in six months or something like that.

Costa: *And some of these structures were religious.*

Williams: The Maya ones are all for the elite priests and priestly class. There is a strong force within the culture just as there was within our own heritage to build the cathedrals. They thought that this was an important thing to commit yourself to, and that's very understandable.

The Nazca lines are another thing. These are the great alignments of stone on the high plateaus in Peru. You have to ask why were they made. Indeed they are very nice to observe from a helicopter. Some archaeologists suggest that they may have had hot air balloons and that they went up and looked at it.

Actually, if one takes a worldwide perspective of human beings around the planet over the centuries and millennia, we have indeed done this a number of times. There are great figures on various hills in the British Isles for example. It's true that, again, the Nazca figures look as if they involved a tremendous amount of time. Actually, it's very easy to do. You just sweep parts of the rock away. It reveals a lighter color, move them along in lines, and pretty soon you have these figures. It is indeed an operation to lay out some of these things but, again, not beyond their capabilities and they tie closely into the Nazca people whose archaeological cultures occur around the time of Christ and shortly thereafter. We have no problem connecting it to them.

COSTA: *They are very large structures, some are in fact miles long, are they not?*

WILLIAMS: Some of the longest lines might be a mile or more, but the complex figures are really not as large as you might think. If you see them without a scale you blow them up on the landscape and think they're covering many, many city blocks. Many of them are not that huge, but they do have long lines. Interestingly enough, the alignment hypothesis that these had something to do with . . .

COSTA: . . . *landing zones* . . .

WILLIAMS: . . . Yes, or also with astronomy. Hawkins went from Stonehenge to the Nazca lines and conducted one of the good pieces of testing. That is what archaeologists or any scientist wants to do is to test that hypothesis. He looked at these alignments and he ran a whole bunch of these alignments through a computer and tried to align them with major planets or risings and he got a 'no' answer. There weren't any alignments.

COSTA: *No match.*

WILLIAMS: No match. That is the best answer I could give.

COSTA: *Even taking into consideration the time that they were built and looking back in time.*

WILLIAMS: Absolutely, that's one of the most important things. The skies today are not the way they were in the past. It's wonderful to see people in New England today say, 'My gosh, here is a structure and I see the sunlight coming through it today right at winter solstice.' Well, if the structure really is a 2,000- or 3,000- or 4,000-year-old building, the light wouldn't have done that at the purported time the structure was built.

COSTA: *I'm curious about some of the techniques of modern archaeology that supplanted some of the old carbon-dating techniques and how archaeology and paleoanthropologists have used the new techniques to obtain finer tuning of the dating.*

WILLIAMS: We didn't have carbon-14 until 1950 and before that there were only a few areas in which we had very precise, absolute dating techniques. We had relative dating—this was older than that, as we do in paleontology and the like—but we had no absolute dating.

No one, just because he puts on a white jacket and walks about a lab, is infallible. Not every carbon-14 date is correct. There are all sorts of reasons why they may not be correct.

Indeed anyone who pins the entire hypothesis on one carbon-14 date is almost certainly doomed for disaster, unless you have a suite of dates, half a dozen to 10, run by different labs. Take a sample, break it in half, have one lab run one, one the other. The labs aren't all perfect. Some of them have been very imperfect as a matter of fact. It is not unusual for people to withdraw dates. Now the withdrawal of the date will appear in some scientific journal, but it won't get into the popular literature.

Carbon-14 goes back to only about 50,000 years, when stretched. The other major dating system, the one that has allowed us to date the earliest evidence of humankind on this planet going back into the 2-million to 3-million year range, is potassium-argon dating, which uses materials from volcanic eruptions. This is what allowed Louis Leakey to date some of his finds and to actually extend humankind quite extensively to an older date at the time, this being the late 1960s and early '70s. Those are the two dating systems. They can go back 2- million or 3-million or 4-million or 5-million years.

Potassium-argon can't come within the last 200,000 years. So we've got a real gap. We've got carbon-14 back to 50,000 and then we have a gap to another 200,000. There is a rather interesting event that occurs—at least according to present thinking—right in the middle of that gap, and that is the origin of homo sapiens.

COSTA: *Isn't there also a method that archaeologists use when an artifact is found, to place* in situ *with the culture, to find some other cultural reference with it?*

WILLIAMS: We call that archaeological context. That is indeed the most important thing. I'm sure many people are familiar with the Piltdown Man fraud [human remains found in Sussex, England, that were the subject of speculation], when what was thought to be a very early specimen of human-kind turned out to be nothing but a confection made up of a human skull, which turned out to be from the 13th century A.D., and a not-too-old orangu-tan jaw that had been put together.

Everyone looked just at the evidence, just at the skull and at the jaw and argued and argued about that. But most people don't realize there were a lot of things said to have been found with it. It was the darndest melange of mate-rial you could have ever imagined. There were all sorts of fossils. There were even some purported artifacts. No one looked at those very carefully and everyone knew they'd been found, it's in their reports, but everyone just focused on the skulls. They did not look at what the skull was purportedly found with. It was ridiculous. There wasn't another fossil assemblage like that in the world. In fact, it was a totally made up one. One of the fossils, it turns out, was found to have come up from the Mediterranean. If one had looked carefully at these other things that were with it, one could have had the blind-ers removed from one's eyes.

Remember, in all of this, one of the things that is most important is perception. We all think perception is so accurate. We know what happens to eyewitness accounts. People have been sent to jail and even to the electric chair on the basis of an eyewitness account which later turns out to be wrong. We also know how easy it is for the mind to affect perception.

This is what happened with Piltdown. The British scientists wanted a fossil skull. After all, the French and the Germans had it, why not us?

COSTA: *It was nationalism.*

WILLIAMS: Oh, yes. That's why the Kensington Rune Stone in Minnesota, my home state, is so important to so many people out there. It can't be declared a fraud. They won't allow that, even though the evidence is overwhelming.

COSTA: *You've written a very funny and interesting line about this. You said, 'Finding a Boston Celtics pennant beside a stone arrowhead does not mean that prehistoric Native Americans worshipped Larry Bird.'*

WILLIAMS: I was trying to put in a more straightforward way this whole message about context. If one is looking for a fossil man and finds it next to a crunched Coke can, one is quite sure that those two are not of the same date.

If, however, in a very careful excavation of a particular level on which one is digging one finds two things or three things or finds an undisturbed burial with these materials together, that is a context that is believable and that is what we build our data on.

COSTA: *Let's talk about paleoanthropology. Now with a lot of revisionist and quite controversial thinking about evolution by creationists and others, what do anthropologists say is our real ancestry, and did we evolve?*

WILLIAMS: As an archaeologist who has been to Olduvai Gorge and worshipped that shrine and has been where Richard Leakey is doing a lot of his work, I'm almost ready to back off that a little bit because I'm not a paleoanthropologist. One of the things I like to tell my students is if someone asks me a question that I don't know the answer to, I'm not ashamed to say I don't know it. I'll give you part of an answer.

The facts are that every piece of evidence we have at present allows us to look at the long history of our fossil ancestors over a period of 5 million or 6 million years. At Harvard we have people like my good friend and colleague David Pilbeam who is working in this much earlier period before any forms that any of us would want to call human existed. What Pilbeam likes to say . . . and I think quite correctly, is that the number of data points between 5 million years ago and today that we have from well-documented finds are so few that one can make up almost any scenario and it shouldn't surprise people to think that there are conflicting views even among well-trained scholars.

I wouldn't give you a simple answer. We think we can see homo sapiens— our own species—arriving sometime before 50,000 or 80,000 years ago, and sometime after 200,000 years ago. Where did this occur? Africa seems like a good place now, although there's new evidence that suggests there might be other sources for the first homo sapiens. What happened in the battle, as it's often thought of, between the resident Neanderthalers and the homo sapiens as they came in? There have been fictionalizations of that. It may not have actually been that way. Some forms of homo sapiens may have been around in some places and may have been there before the Neanderthalers. So we're still very much arguing about . . . the simple answer to the creationist questions. I keep up on that literature and I'm on mailing lists just because I feel I ought to know a little bit about it.

COSTA: *Is it going to be more difficult for archaeologists of the future to look back at our culture with all of our culture covered with asphalt and concrete? Nothing seems to be deposited too deep in our garbage heaps.*

WILLIAMS: There's a whole field, you can rest assured—I've been part of it, I teach a course on it—historic archaeology. I like to say that when I give my course on historic archaeology and am asked what is my timespan, I say this course stopped yesterday afternoon in terms of the garbage being deposited out there. Yes, we're looking at our own history a lot more carefully.

A *conversation with*

Alex Krieger

*Alex Krieger is adjunct professor of architecture and urban design, and
director of the Master of Urban Design and Master of Landscape
Architecture Design programs. Krieger, an AIA award recipient, is a
principal in the firm of Chan Krieger Levi, winner of eight national
design competitions. He consults with the Boston Civic Design Board
and the New England Holocaust Memorial.*

COSTA: *In your design primer for cities and towns you write, 'We now find
ourselves planning communities in which it is necessary to own a car to travel
to the store, work, and neighborhood institutions. Children and the elderly are
particularly victims of this car dependence, needing to be chauffeured about
for even the simplest of their needs. Ironically the car, which promises so
much freedom and choice, has diminished the accessibility and choices available within town environments.'*

KRIEGER: It's deeply ingrained in our culture. What will change it? I think
what will change it is an increase in gasoline costs; this is something that is
very topical. The cost of owning a car and maintaining a car. But I wish I had
panacea for this, which I don't. I think we have to keep making more and
more people aware of the trade-offs involved. If a car costs you $5,000 or
$6,000 to maintain annually—which people don't even always assess—people
might think about a larger mortgage in a suburban or a more urban neighborhood closer to a set of facilities, where you would need the car less. People
are not yet able to make such trade-offs but I think they're starting to.

COSTA: *But the car is so much a part of our culture and for many represents a symbol of our freedom.*

KRIEGER: That's where I think the planning community has been fighting the wrong battle for the last 20 or 30 years or so, because this is not news: the dominance of the automobile culture and the constraints of suburbanization as opposed to its benefits. That's old news. People like Lewis Mumford were battling against the suburbs in the '30s and '40s and '50s, even though people like Mumford themselves lived in a somewhat suburban or exurban environment.

Mumford said we have to eliminate the car. I think that has been foolhardy. What we have to do is make peace with the car. Planning theory has said, 'There will be no cars, we will all go back to living in towns, and so forth.' I think that's too utopian. And people haven't listened. People have built suburbs whereas we should have been building *better* suburbs, to design the suburbs as if they were really small towns, which they are, as opposed to something else. For many years they were simply something else, something untown-like. I think now among the more enlightened developers and planners, they are being designed as small towns, which therefore leads to more concentration of activities. Segregation of activities is the principal thing that requires us to use cars all the time.

COSTA: *I'd like to talk about two things, first the concept of the shopping mall and, secondly, strip development. Shopping malls are now taking the place of main streets across America. The elderly, teenagers, and couples all walk the mall, and for many of them shopping is a secondary activity. The primary activity is a social one. Will this continue—the malling of America, so to speak?*

KRIEGER: There's a wonderful cartoon, which I believe we even reproduced in the primer, which has a scene that is called 'The spike is driven to connect all the malls in America.' We may be closer to that time than we would like to believe. I think that the success of malls has to do with the abysmal state of our main streets and town centers. You're absolutely right: people go [to malls] because other parts of our town environments and town centers are so divorced of social activities and interaction that people flock to the suburbs. I think that will continue. I think it's still increasing as people are being introduced to the shopping mall.

However, in places like Boston or Cambridge or Washington, D.C., in places that have now lived with malls for 20 or 30 years, we are starting to see a difference. We're starting to see that [the mall] seems to be thought of as ordinary, and an alternative to it seems to be better. Like going back into a small town, or like Boston's own Quincy Market, which is a mall in every sense of the term, except that it's not enclosed and it's within the city rather than on the outskirts of the city.

Everything is subject to a certain fashion, including town planning and settlement patterns and so forth. The mall was a great idea because we had been negligent about our town centers for a longer period of time than since the rise of the mall, so it seemed like a great idea to build such malls, economically. And, in a way, socially, although that was not always the foremost motivation on the part of those who built them. But in cities or suburbs where malls have become commonplace you're now starting to see less of an intrigue with them and an intrigue for something else and that something else hopefully—and I believe this—is a return to a more time-honored way of behaving in common places and social places along streets.

COSTA: *The thing about malls is that they have the appearance of being a small town on a main street except, as you point out, they are enclosed. You don't get a feeling of oneness with the environment and you don't know the people the way you do on your main street. The other people in the malls are strangers.*

KRIEGER: There's a slightly even more insidious aspect that they have, which is not talked about very much, and that is that they're ultimately private. There are people in green suits there who question you [if you] misbehave. Also, have you ever seen a panhandler at Quincy Market? Not really, and yet if I were a panhandler, where would I go? Where the most people are—and people with means. But, clearly, somebody at Quincy Market shoos them away.

In a mall [there's a] programmed social life. Many malls are going to some length to program in concerts and circuses and incorporate activities and so forth. Yet it's always on the terms of someone—an institution to which we do not have direct access. It's not like the mayor. It's some developer with a lock on the door of the mall. I think that's an issue that's tougher to get at, but it's more significant than the fact that malls are full of strangers, because malls are probably not more full of strangers than a main street.

COSTA: *Is this so-called privatization of land and ownership of larger and larger parts of the landscape leading to a disintegration of the community? What can be done to stop privatization and yet allow development to continue, which seems to be necessary?*

KRIEGER: Part of it has to do with overcoming the belief that bigger is better and that contemporary economies require larger concentration of capital, otherwise it's not economically feasible to develop and build and so forth. Some of this may be true, some of it is kind of common knowledge right now. I think that what has to happen—and maybe a downturn in the economy is a good way [to learn this]—is the realization that people can build smaller things and still make money. People don't have to garner 50 acres to build a mall. They can do well by developing smaller things or communities instead of allowing large-scale land ownerships to be assembled. . . .

There is no panacea in this, but part of it has to do with starting to believe that one doesn't have to always build at a larger scale. That's just the way that we've become accustomed to doing things in this country. One doesn't have to always think in large terms: large office buildings, large shopping centers and so forth. For a long time, office buildings were thought to need to be as big as they are because developers had a formula that you need so many square feet per floor to accommodate uses. We have conventional wisdom—some of which is useful, a lot of it is simply not so useful. Among the most conventional wisdom that has to dissipate is the belief that we can only deal with things at a large scale, which produces things like shopping malls, rather than streets of, say, a dozen stores.

COSTA: *Let's get to the development of the strip culture. One can go all the way from Cambridge to San Francisco and see this nonintegration of service stations, fast food places, you-name-it. Why does that kind of chaotic development continue to exist—because it's easy?*

KRIEGER: It's easy, and I think some people find it appealing. It still is probably the best way to capture an audience, if you believe that the audience is in a car. A century from now, wherever we are, we're not going to look at such strip developments purely with critical eyes. They will be associated with our culture and will be believed to embody our culture to some extent. We have already seen novels written about it and movies made about it that tend to romanticize it.

I think we need to find ways at a regional scale to create pauses within such strips. Towns ought to designate some areas in which this may happen, but other areas in which this cannot happen, rather than having it be somewhat ubiquitous. So my own sense is not to come out in opposition of it, to say it's just 'bad.' We've been saying this for half a century and the rest of the citizens in this country are saying, 'Big deal, we still enjoy it because it serves our interests in some way.' I would like us to say, 'Here's how it can be better, here's how it can be more attractive, here's how it can be more efficient' without necessarily evoking a revolution.

COSTA: *There may not be any room left to develop along the ways you recommend. For example, you say that with all these cars the best thing is to hide parking areas behind buildings or place them underground or build a garage for cars, and in most instances none of those options are available simply because there is no space left to put these cars. What do you say to that?*

KRIEGER: I say 'bunk.' For one thing, I think because we love our cars—and we have been aware of the car being both an asset and a problem for many years—there's another bit of conventional wisdom that doesn't really hold: that there is not enough parking. I think that there's a lot of parking. If you fly over a metropolitan area all you see is half-filled parking lots. You hardly ever see full parking lots.

One of the ways in which we have provided for parking in a very inefficient way is by legislating that each user provides a set of spaces for its own use, without worrying about whether the neighbor might have more or less [capacity for access]. So, as a result—to return to the strip—each little HoJo's and the other stores has its own parking lot, each one is half-full, and yet it is occasionally easier to walk from the HoJo's parking lot to, say, McDonald's. It's not any more distant than from the farthest recesses of the parking lot at McDonald's. We never think of it that way. There are usually some barriers like hedges or other things and we simply don't think that way in terms of planning.

I don't think it's so much a lack of parking space that afflicts us. Only in some instances, like the day before Christmas, it certainly is. I think mostly it's an inefficient use of parking spaces. A parking space should be like the MBTA. I think that it's a civic responsibility, something that is shared or communal, rather like a sidewalk. You don't think of a sidewalk as belonging to the building that it faces, though you hope the people in the building will sweep it periodically.

COSTA: *But even sidewalks are casualties these days. A lot of developers don't even put them in because they think people are arriving by car.*

KRIEGER: I'm trying to bring back into the foreground all the things that cars tend to displace, like storefronts, sidewalks, benches, entrances and so forth, not to mention more gracious spaces like yards and lawns and so forth. It's a matter of allowing these things to get back into the foreground and let the background—the serving mechanism, the car—recede into the background.

In terms of whether developers [want] sidewalks or not: developers will do almost anything to get their projects built and they're as fashion-conscious, even more so, than the population at large. They will do exactly what the last successful developer did. And if the last successful developer put sidewalks in or was forced to put sidewalks in by the municipality, the next developer surely will as well. So that's part of the real revolution that I believe ought to take place, which you have not asked me about yet, which is municipal zoning ordinances.

COSTA: *There's a lot of talk in the Northeast about linking new development to better parking and making developers provide low-income housing options, all kinds of things. Could you tell us about the zoning possibilities?*

KRIEGER: What you refer to as linkage is among the most creative forms of zoning that has come about in the past couple of years. It's somewhat dependent upon a healthy economy. It's dependent upon an economy where there are many people who want to develop in an area and therefore the municipality is able to exert some pressure or extract some benefit from the developer by asking or mandating that they do other things for the public welfare. So while linkage is terrific, it's somewhat dependent upon there being a demand for development. It works a little bit less well when no one comes knocking on your door. If no one comes knocking on your door you can't so easily get them to do things beyond what they wish to do.

When I say zoning, I am referring to the conventional zoning ordinance that governs most towns and suburban areas. In that zoning ordinance, it is never [made explicit] but in a ghostly fashion you can see written into that zoning ordinance precisely the kind of environment that we have been building. Most zoning ordinances have stringent regulations about mixing use, most zoning ordinances favor large parking lots in the belief that we need them, most zoning ordinances favor broader streets because we believe that the more lanes you have the easier traffic will flow—that is not always the case either. Most zoning ordinances were developed in the '20s and '30s and based upon an environment that no longer really exists and yet they have not adapted themselves. To make a caricature of it, what governs most zoning ordinances is the fear of the tannery moving next door to you. But there are fewer tanneries right now.

The problem is not so much segregation. That may have been the problem towards the end of the 19th century or the beginning of the 20th century when noxious factories and other things required a mechanism by which residential uses and family life [were afforded] some separation from other sectors of society. I think that's less the case now, and I think that the zoning ordinances have not yet become cognizant of our change of life. I actually blame developers less these days or citizens fleeing the suburbs or architectural teachers like myself. I blame the zoning ordinances because they're based upon a no longer pertinent model of habitation, which is the idealized suburban model of houses here, places of employment here, places of recreation there. I believe that in the next 10, 20, 30 years you will see a great deal of change . . . to move us away from the kind of thinking that we've had about a segregated society.

COSTA: *Isn't it also a matter of scale? I'm thinking of the well thought-out and well-received redevelopment of downtown Boston and Baltimore. If you have these megalithic projects—which require funds that would daunt a Pharaoh—you can make real change and revitalize the core of an entire city. But in a smaller town situation, away from these huge urban centers, you don't have enough funding to do the kind of changes that are necessary, so the small-town main street continues to be left abandoned.*

KRIEGER: American culture has had a love/hate relationship with the town. You can evoke novelists and romanticizers of small-town virtues and you also can evoke Sinclair Lewis and *Main Street* and the kind of fear, boredom, and dislike of small-town mores and values. It's not as if we have always supported small towns, but somehow we don't have the means by which to maintain them. Oftentimes in our history we tended to reject that as a way of a life in favor of the big city or, say, during this century, in favor of something on the outskirts of the city. I think most zoning ordinances right now don't allow you to build—literally, I'm not exaggerating—the kinds of things that I'm talking about or the kinds of things that some people value. I want a nucleated form of community. It's not funding. Of course, funding is a problem, of course resources are scarce, but it's not just that. It's a confidence in doing it in a particular way and making sure that your land-use legislation still allows it to be done that way.

COSTA: *Recently you and your group have done two planned communities, one in Maryland and the other on Cape Cod.*

KRIEGER: They're in the planning phases. They're not really there yet.

COSTA: *How do these planned towns represent what you're saying? Did you have to go through variances for land use?*

KRIEGER: Some of the most innovative communities that are being built right now are being built by private developers rather than in towns, so that goes counter to the argument about avoiding large scale. The reason is that if you assemble a large enough piece of land, you can create a special zoning to govern that piece of land, which excuses you from some of the constraints of normal zoning in favor of some other constraints that are imposed upon you. So in both these cases, I wish I was working with towns more directly. Among people like myself—and, by the way, there are people who have been at this longer than I and who have worked with developers around the country to try to reform suburban building—all of us wish we could work more for towns as opposed to developers. It's actually tougher to work for towns because in towns you encounter the great complexities of many land owners and zoning ordinances and other constraints and requirements.

A conversation with

Seamus Heaney

Seamus Heaney is Boylston Professor of Rhetoric and Oratory, and, at Oxford, professor of poetry. A member of the Irish Academy of Arts and Letters, Heaney has received numerous awards and honors which attest to his status as one of the world's greatest poets. Among his many publications is Selected Poems 1966-1987 *(Farrar, Straus, Giroux).*

COSTA: *In Richmond Lattimore's beautiful translation of the* Illiad, *there are some lines about Odysseus that he wrote that have remained with me since I read them as a freshman 25 years ago in college. Lattimore wrote—and I'm paraphrasing—that Odysseus is not the strongest of the Greeks, nor is he the bravest or the wisest or the best orator. Rather, he uses a hundred percent of what he has, and therefore triumphs over all and survives. Is that what makes him so special as a Homeric hero? The reason I ask is because we're going to talk about your Sophocles play.*

HEANEY: I think that that is one definition of triumph and of fulfilling a destiny, to make use of everything you have. The sense of susceptibility, mixed with the sense of opportunism, and also the resource with words—I think that makes Odysseus extremely attractive to the artist in Homer. He has a bad reputation in some ways, because that political adeptness, which I think the Greeks rather valued, has been devalued a bit, and understandably, I suppose. Odysseus would represent a committed sense of service to the whole thing—the polis—and the sense that we have of political opportunism is rather more self-serving than that. There is some kind of disjunction between the

Greek notion of political service and the more demeaned reputation that politicians have in our own time.

COSTA: *In your play,* The Cure at Troy, *which was performed last year by the Field Day Theatre Company in Ireland, you have your own conception of the quintessential Greek hero. Tell us about it.*

HEANEY: Well, it's got three very different characters in it. I received that play from Sophocles, and I returned it to him, passing it through my own version of English. I regret very much that I don't have Greek. I did attend a school where the classics were taught, but in my first year there we had to choose between Greek and French. If you chose Greek, that signified your vocation for the priesthood, and if you chose French, it signified your readiness for 'the world," as it was still called in those days. So, I'm afraid I stumbled towards the world and French.

The play is *Philoctetes* and it is about the wounded hero, the wounded Greek whom the Greek force maroons on Lemnos Island, where he is abandoned for 10 years. He has 10 years in which to feel betrayed and to generate his resentment, and firm his resolve against the leadership. This leadership then discovers they need him: in order for Troy to be taken, Philoctetes will have to return of his own free will, with his magic bow, and join up with the force. So, the play begins when Odysseus, the great tactician, the man who is there to serve a cause, and Neoptolemus, the neophyte, the young warrior completely in thrall to warrior honor and completely the son of his heroic, open-faced, chivalric father, come to the island. What ensues is a kind of political debate. It's a debate in which personal morality and public morality are urged upon each other, and urged against each other. Neoptolemus says, 'You can't tell a lie.' Odysseus says, 'This isn't a lie. This is a larger truth. We must deceive this hero—we must deceive Philoctetes. Otherwise he won't come with us, back to Troy.' Neoptolemus says, 'I hate winning by telling lies. I prefer to tell the truth and have a collision.'

The play is resolved only by the appearance of the god. In the original, the god commands the wounded hero, Philoctetes, to return. And there, I made a change—I allowed the Chorus to speak for the hero at the end, to speak for Philoctetes, and to represent, to externalize what is going on in his mind.

COSTA: *I am reminded of* Antigone, *and, again, the wonderful Chorus. I'll paraphrase it, because I don't remember it exactly—the Chorus says, 'What a wonderful thing is man; he has tamed the earth, ensnared animals, and captured fish in nets; and is triumphant over all except death,' which is always a Greek theme. I was wondering if you might read the chorus that you wrote for your play.*

HEANEY: Happily. Actually, I added in a couple of choruses. This play was performed in Northern Ireland. It was written for the Field Day Theatre Company, which tours the country, north and south, for 10 weeks. I [felt that] a play about a person with a wound, who is resentful and refuses to yield up the wound, who hugs the wound, and hugs the resentment, and hugs the isolation, and hugs distrust, obviously a play like that has applications in a situation like Northern Ireland. There each side, Protestant or Catholic, feels itself in different contexts [to be] a minority, feels itself ill-done by, feels itself betrayed. The Unionists, especially since the Anglo-Irish Agreement in 1985, feel that England has betrayed them—not quite into the Republic—but has betrayed them into a situation where the Republic has some say over them. Of course, the Catholics feel immemorially betrayed and ill-done by in the Northern situation. So, what you have is the sense of identity getting tied up with the sense of betrayal, and the sense of fidelity and integrity getting tied up with the refusal to be healed. The dream is that you might loosen all that, that it might thaw. This play was written—I mean I translated it—just after the events of late 1989: the Berlin Wall, Czechoslovakia, Rumania, and so on, so there was a feeling of possibility in the air. So, this is the Chorus speaking about the possibilities of changes after the psyche has got hardened:

Human beings suffer,
They torture one another,
They get hurt and get hard.
No poem or play or song
Can fully right a wrong
Inflicted and endured.
The innocent in jails
Beat on their bars together.
A hunger-striker's father
Stands in the graveyard dumb.
The police widow in veils
Faints at the funeral home
History says, *Don't hope*
On this side of the grave.
But then, once in a lifetime
The longed-for tidal wave
Of justice can rise up
And hope and history rhyme.
So hope for a great sea-change
On the far side of revenge.
Believe that a further shore
Is reachable from here.
Believe in miracles
And cures and healing wells.
Call miracle self-healing:
The utter, self-revealing
Double-take of feeling.
If there's fire on the mountain

Or lightning and storm
And a god speaks from the sky
That means someone is hearing
The outcry and the birth-cry
Of new life at its term.

COSTA: *That's beautiful. That's the kind of lyrical chorus that only a poet could write—the fusion of poetry with drama.*

HEANEY: Well, I felt freer in this adaptation when I was moving in the choruses, because I was swimming the laps I was used to swimming. The formal line of the Chorus is a dance, after all, fundamentally. It was—in the beginning, it was the dance step returning upon itself. And, of course, the poetic line is the verse, which represents the turn, 'versus' meaning 'the turn.' The traditional stanzaic poem turns and returns upon itself, so that you are both opening and returning all the time. And I know where I am when I am writing verse like that. But I was very much a beginner in dealing with dialogue, and so on. I have to say, in all honesty, that there was a touch of classics homework about parts of the actual play. I was blessed with a study in Widener a couple of years ago, and I used to go in there, and it had the feeling of settling down to do the prep.

COSTA: *Homer and Sophocles are easily our most accomplished storytellers. Are the two forms linked; is a poem a story?*

HEANEY: More and more I am attracted to the story-poem, but is a story a poem? A poem—what is it? It's a symbolic retelling or a symbolic redoing or a symbolic enactment of things as we know them, things as they are. I like to think of Robert Frost's poem, 'Directive,' as being a kind of allegory of what's possible in the world of symbol, or the world of make-believe, the world of play. In that poem, somebody goes back to a typical old, New England farmstead, deserted. And the person discovers, first of all, what Frost calls, 'the playthings in the playhouse of the children.' 'Weep for what little things can make them glad,' he says. And then, just across the yard, there is the ruin of the house, which he calls 'the house in earnest.' But in the actual locus of the poem, and within the poem's world, the playthings, the children's playhouse, are as potent, and mark time, and mark history, every bit as much as the ruined house, which was the historical place, 'the house in earnest.' So I think that that says the story which is retold, which is made up, equals the story which was endured historically.

I don't think that poetry needs to be specifically story. Drama has to have some story. Poetry can be the outcry. It can be the equivalent of, 'Hah!' as well as storytelling. Obviously, Homer and epic poetry are a different matter. But we have got used to a poetry which does without story. It's just a different kind of representation. Even so, I find myself happier writing down tales now than I was, and wonder tales at that, miracle tales.

I recollect one evening in Belfast—this is kind of parable also, and I've always remembered it—in the early '60s, a summer evening, it was nine o'clock. Two men came into this cafe, where I was sitting. It was very still at that time of the evening. They had been to a prayer meeting, some kind of evangelical event, and they were working-class chaps from the Belfast ship-yard. But they were earnest fellows, and they sat down, and they had their tea, and one said to the other, 'What did you think of that?' and the other said, 'Well, it was all right,' he said. 'But the message, it was a bit soft,' he said. So, in the beginning, I would have thought tales of transformation, wonder, and miracle were a bit soft. But I've changed.

COSTA: *How do poetic phrases come to you? Do they just pop into your head while walking through the Yard or while looking out the window, or do they arrive somewhere deep in the occipital region of your brain, and are only pried out after hours of actual writing, or crafting a poem?*

HEANEY: Typically, there's an onset of possibility, which isn't usually, with me, in a phrase. It might originate in some off-center way, with a single word or an image or a memory. But, to tell you the truth, until that onset of possibility occurs, either momentarily, or over a set of days or weeks, I am as poetically inert as the next person. And I think that that is one of the fundamental truths about being a poet. It's easy to be a poet, it's easy to write—when you're writing. The test is in the in-between times. And different writers have different ways of dealing with their silence, or their dryness. There are those who operate industriously against it, who take the plow of translation, or the plow of doing adaptations of Greek plays, or whatever, and they stick that into the dry ground of their being, and they turn up something.

On the other hand, there is another discipline, a discipline of waiting. One thinks of Rilke waiting for it to happen to him in the castle. I tend to be of the risky waiting sort, and it's very panicky. The best time for me almost is the first weeks after I return to Ireland from Harvard in the summer. I've been coming here now for the last—well, I started in 1982—so for nine years. In Cambridge, my experience is of the engine getting overrun and overheating as I go through marking theses, and grading, and so on, and just the busy-ness of life here. But there is a sense of possibility and a sense of release and a sense of stepping into potential in the first couple of weeks at home. Typically I've got notions for poems then, and they open up, and then the ideal thing is that, like a chain smoker or a binge drinker, you light one off the other. And you can keep it going. The phrases, whatever they are, come in the process of sitting down and doing it. I'm not one who walks around with a quiver full of orphaned phrases, waiting for the family of the poem to adopt them.

COSTA: *You've reached a point in your career now that is very much like the point that, let's say, Ernest Hemingway reached as a novelist. That is, you're regarded as one of the best—if not the best—poets writing in the English language today. How does that celebrity status affect you, or pressure you?*

HEANEY: I respond to this question sometimes jocosely, but half in earnest, by saying, first of all, that everybody in Ireland is a celebrity. It's a small country, and the pressure to perform, and to masquerade as yourself, is there for every person, whether they're writers or not. A second thing I would say is that I felt from my first book, which was published by Faber & Faber, a strange kind of ahead-of-myselfness. My first poems were published when I sent them out. I sent them out first to the *Belfast Telegraph, Irish Times,* the *Kilkenny Magazine,* small magazines, then to the *New Statesman* in England, and after three of them appeared in the *New Statesman*—there were several rejections, but eventually they appeared—after three of them appeared, I had a letter from Faber & Faber, and that was more or less like receiving a letter from Elysium. I would never have sent my poems to Faber's, because on the back of Faber's books appeared the names T.S. Eliot, Wallace Stevens, James Joyce. And even though Eliot was alive at that time, and, I think, Stevens, they were still, to me, like figures from the Pantheon. They had the same force as names like Odysseus, or whatever.

So, I regarded myself as astonishingly visited by the wing of fortune and the brush of fame, even though it was not celebrity of any sort. And I also, there-fore, of course, experienced the wing of resentment among peers, and over the years, an increasing volume of backbiting. So, I have retained, I hope, both skepticism and gratitude. And I have half-successfully ignored all that, I think. I've been very lucky in having friends who are good mockers, and at the same time good supporters. People who would knock the halo off or knock the scepter out of your hand. It's O.K. to carry a small walking stick, but if it turns into anything of a scepter, it gets knocked down.

COSTA: *There's a question that I ask every poet I have the good fortune to interview: Why is it that poets write so often about death or mortality—although you write less about death than other poets.*

HEANEY: First of all, it's a big marker. It's one thing that is certain to hap-pen. So, in terms of prospect, it does, as Samuel Johnson said, concentrate the mind. In terms of retrospect, in terms of memory, the formative, definitive moments in many's a life, are moments of loss, and the elegy for the lost one, for the dear one, which turns out to be an elegy for a part of yourself, that is very much part of the shape of human life.

Writing about death is also, of course, a convention. It's established. Poetry is a learned behavior, too, and the themes are, if not culturally determined, at least culturally suggested. And the elegiac is an established mood of sensibil-ity. The lament, the requiem note is a formal note, and it's an agreed formal note: it's one of those places of the utterly shared experience—loss of loved ones, sense of death—one thing that brings the race together. So, if the poet is desirous of striking a note that belongs intimately and authoritatively to the inner theater and the inner acoustic of his or her individuality, and at the same time, wishes to speak with and for the bigger group, I think the death theme is a mighty one.

Also, I think, as poets get older, death may not be an explicit subject, but for those poets who continue to develop, poets with the great finish, as it were, like Wallace Stevens or Yeats, or artists like Monet or Beethoven, the medium becomes implicated with a freedom and a freed readiness, a readiness to go, a readiness to say anything, almost. It is as if the death theme disappears as subject, but is present as an utterly sensitized gratitude for and susceptibility to things in time. Like those last poems of Stevens', like "The River of Rivers in Connecticut," or Yeats' poem like, "Cuchulain Comforted," or "The Man in the Echo." They have a sort of buoyancy that relates to the ship of death itself, the little ship carrying the soul off.

COSTA: *Is there a poem that you would most like to read to an American audience?*

HEANEY: I would like to read this little twelve-line thing. I referred to it earlier on as a story. I've begun to think of it as an allegory, yet it did not begin life as an allegory. It began life, I suppose we might say, as a fantasy or as a vision. But it is entered in the Annals of Ulster as a historical fact. It's about an imagined thing, about a lightness that happens—lightness in the sense of a brightening, an illumination and also in the sense of something unburdened arriving. It's about the perviousness that can exist between the imagined world and the earthly world, between the heavenly world and the earthly. I think of it as an allegory for the parallel lives that imagined things like poems, plays, pictures, words, and music possess. The parallel life that a spiritual, symbolic reality possesses in relation to our historical quotidian, domestic lives. It's untitled and it goes like this:

The annals say, when the monks of Clonmacnoise
Were all at prayers inside the oratory,
A ship appeared above them in the air.

The anchor dragged along behind so deep,
It hooked itself into the altar rails
And then, as the big hull rocked to a standstill,

A crewman shinned and grappled down the rope
And struggled to release it. But in vain.
'This man cannot bear our life here and will drown,'

The abbot said, 'unless we help him.' So,
They did, the freed ship sailed and the man climbed back
Out of the marvelous as he had known it.